Superstitionism

The Psychology of Sport

David White

First published by Thought Department, 2018

Printed in the United Kingdom

First Printing, 2018

ISBN 978-1-5272-2291-5

Contents

Foreword

"Superstition in sport; is it the secret of success or is it a load of old codswallop? What makes a player sit on the same seat going to training every day? What makes a player come out of the changing room third every single game, and what makes a player put his shin pads on last, because if he doesn't his world's going to fall apart? Superstition, let's find out a little more from people who know."

- Colin Murray, Radio and Television Presenter

Genesism

"I won't give their names away, but I did see superstition leading to a fight, and I have to say it was one of the most surreal experiences of my life. I'd just left university and signed on for a new club. I was 18, and the second day I was there a six-foot three-inch black man and a six-foot two-inch white man were standing in an open bath, nakedly punching lumps out of each other because they both had the same superstition about going into the same bath at exactly the same time, and I looked at it and thought, this is just too weird for me. So yes, I have seen it."

- Pat Nevin, Football writer and pundit

'Superstitionism - The Psychology of Sport' unleashes a unique and inquisitive brand of curious insight to unearth the blueprints lying secreted within superstition's metaphorical DNA. The author's playful sense of purposeful inquiry and comedic instinct for witty discourse is designed to encourage a shared interaction, whereby we each may discover the hidden genius lying currently dormant within us all.

Our attitude towards sport is built around mesmeric metaphors and subtle templates; each of which forms the crux of how we choose to assemble and circumnavigate our world. Perhaps now is as good a time as any for the gloves to come off as we bid to reclaim our unique capacity to assert curiosity and spontaneity, both of which are deemed as sacrosanct and as the sacred cows of expressive free will.

This book uses words as a guide to elicit a form of awareness which we must ultimately fathom for ourselves. Words do not have meanings, merely usages. This significant difference issues fair warning that superstitions offer no plot and no happy ending as they possess no explanatory power. Instead, this information is open-ended, and it's up to us to fill in the blanks.

Each of us possesses the capacity to think independently. Hence, the author submits information which he hopes will lead to the expansion of human potential. So now it's up to us to draw whatever conclusions we deem appropriate since each of us is wonderfully unique. Moreover, the insight of every contributor is equally valued, irrespective of how absurd their contribution may appear.

As and when this book makes reference to 'we', the author seeks to imply a collective perspective. It's not implicit however that any contributor or reader share his projected point of view. The author's approach aims to be objective but also challenging and thought-provoking, just as any process of questioning beliefs founded on faith ought to be.

Decoding superstition's metaphorical DNA

To discover the causes of superstitions, it's essential to search in all the right places. Therefore, over the course of this literary experience, we shall seek to dissect the elusive and yet all-encompassing topic of superstitious beliefs by exploring real life case studies, interviews, stories, humorous anecdotes, tales, omens, and myths. Our purpose is to unearth the underlying psychologies of which sport is so painstakingly comprised; and who knows, perhaps somewhere in the void between appearance and reality, we may even discover that the key to unlocking personal genius is realising that genius isn't locked.

> *"It's not the strongest of the species that die nor the most intelligent,*
> *but the ones least responsive to change."*
> - Charles Darwin

Consider the story of a driver stopping his car on a miserable, dark and rainy night to assist a fellow driver who was down on his knees under a street lamp searching frantically for his keys. The weather was treacherous and the wind and rain drove fiercely into their faces as they searched diligently for a further ten minutes or so, before finally, and soaked to the skin, the second driver demanded to know, *"Where exactly was your car parked when you discovered your keys were missing?"*

"Over there!" the first driver replied, pointing to his car almost ten metres away.

"What?" gasped the second driver exasperated. *"Then why on earth are we searching over here?"*

"Well," said the man, *"I happened to notice more light in this direction."*

One can only imagine the extent of frustration experienced by the driver of the second car. This tale is a quintessential example of the metaphorical blind leading the blind. Whereby, irrespective of any attempt at good natured humour, this dovetails perfectly with the logic required to comply with superstitions founded in faith. It is a human compulsion to trawl through the shadows of ambiguity, fumbling clumsily in all the wrong places while searching for answers which, despite our endeavours, are nowhere to be found. Perhaps it's not just the street lamps that were dim.

3

Next, consider Manchester United footballer Paul Pogba who trawled through the least likely possible causes of practical dilemmas experienced by his team, and seemingly concluded 'curses' and 'luck'. In other words, he accused superstitions of hindering practical solutions, when in hindsight, the team's problems lay a little closer to home.

"We're going to start to think we're cursed. It doesn't matter which team comes here; we dominate them, be it Arsenal [or West Ham]. Our luck will change at one time or another."

- Paul Pogba, Manchester United Football Player

Pogba was reported by *Mail Online* as stating: *"We just have to pay attention to the small details. We conceded a daft goal [against West Ham]. Against Arsenal it was also the small details. We are dropping silly points."* So in retrospect, it appears the real cause of Pogba's ire was his team's inability to correct the 'small details', none of which were a result of curses or luck.

There was nothing flippant about Pogba's initial superstitious remarks. Nor, in retrospect, was it said in jest; since prior to and following Pogba's superstitious remarks, almost every post-match interview conducted during that period with players and manager alike made some form of discreet reference to the cause of United's poor run of results being linked to curses or bad luck.

Later in the book we shall endeavour to explore luck as a concept in more detail. For now, however, let's consider the origin of when citing 'luck' first became habitual and ask why it's so hard to quit superstitious rituals, compulsions, and traits? Are we searching for answers in all the wrong places, when in reality the supernatural has no demonstrable bearing on sport at all?

What if I were to suggest that superstitions are as addictive as cigarettes? Or that superstition's erratic and addictive behaviours are also chemically induced since a primary function of sports superstitions is helping to eradicate anxiety and fear. Both anxiety and fear release cortisol and adrenaline into our system and add excess glucose to our bloodstream, thus ensuring that superstitions (like cigarettes) induce a chemical threat.

What do we actually know of sports psychology? Is it that no such thing actually exists? Instead there's only psychology modified or adapted to specifically compensate for sport. The types of competitiveness we experience in sport are no different from the cut throat demands experienced in business, personal relationships, or during the cut and thrust of living our everyday lives.

Our experiences within sport do not make us unique. Consider, for instance, the following snapshot from an article in *Fast Company* magazine which reported the findings by Dr Edward Miller, Dean of Johns Hopkins School of Medicine in Baltimore. He calculated that every year, over 600,000 people in the United States who have coronary bypass surgery are told they need to stop smoking, start walking, eat less, and cut down on alcohol if they wish to survive.

Quite incredibly, only 10% of those 600,000 people could sustain the lifestyle changes necessary to avoid the threat of future heart failure or coronary attacks. This gives rise to the following question: if 90% of coronary bypass patients cannot alter their actions to save their own lives, then what chance have we of executing the changes necessary to nullify the effects of superstitious beliefs?

Why is it so hard to implement changes when change is both necessary and in our best interest? The answer is relative and simple! It's because human nature is resistant to change. Likewise, part of the reason why change appears painful is because we often lose our motivation to change before the process of change ever got to begin.

Change, nonetheless, remains integral to growth. So too is the importance of which 'types' of methodologies we adopt to bring about behavioural change. The human brain operates from within a continuous state of flux where it seeks equilibrium by attempting to avoid unnecessary forms of turmoil, disruption, chaos, or change.

The human psyche is pliant and adaptable and has long since figured out that the easiest route to achieving equilibrium is simply to believe whatever we like, irrespective of verifiable facts. The placebo effect is yet a further behaviour whereby the brain tricks the superstition called 'ego' into justifying anything we choose to believe.

Ego is primarily superstition as, despite the placebo effect appearing to work in certain scenarios, it is merely the effect which carries some potency and only the deception which makes it seem real. Being told all the answers is not as mentally exhilarating as discovering answers for ourselves since the brain pushes back in the form of regression when told what to do. This process is attributed to homoeostasis, which is the movement of organisms in the brain *towards* equilibrium and *away* from change. So what are the de-motivational drivers behind the human aversion to change?

What stops us from disbanding superstitious convictions the moment our performances start to dip? Why get irritated by other people's opinions of our superstitious beliefs when we can't prove to the contrary that our beliefs are valid, practical, or real? Why not apply scepticism to all beliefs founded on faith, irrespective of whether our superstitious preferences are generic or simply seen through the eyes of willing acolytes who seek divine intervention in sporting affairs?

Why remain so guarded of superstitious beliefs when experiencing a losing streak? Is it because we're subconsciously aware that superstitions are completely reliant on luck and that luck remains a mystery to us all. No one has categorically deciphered luck, nor does evidence exist to prove luck's existence; so what then is the cause of superstitious beliefs?

Superstitions, although seemingly complex, are merely anxieties on a continuous loop. Consider February 2016 in front of a sell-out crowd at the MEN Arena in Manchester, as WBA World Super-Bantamweight Boxing Champion Scott Quigg entered the ring to tumultuous applause. The crowd uttered a collective sigh of relief which reverberated throughout the whole building following weeks of wrangling and bickering between both boxing camps.

During this electrifying encounter of boxing history-in-the-making to unify the WBA and IBF belts, boxing's now customary verbal-posturing and psychological jockeying-for-pole-position kicked into overdrive. Immediately the stakes were upped as Northern Ireland's IBF World Super-Bantamweight Champion, Carl 'The Jackal' Frampton threatened to pull out of the fight.

Frampton's gripe was not due to money, venue, choice of referee, or weight of the gloves. Instead, the media storm centred around Frampton's stubborn demands to occupy the home dressing room. His manager, former WBA Featherweight Irish legend Barry McGuigan clarified, *"The bottom-line is it's a point of principle; we're not willing to relent on this because it's important. If we don't get it, we'll lock it up, and we can both use different dressing rooms; there's loads of them in the place."*

In response to his somewhat aggressive comments, the disgruntled public who had watched proceedings from afar began questioning why all the fuss and hullabaloo? They were sceptical as to whether either camp really wanted the fight to happen at all, which was understandable from a punter's perspective. Yet, what were the *real* reasons behind Frampton's persistent demands?

Was Frampton's camp simply nit-picking as Quigg's camp was quick to imply? Or did a more calculated strategy lie beneath their outright refusal to budge? We didn't have to wait long to find out since, widely-reported by the tabloid press one day prior to the fight, came the answer perfectly laid out as if on a plate. *The Sun* reported that Frampton believed he had already drawn first-blood in the battle-of-wills by flushing Quigg out of his comfort zone.

Frampton stated that his rival's superstition showed he is weak of mind. Ah-ha! Now we're getting somewhere. It began to emerge that beneath Frampton's posturing was a calculated attempt to heighten Quigg's superstitious anxieties, trepidations, and fears. Bingo! Consider the psychological impact of Frampton's well thought out verbal sparring attacks or of McGuigan's less than subtle barbs stating, *"The wrangling will knock the Englishman off his stride."*

McGuigan further asserted, *"I think it's important for Scott Quigg. He's got so many idiosyncrasies and superstitions. Everything has to be aligned for him or else he gets jittery and out of kilter, and we know it's upsetting Scott more than it's upsetting Carl."* Frampton then interjected and delivered the final coup-de-grace to Quigg's fragile mentality by remarking, *"This is just stupid stuff. I have visions of Scott sleeping in the dressing room on a camp bed, [just] so that he gets the dressing room [he wants]. I would not put that past him because he is that superstitious."*

Next Carl began to question, *"If he backs himself so much and believes he's the fighter that he thinks he is, then why does it matter what dressing room he gets changed in? Scott has been saying things to get under our skins from the very start. I'm just playing the game, but these guys are losing it. You saw that today, it has worked against them; I'm just sitting back and laughing. If I'm honest, it's all a game and I'm playing the game."* As if to emphasise his point, Frampton's camp then reportedly blasted Stevie Wonder's classic song 'Superstition' through the speakers, just to wind Scott up.

Quigg's camp wasn't amused, but if superstitions are truly as innocuous and truly as ineffective as they tried to portray, then why did Scott take the bait and allow himself to be offended? Why not simply dismiss any talk which suggested that securing the home dressing room could in any way impact the final result? Why not let Carl have the dressing room and be done with the whole sorry saga once and for all?

Superstition in sport is not new phenomena. Consider the words of former Bury FC manager Alan Knill who, during a 2009 league two play-off game, was widely-reported as accepting he may be accused of madness for relying on his baggy trousers to help Bury clinch a place in League One.

The 'Shakers' boss had apparently worn the same tatty tracksuit bottoms throughout a 12-match unbeaten run which propelled his team into the end-of-season play-offs as promotion favourites. Yet, as Alan meticulously prepared his team for the first leg of their semi-final against Shrewsbury Town FC, he explained:

"I'm no different to any other manager. We say we're not superstitious, but we are. I have these scruffy training bottoms that were black when I got them, and you wash them once and they come out grey. But we haven't lost when I've worn them for the last 12 games. So I can't not wear them; I would hate to think that if I changed my trackie bottoms and we lost, it would be my fault [and] would be down to the trackie bottoms, and not the players on the pitch."

This is a startling indictment of the hidden undercurrents and psychological intransigence inflicted by superstitious beliefs which suggest they either work for us or against us based solely on the strength of our faith. Such delusions were evident during the 2014 Formula One season, where a very public spat between warring Mercedes drivers, Lewis Hamilton and Nico Rosberg, saw a curious twist of reasoning occur.

Stories leaked to the media of a no-holds-barred psychological skirmish whereby, like a bolt out of the blue, Lewis bizarrely requested his Mercedes Team Chiefs to put an end to Nico's pre-race ritual of football keepie-ups. Lewis seemingly believed that keepie-ups were a ritual the German had refined to improve his reactions before climbing into his car to race.

Lewis shrewdly complained that the sound of the ball bouncing continuously in the garage was affecting his concentration and driving him mad, so he wanted it stopped. But what was the real motivation behind his peculiar request? Was it really to curb the irritation factor or was he seeking to engineer a definitive edge by disrupting Nico's psychology?

Superstitions are habit-forming diversions which we wilfully embrace as convenient distractions to counter sport's many anxieties and fears. To detach from superstitious rituals and routines can infuse us with a sense of paranoia and of feeling exposed and ill-at-ease. What if Nico was subsequently banned from performing his pre-race routine? How unsettling might any knock-on effect prove to be to his confident demeanour or to his pre-race preparations regarding the equilibrium of his state of mind?

Could such a subtle disruption of Nico's psychology influence the outcome of a race? Lewis clearly felt it was worthy of a try, which led me to question whether he was 'double jobbing' as a proficient psychologist on the side? Was he practising gamesmanship in a deliberate attempt to force Nico Rosberg to resort to Plan B?

Superstitious beliefs are highly obtrusive, uncomfortably intrusive, and often hidden in plain sight. The most practical means to avoid superstition's all-encompassing gaze is to cast our eyes in the direction of scepticism when the threat of ambiguity stares us right in the face. There is a wonderfully stylish phrase which suggests that 'thoughts have the ability to manifest as things'. It is linked to the pseudoscientific superstition called 'Law of Attraction' which is relatively simplistic in terms of reasoning but is not supported by falsifiable facts.

The Universal Law of Attraction is an interesting hypothesis, and for that purpose alone it's important as we go forward to consider 'universal law' in a little more depth. The Law of Attraction gives rise to many sayings, the most common of which is: "Be careful what you wish for, you just might get it." This is an assertion that our thoughts have the capacity to manifest as things.

If the Law of Attraction is to be believed, then we are bound by its immutable premise that repeatedly thinking of specific outcomes causes the energies we release with every thought to interact with the synergy of the universe. The same energy (seemingly enhanced by our wishes) then manifests as a physical thing. It is effectively a claim that 'like attracts like', whereby maintaining a positive state of will attracts positive results. The importance of such thinking cannot be overstated since, minus Law of Attraction, a belief in superstition cannot be said to exist.

All superstitions are rooted in the Law of Attraction; as indeed is prayer. Both imply that positive thinking will supernaturally enrich our state of being. The difficulty, however, is that Law of Attraction, if it exists, cannot discriminate in terms of attraction. It must therefore carry a health-warning, as the same definition of warm and cosy optimism must also exist in equal measure from a negative standpoint. If like attracts like, then surely a negative state-of-will attracts equally negative outcomes. Perhaps we should put it to the test.

Consider the impact of negative thinking as conveyed at the greatest show on earth. The story begins in the wake of a humiliating defeat at the 2014 World Cup Finals in Brazil, with Brazilian Sports Minister Aldo Rebelo widely acknowledging that Brazil's 7-1 loss to Germany would leave a deep scar on the nation's footballing psyche. He stated that *"the manner of the 7-1 defeat was a terrible blemish. It was an accident; but if you analyse the causes of the accident, that's a different story."*

Rebelo suggested with apparent concern that *"Perhaps the psychology of a nation should not be so deeply ingrained and inter-dependent upon the result of a football match."* It was an interesting observation, especially if we consider that during one particular game, 80 fans were reportedly treated for stress inside the stadium and one even died of a heart attack.

An incredible weight of expectation hung around the neck of host nation Brazil to win the World Cup on home soil. So much so, it emerged that the visibly rattled Brazilian Manager, Luiz Felipe Scolari, had called in a leading psychologist to implant mental resilience into what the media referred to as his cry-babies, so that they may do their nation proud.

Scolari's cry for help followed an earlier performance which was marred by the Samba stars' seeming fragilities, where they appeared before the public as emotional wrecks, yet still managed to successfully negotiate a tense but dramatic penalty shootout to register a win over rivals Chile. However, fears mounted for player welfare as eventually the pressure started to tell and doubts began to escalate over the state of their mental health.

Questions were raised as to whether the squad possessed the psychological toughness required to cope. Yet, had Rebelo's assessment been ever-so-slightly disingenuous? Why had he not anticipated the prospect of national mass hysteria prior to hosting the largest sporting event in the world? Surely there must have been awareness of the potential for fragility to grip an adoring nation's tournament psych? Yet where was the foresight to recognise a nation daring to dream but strung out on hope?

What form of contingency was put in place to manage Brazil's growing expectations which were being projected from every billboard, media outlet, and advertisement on public transport? Moreover, what plans were in place to counteract the effects of the superstition called luck pulling against host nation Brazil? In the end luck turned its back on the Samba stars, thereby leaving their aspirations in tatters as their dreams fell apart.

If Sports Minister Rebelo was correct about one thing, it's the extent to which many fans were left deeply scarred by the whole experience. So much so, that Brazilian National pride would much prefer that the whole episode be wiped from the annals of history. Instead, the result may continue to haunt the collective consciousness of those who witnessed the event, for the rest of their lives.

It may prove difficult to erase lasting iconic images such as Brazilian central defender David Luiz falling to his knees with both index fingers pointed skywards towards his god. This was a public display of superstition as he shed floods of tears to relieve the tension and prayed to alleviate his emotions prior to the impending demands of each match.

Certain sections of media implied that this show of emotion was a good thing since it was Brazil's visibly emotional players who had performed best up to that point. The fervour among players became further intensified as Brazilian fans belted out the national anthem with passion and zeal, while many players saw fit to cross themselves with startling regularity to summon supernatural assistance from somewhere beyond this mortal coil.

Unbeknown to a captivated global audience, the psychologist and support staff were working tirelessly to instil whatever magic they could muster to erase the culture of fragility which clearly existed within the group. While, somewhere on the cusp of the deep-seated madness which collectively ensued, a new generation of dreamers emerged seeking favour from benevolent gods with a weakness for sport.

Welcome to the dawning of a brand-new age, the age of *Superstitionism*, aided and abetted by ambiguous beliefs. *Superstitionism* was prevalent in the actions of every player who pointed and gestured towards the sky for divine inspiration and intervention. Many also reverted to the usual suspects such as crossing-their-hearts and the rubbing-of-rosaries etc. Yet this was merely a case of special pleading, whereby they appealed to superstition in a bid to experience intermittent relief.

The Brazilian players sought mental respite by attempting to coerce supernatural phenomena; but coerce to do what? Seemingly, to interfere and meddle in Brazilian footballing affairs. All it took was some patriotic nationalists in floods of tears to coerce the god of Brazilian soccer to be filled with compassion, enough to nail his divine colours to the Samba mast (if God is a 'he').

Sadly, despite their best efforts, it appears that the supernatural essence on the ascendancy that historic day turned out to be German and not Brazilian. Irrespective of the players' public endeavours to elicit favour from an invisible god, all they got to experience were feelings of desolation due to a result which was more apt to reflect a German god at the helm.

Faith is not a reliable pathway to establish truth. It's not reasonable to apply never ending faith to things which we cannot hear, taste, touch, smell, or see. The Brazilians were not only beaten, but publicly humiliated; and therein lies the crux of all superstitions. It's that irrespective of deep-seated hope, eternal optimism, and even the most vivid of imaginations, no superstition has ever been demonstrably proven to work.

"Mysticism: starts with 'myst' centres on 'I' and ends in 'cism'."

- Unknown

The moment superstitions are granted the gift of impunity and free-reign over human emotions, we fall into the clutches of mental discourse; whereby aspects of the mind enter constant dialogue with itself (self-talk) in a bid to alleviate sporting anxieties. If left to its own devices, the brain by way of self-talk will seek to reignite previous superstitions by grasping at anything it recalls as having swung matters back in our favour in the past.

Activating a superstitious belief, similar to rolling a dice or tossing a coin, requires the psychology of a gambler. The superstitious punter is equally willing to stake their reputation on irrational behaviour and bizarre characteristic quirks, or even on prayers to invisible gods despite prayer and the Universal Law of Attraction being primarily one and the same.

Once we no longer care if the things we believe are true, we give rise to the birth of *Superstitionism*. At which point, we fall hook, line, and sinker into the vastness of an even greater mystery called luck, which stretches further again into mystifying tributaries such as hope, faith, and belief. None of which is a rational foundation for claiming to know anything at all.

"It takes a very unusual mind to undertake the analysis of the obvious."

- Alfred North Whitehead, Mathematician

Our brains are hardwired to accept information in whatever shape or guise our earthly gurus would have us believe, but too often our brains lack urgency and curiosity when pursuing the thrill of daring to explore less obvious thoughts. Many athletes no longer seem to care for the whys or the wherefores of whether the superstitions to which they subscribe are true or false. Instead, for all intents and purposes, they appear to accept that they just 'are'.

"Religion comes from the infancy of our species, when we didn't know that the earth went round the sun, we didn't know that germs caused disease, we didn't know when we were told in Genesis, 'you're given dominion over all creatures,' that this did not include microorganisms, because we didn't know they were there, and so we didn't know they had dominion over us. So when diseases broke out it was blamed on wickedness."

- Christopher Hitchens, Author

Superstitions from biblical times were constrained by ignorance due to the lack of scientific knowledge available at the time. Science has since increased our understanding in areas such as meteorology, astronomy, and biology, yet ancient and medieval superstitions continue to pursue us like time travellers into modern sport.

Consider how many natural occurrences our ancestors saw fit to attribute to the moods of the gods, purely because they lacked knowledge of the scientific breakthroughs available today. Superstitions are remnants from a bygone age. They are surplus to requirements and even day-old superstitions have already lasted a day too long.

As we continue to learn more about the physical composition of the observable universe and of the natural cycles of life within, the need for gods becomes ever increasingly redundant. This is because every superstition debunked by science renders the superstition called 'god' further obsolete, and leads us to question whether it's plausible to commit time, energy, and resources to superstitious placebos known commonly as gods?

Superstitions lay claim to things we don't know. Yet, how radically different might our outlook be if, from this moment onwards we agreed to believe as many true things as possible and as few things that are false? The human instinct intuitively searches for answers and context to life's biggest questions; but until answers are forthcoming, superstition continues to act as our favourite 'god of the gaps' to make sense of the things we can't comprehend.

What justification is there to assert supernatural explanations for things which we cannot yet explain? Who can categorically define the term 'supernatural' in its entirety or demonstrate how it exists or why? We can all have a stab at what it may entail, or as to how we believe it relates to us; but in the end, we must all capitulate to ignorance until someone can demonstrate that it actually exists.

It's important to keep reminding our minds that concealed in our thoughts are our true identities, lying smothered beneath an illusionary continuum of faith. The fact that we assert superstition as a sporting reality is a vivid reflection of the many gaps which exist in our subconscious, and these gaps need to be filled before we can feel comfortable in our own skin.

Superstitions exist in a void between appearance and reality in situations where convention, tradition, confirmation bias, custom, ritual, and routine are rife. All of these are potential characteristics of a weakened state of mental resolve. Our mentalities act as the personal glue which either binds us together in mind and body or inadvertently prises our emotions apart, thus creating a state of disconnect between our emotions and our instinctive and intuitive sense of self. To experience self-awareness is illuminating but often complex as illustrated by the following enlightening true story:

A very devout Catholic woman once entered a religious retreat. As time passed, the woman experienced states of self-reflection and mindlessness in a bid to remove all prior illusions of her former self, whereupon she came to believe that she had experienced the divine.

She returned to her domestic circle of peers and declared, "I have changed. I am no longer the person I used to be." To which her family and friends sarcastically whispered, "She is definitely different, but she hasn't changed." As time passed, the woman's demeanour became more distant.

Still, her family and friends continued to accept that she was definitely different but refused to acknowledge any change. Finally one day, with her repeated efforts failing to convince them and her protestations once again falling on deaf ears, she abandoned her epiphany and reverted back-to-type, thus denouncing all previous affiliation with the divine.

Infuriatingly, and almost as quickly as the woman began to reconcile with her

*former-self, the annoying response of those doubting sceptics was simply to say,
"We told you she hadn't changed. This proves we were right all along."*

The sad irony is that the woman *had* changed. Her family, however, were unable or simply unwilling to countenance her transformation due to their personal reluctance to transition beyond the rigid confines of their fixed beliefs.

The woman felt constrained by the collective ignorance of her family and friends. She was deprived of expressing her newfound identity and of the chance to celebrate her brief emancipation from the woman she'd left behind. This story leads to the question of how the bias perpetrated by her family members differs from the types of bias projected by you or I? After all, how many of *us* display the mental resilience required to transition beyond superstitious bias by leaving our superstitions behind?

Superstitionism - The Psychology of Sport aims to celebrate the uniqueness of human potential, far beyond ideologies and dogmas imposed at the behest of superstitious fairy tales and myths. It's time to re-engage with curiosity, spontaneity, and personal genius so that we are no longer owned by the past. We are not free to unleash our untapped potential until we are first aware of the gifts, talents, or debilitating traits we uniquely possess. So let's stop tiptoeing around superstitions and instead feel encouraged to open the topic for further debate.

*"What lies behind us and what lies before us, are tiny matters compared to what
lies within us."*

- Ralph Waldo Emerson, Philosopher

All psychology is corrupted by the indoctrinations of whatever cultures ultimately prevail. The greatest renaissance of personal intelligence tends to occur once we stop seeking to emulate the characteristics of cultures and finally wake-up to being us. This can begin by examining our motivation for activating a superstitious belief. For instance, do superstitions act as our alter egos, as if pulling on a cape or hiding behind a mask?

Perhaps the 'out of body experiences' occasionally proclaimed by those close to death are the nearest comparisons to superstitious athletes who sense 'out of character' experiences. Such experiences are triggered by alter egos and based on an almost hallucinogenic understanding that only ghosts, apparitions, or an invisible friend in the sky can get the job done?

Sports psychology transcends academia, is much wider than educational add-ons, and stays with us too long to be considered a fad. We draw on psychology to interpret life, and how we think is of vital importance since we cannot escape from the thoughts which go through our minds unless or until we replace each thought with alternative thoughts, which is often easier said than done.

Consider June 2014, as manager Liam Bradley appraised his Antrim Senior County Gaelic football team's unexpected passage into an Ulster semi-final following a dramatic and pulsating win over Donegal. *"Nobody gave us a chance coming down here,"* he stated, *"But I knew in training on Friday night that we were going to win this game."*

Liam seemed understandably elated, but were his post-match assertions overstated regarding the means of his historic win? What if we were to apply a more rigorous form of inquiry to the mysterious nature of Liam's words? Would we uncover a superstitious conspiracy, or did Liam initiate the Law of Attraction by using the power of intentionality to engineer a win?

Is it wise to dismiss Liam's overarching sense of intuitive prophecy or did he truly possess the ability to foresee the outcome of future events? Was Antrim the beneficiary of a wonderful team performance or the clear recipients of luck? Antrim player Kevin O'Boyle provided invaluable insight regarding his match-winning goal line clearance in the final seconds of the game. *"I just covered the keeper,"* he enthused. *"I didn't realise that it was the last kick of the game. I was very fortunate I was in the right place at the right time."*

Was it luck, fate, destiny, karma, or sheer coincidence which dealt Antrim the winning hand of success? Or was Liam's sincerity, unerring accuracy, and sixth-sense of impending success the result of his mind playing tricks? Might there be more to instinct and intuition than often we care to admit? What if Liam's winning contention was a valid reflection of the fact that somehow he instinctively knew?

Imagine if such a phenomenon was possible? How might we even begin to comprehend or to explain that we have powers which can harness intentionality for our own ends? Might it lead to a breakthrough regarding how we approach future preparations for competing at sport? Conversely, if intuition is telling us we're going to lose, then why bother turning up? Should we pay more attention to intuition?

Liam's assertion typically reflected the myriad of throwaway comments being tossed around sport every single day. Yet, something had to be feeding his conscious awareness. So what caused his prophetic assertion to be correct? Did it stem from an omen or premonition? Was he universally attuned to his subconscious self? Or were his assertions mere pie-in-the-sky?

What if Antrim had lost? Would a losing scenario present Liam with just cause to never trust his instincts, intuition, or spontaneous impulses ever again? Sport opens us up to many questions; fortunately there are no better means to elicit answers than to search and explore the contrasting insights and experiences of sporting elite.

Every athlete has their own unfolding story complete with chapter and verse of a series of events which they interpret as consummate truths. So much so, that to athletes who regularly engage in superstitious behaviour, any deviation away from ritual and routine just feels downright weird.

Superstitious athletes are wary of scepticism and susceptible to confirmation-bias, yet they rarely permit others to share the same mental concessions as they grant to themselves. To experience life to its fullest potential requires meaningful insights, since minus meaningful insights we may never fully realise our true potential and purpose at all, which is not to be dead.

Each of us has been gifted a unique set of skills and the necessary characteristics to make meaningful impacts, and where better to start than at the crux of all reasoning within our own mind? Let's begin by questioning our earthly purpose? Some of us exist primarily as a warning to others, while some of us may die never once having realised the full extent of our purpose at all, and yet still made a telling and meaningful contribution towards our collective wellbeing.

A new beginning requires a new *us* who is free from superstition. Yet, superstitious beliefs form their very own death knells for even the most basic of human tenets, which is the psychological freedom to disregard, disavow, or reject unverifiable claims which are founded on faith.

We don't have to believe everything that we think, nor subscribe to the essence of all that we read. But every book should endeavour to give up its secrets using words and the power of suggestion to court even the most sceptical and intransigent imagination, while drawing from unique sporting insights and revelations designed to enrich its unique reading vibrancy and tone. This book aims to create a thoughtful environment to reappraise the practical impact of faith-based delusions on athletes' competitive state of mind.

During the turning of each crisp page or with each effortless scroll across a screen, we open our mind to being questioned why we concede emotional value and false kudos to strange habits, eccentricities, and actionable quirks which so often precede our endeavours to excel at sport. Superstitious psychology in its primary state manifests as an accumulation of stories, all of which are enchanting but none of which are verifiably true.

Consider this illuminating quote by author and humourist Don Marquis: *"An idea isn't responsible for the people who believe in it."* As if to validate this parody of satire, here is a contrasting parody of superstition from the delightfully sumptuous Garden of Eden:

The story begins with the Bible's femme fatale, Eve, who saw the forbidden pomegranate and found it was pleasing to the eye. Not only did it look tempting and potentially delicious, but she also believed this enticing fruit could induce great wisdom, awareness, and power. So, she hastily ate some fruit from the tree before sharing the rest with her hapless partner in crime, Adam. This altered the course of humanity forever, or at least until the much-prophesied extra-terrestrial known as Jesus came to earth to save us all from our pomegranate induced sins.

When compiling this chapter, I politely requested passers-by in random locations to explain why they had chosen to hitch their wagons to the idea of an apple being cast in the role of the pantomime villain (aka the forbidden fruit). Why did no one mention a pomegranate, date, or fig, all of which are equally native to the middle-eastern region often associated with Eden's location? Nowhere in the Bible or other scholarly literature is an apple stated as being an absolute categorical fact.

Not one passerby could recall being taught anything other than an apple appearing centre stage in the whole alleged Eden affair. Yet, pomegranates, dates, and figs were equally as likely to provide the tantalisingly and tempting fare facing Adam and Eve that fateful day. So began a most curious superstitious odyssey, whereby the apple's mythology spread East and West as its legend sprouted legs to become one of the world's most enduring beliefs, and one of the greatest myths ever to be sold to humanity under the guise of an actual fact.

So cataclysmic were its effects, that it currently impacts an estimated 2.2 billion people of Christian persuasion by way of superstitious ideology founded on faith. The superstition suggests that all humans are born with inherent sickness and are subsequently commanded to be well by a construct of human imagination called God. This story perpetuates the unreasonable myth of infinite punishment for finite crimes. All because of a woman charmed by a talking snake and a guy who bit off more than he could chew.

Many are mentally scarred by this fairy story, which is neither demonstrable nor has it been proven to be true. Faith is not a reliable pathway to establishing truth. It is therefore not rational to claim, using only faith, that we possess the capacity to understand the inner-workings of an invisible apparition called God. Irrespective of whichever god is our personal brand.

Questioning the existence of gods is neither irrational, offensive, nor arrogant. Laying claim to knowing God's mind, however, is not only arrogant and preposterous, but screams of superstition masquerading as faith. Worse still is the scurrilous belief which accompanies the myth of the hypothetical apple. It's the superstition called 'sin' which creates an illusion, to non-sceptical minds, of needing to be governed by an arbitrary figurehead called God who apparently 'is' visible, but only to certain sets of eyes.

Faith is unreliable. Consider the impact of attributing faith to routinely kissing a lucky talisman before competing at sport. Visualise the scenario, prior to a race, of one athlete kissing a lucky necklace while another points to the sky in acknowledgement of a god; then ask yourself, what do both parties truly expect to happen as a result? Who is arrogant enough to believe that such actions have any supernatural bearing on how they are about to perform? Both chose to act that way for a reason, yet, in the cut and thrust of competitive sport, behaving erratically is nothing new.

Psychological Warfare

Superstitious beliefs are profound, but are they practical? Consider the start of the 2014/15 Formula One season whereby World Champion Lewis Hamilton reportedly sought to avoid being allocated No. 1 as the official number of his Mercedes car. Lewis was the number one driver in the World at that time, yet when asked by reporters why he declined such a prestigious honour, he conveyed his desire to seek permission from team officials to stick with his lucky No. 44.

The number 44 was allocated to Lewis when he won his first karting title and is reportedly tattooed behind his right ear. Yet, from a corporate perspective, displaying number 1 set both Lewis and Mercedes apart as the premier marketing brand within Formula One. He already admitted during a very public spat, which came to light as a result of his deteriorating relationship with teammate and fiercest rival Nico Rosberg, that *"It did reach a crisis point and it was very tough. It has been the most intense battle and there was lots of psychological warfare."*

To purposely activate a superstitious belief qualifies as psychological warfare, but how far did their superstitions extend? The human brain, it is said, cannot accept two separate thoughts at the exact same time and simultaneously struggles to evolve beyond whichever thought is predominant at any given time. This was perfectly demonstrated by two-time Formula One World Champion Fernando Alonso's reported insistence on wearing and displaying the number 14.

Fernando's insistence was predicated on the sentimentality of prior success since it was kart number 14 which he had driven to his first ever world title at just 14 years-of-age. Consequently, he drew a mental correlation whereby the prospects of winning and the number 14 formed a seemingly unbreakable alliance in the inner recesses of his mind.

Fernando's emotional attachment to the number 14 appears to have sprouted its own set of legs and formed a new reality with 14 at the helm, despite a distinct lack of credible evidence linking his first ever world title win to anything supernatural or divine. The lack of practical evidence to substantiate his belief was highlighted by race statistics from the previous season, where despite wearing his lucky number 14, he lost more races than he won.

It transpired, on the basis of statistical evidence, that there was nothing lucky about number 14 since Fernando failed to secure the Driver's Championship title and failed again the following year. His relationship with superstition was robust, however, as not once did he contemplate ditching his allegiance to wearing the number 14.

Superstitions exist in the space between appearance and reality, while the concept of supernatural relates to things which violate natural laws. Superstitious beliefs are contingent on claims that intelligent agents somewhere in the ether are either working against us or pulling in our favour. Or that two complete strangers from antiquity who bit into an apple somehow empowered self-serving spiritual leaders with some form of dominion over us all.

There is no greater myth than the superstition called sin. This myth is perpetuated by the idea that superstitions are thinking and reasoning agents, yet, it is only a failure to apply scepticism which makes superstitions seem real. The superstition called sin is designed to erase spontaneity, scepticism, and curiosity from occupying the forefront of our mind. Otherwise, it is at best hypocritical to feel compelled towards subservience while claiming, in contrast, that we are the masters of our own free will.

Superstitions create the appearance that there is nothing 'free' about human 'will'. Why subscribe to unfalsifiable mental constructs, knowing in advance that many of our peers have been sectioned on the grounds of fragile mental health for considerably less? The superstition called sin exists to prompt fear, and fear permeates every aspect of our lives including sport.

If we cast an inquisitive glance in the direction of the Hebrew root of the word 'sin', we discover its meaning is simply 'to miss'. It does not refer to, nor does it specify the myth of wrongdoing. Yet, superstitious beliefs do not allow facts to stand in the way of a damn good story, such as feeling we are born with an innate sense of abject failure, and the only way to erase such an inherent sense of failure is to win.

The superstitions we cling to in sport are mirrored by the superstitions we cling to throughout life. 'Sin', for instance, is a means to expose human fragility by projecting emotional blackmail into the human psyche in order to cause 'shame'. The idea of an 'afterlife' is also superstition since scientists still wait in anticipation for the honour of awarding a Nobel Prize to anyone who can demonstrate an afterlife which exists beyond mere belief.

"When I do good, I feel good. When I do bad, I feel bad. That's my religion."

- Abraham Lincoln, 16th U.S. President

How's that for a practical discipline to which we can all aspire, with no talk of superstitions or gods in sight? Superstitions are subliminal forms of mind control, and each one leaves a scar deeply engraved in our personal psyche. Whereupon, we are left to question whether we have control of our superstitions or whether superstitions are controlling us?

Are we being controlled at the whim of others, using superstitions to induce us to comply? This, it appears, is a real possibility recognised by many esteemed luminaries. One example is author Mark Twain who famously said, *"Let me make the superstitions of a nation and I care not who makes its laws or its songs."*

If we care to elicit a clearer understanding of how the same methodology is being used to control the minds of many by very few then consider the following quote by Mayer Amschel Rothschild. *"The few who understand the [monetary banking] system will either be so interested from its profits or so dependent on its favours that there will be no opposition from that class. Let me issue and control a nation's money and I care not who writes the laws."* You've got to admit, it's bloody genius.

The exact same methodology is being exploited by cunning gurus of theism to promote superstitions such as gods and sin. If we recall, however, the Hebrew root of 'sin' is separate from the idea of a divine overlord with an inferiority complex dispensing infinite punishment for finite crimes. Superstitions decree that the space between appearance and reality is marginal, yet their only means to determine which from which is by taking a punt.

If we are observant we can at least measure the detrimental effects of superstitious ambiguity on modern sport. An example of which is the effects of guilt attributed to sin, such as beating ourselves up at the idea of letting others or ourselves down. This behaviour is evident each time we 'miss out', 'miss the mark', 'miss our projected targets', or fall short of our expectations and goals.

Theism hardwires guilt into our brains from birth as a symptom of sin, but if we reframe sin as meaning 'to miss', given guilt is a subset of sin, we can transform the experience of participating in sport. The collective psychology of the culture into which we were born has ramifications on how our emotions are distributed throughout sport. Every failure to translate the Hebrew root for sin as meaning 'to miss' has similar ramifications which leave us vulnerable to popular metaphors such as 'drowning in guilt' just because we 'missed out' on achieving a target or reaching a goal.

Irrespective of whether we view the superstition called sin as credible or lacking in sense, in the end, it all stems from the tale of a mythical apple which might not have been an apple and a dodgy liaison between a woman and a talking snake. Superstitions spark unique conversations inside our brain; one example is sin, which minus its literal translation 'to miss' causes subliminal guilt in sport. This manifests as performance *mis*givings or feeling as though we have *mis*calculated, *mis*judged, *mis*fired, been *mis*guided, *mis*informed, made *mis*takes, or *mis*sed the cut.

All of these experiences emotionally equate in a sporting context to a sense of having done something bad, disappointing, or wrong. Hence, as a result, athletes and coaches tend to experience subsequent guilt and feel the need to atone. Guilt increases anxiety and decreases self-belief, leaving us feeling discombobulated and socially inept.

Sin primes human emotions to fear *missing out* on promises of receiving bountiful rewards. Losing conjures up similar emotions and a similar sense that we cannot be happy until first we atone. We may debate sin's translation, but its impact is guilt. So let's backtrack a little; how did an apple manage to wangle its way into the collective human psyche? It didn't get there of its own accord, someone purposely implanted the idea of an apple into our thoughts.

Perhaps we take such fairy tales too literally at the expense of alternative variations of truth. Is Eden, for instance, a metaphorical tale of genetic engineering by extraterrestrials and not the divine will of a god? Perhaps the tale is just a metaphorical oversimplification of The Big Bang Theory? Either way, the premise of an apple and unparalleled guilt is relayed to us by contemporary intermediaries, courtesy of those who are long since dead.

Through time immemorial, civilisations have fashioned gods and afforded them the temporary privilege of a limited shelf life, during which they were worshipped in vogue as the current fad. Very quickly, however, as with all fashion, Yahweh became the new Zeus, just as orange became the new black. Yet, centuries ago, who would have dared to imagine a reality without gods such as Apollo, Osiris, Poseidon, Odin, Quetzalcoatl, or Zeus? What became of those gods?

Where are the gods of antiquity right now? Are they utilising their leisure time meaningfully? Is one god more powerful than the rest and when did they pass the baton to the newest gods on the block? Did they simply roll over and agree to concede their powers to 21st-century gods, and if so, how very accommodating? Most theists are atheists by default, by choosing not to believe in the gods of alternative faiths.

The legend of Eden is popularised by an apple and its repercussions negatively impact modern sport. The reason is twofold. First, our beliefs don't exist in a vacuum. To be spoon-fed the idea that we are failures at birth and to then reinforce the idea through centuries of saturation leaves us subject to a heightened sense of guilt by association, which spills into every avenue of our lives including sport.

The second reason revolves around the failure of sports governing bodies to implement contingencies for unlearning the idea that guilt is a disproportionate symptom of losing and a coachable component of competitive sport. To the sceptical mind, there is no justification for cutting corners when outing superstitions which permeate sport, since there are no means of measuring the outcome of beckoning to gods to intervene in terrestrial sporting affairs?

How practical is the internalisation of guilt in sport? The answer lies in observing athletes of all ages, cultures, and denominations during the aftermath of having lost. Observe them acting as though their world has come to an end and consider whether the value of the prize on offer is proportionate to the degree of guilt they inflict on themselves.

Here is a question we rarely ask. Is any winning prize proportionate to the traumatic effects on an athlete's health, or to any breakdown in relationships caused by the athlete venting underlying frustrations towards family members in close proximity, who have little choice but to bear the brunt of their angst? Perhaps it is *us* who struggles to cope with the idea of losing, due to yet another superstition called ego and a hardwired predisposition for accepting guilt.

Where are the specialists in competitive sport to coach athletes how to utilise spontaneity and eliminate guilt? Sport mirrors our lives in microcosm and so whatever experiences are prevalent within sport are equally prevalent in other aspects of our lives. Therefore, it's time to start seeing superstitions for the placebos, nocebos, and unfathomable truths that they are. They have no credible means of authentication to separate the ridiculous from the sublime.

Imagine if during this reading experience we unlocked the truth behind sporting fallacies by revealing the secret sauce by which superstitions are primarily comprised. Or perhaps we may discover a living template which reverse-engineers superstition's precise inner-workings and, as a result, helps us to better understand what makes athletes tick.

Faith is not a virtue. The reason athletes appeal to faith is because faith justifies the idea of superstition acting as a convenient god of the gaps. This then raises the question as to who or what is calling the shots? Are we in control of our superstitions or are superstitions controlling us? To gain further insight, I asked Irish goalkeeping legend Shea Given why he crossed himself walking onto the pitch and what was the origin his ritual?

In response to what is clearly an orchestrated behaviour, Shea looked somewhat bemused as to whether or not his action qualified as a superstition. Yet, the sheer regularity, ambiguity, and unscientific nature of his meticulous action suggests that it most definitely does. Shea appeared to believe at some deep, intrinsic level that crossing himself affected his luck.

If luck wasn't Shea's motivation, then why bother to cross himself at all? He expressed no desire to reverse this recurring action; it was an adopted trait and he had to do it, just as he always did it for as far back as he cared to remember, and he will most likely continue to do it for as long as he plays football at any level. Tell him to stop and he probably won't. Ask him to stop and it's unlikely he can. Challenge him to affirm the exact percentage which superstition played in his meteoric rise to become a world class goalkeeper and he is unlikely to succeed.

During the 2012 European Championships in Poland and Ukraine, despite routinely crossing himself while walking onto the pitch, neither Shea or his Republic of Ireland teammates experienced their finest hour. Shea even admitted, in retrospect, how on numerous occasions he could've done with a bit more luck, but instead luck went missing when he needed it most. This poses the question that if a superstition isn't working, then why bring it into the sporting arena, and if it's merely a habit or religiously symbolic, why integrate such an action into sport at all?

"Sometimes I get confused by what I think is really obvious, but what I think is really obvious, obviously isn't obvious."

- Michael Stipe, Lead Singer of R.E.M

If Shea's goalkeeping gloves should fail to match his expectations, he would surely discard them with immediate effect and request that his sponsor supply him with a different pair ASAP. So, why then did he find it so seemingly difficult to apply similar logic to his superstitious belief once it failed to comply with his sporting expectations and demands?

In a bid to compile sporting insight, I interviewed athletes from various sports to explore the origins of their superstitious beliefs. I encouraged them to shed light on the motivations behind any sporadic and haphazard act. Yet, despite their best efforts to remember, many struggled to recall the source of their addictive beliefs with any precision. The most common response was a sense of bemusement and utter bewilderment as to how such an eclectic-mix of absurd behaviours were ever allowed to infiltrate their prior sense of reasoning at all.

Few understood or elaborated on how their actions became so far removed from their original intent. Yet, every athlete who engages with any form of superstitious behaviour believes, either consciously or subconsciously, that superstitions cause premeditated outcomes or act as catalysts for paranormal shifts. Speaking metaphorically, by invoking superstition we are subsequently invoking the supernatural to fight on our behalf. So, are we ready to rumble?

Rarely do athletes dare speak to others using the same self-demeaning manner, self-defeatist philosophies, and self-depreciative tones which they so often see fit to communicate to themselves. Despite superstitions waging psychological warfare for overall control of an athlete's mind, they are often mistaken as somewhat benign. Yet, nature manifests within cycles, and any cycle with influence over our nature cannot be considered benign.

Nature's cycles are self-perpetuating, as are the behavioural cycles of superstitious protagonists who concede to illusions governed by faith. So, what are these self-perpetuating illusions of which I speak? The answer does not make for pleasant viewing, as somewhere deep within the murky depths of every superstitious belief lurks even murkier mysteries with untold psychological repercussions.

No mysteries are murkier than illusions such as coincidence, serendipity, destiny, providence, kismet, karma, fluke, fate, and luck. All of which are immeasurable and of high consequence, but none of which are reliable components on which to base sport. The superstition called Law of Attraction implies that a projected thought can manifest as a physical thing. This sounds eerily similar to the optimism projected by human will when activating a generic superstition or the seemingly divine process of prayer.

Even sporting novices are increasingly aware, despite their best will and intention and outside of cheating, that there is no such thing as guaranteed success. So irrespective of whether their preferred superstitions adopt the guise of a prophetic omen, premonition, invisible god, ambiguous ritual, or myth, they should qualify each thought with a resounding 'perhaps', since 'perhaps' is as near as they're likely to get to demonstrating supernatural causality.

To this end, *Superstitionism - The Psychology of Sport* advocates for curiosity as a practical means of unearthing the untapped human potential which lies dormant and buried beneath a landslide of faith. Scepticism is grossly undervalued as it draws on the most natural form of reasoning available to us all. Evidence is the sceptic's tool-of-choice to debunk supernatural claims which are not demonstrable, so that we may believe as many true things as possible and as few things which are false.

We cannot transition from 'unknowing' superstitious states towards 'knowing' states without curiosity. Superstitions give rise to poetic licence and carry the potential to affect health and well-being due to cause and effect. Too often the *cause* of underperforming at sport slips undetected beneath hidden ego, causing us to dwell disproportionately on superstition's *effects* and less so on its *cause*.

No outright belief in the paranormal is ever as clear-cut as perhaps we first imagine. This gives rise to the cult of 'Superstitionism' and raises questions such as why, in retrospect, do the outcomes of superstitious actions rarely work out according to original intent? How can anyone tell if a superstition is reasonable without proof of a paranormal event ever having occurred? So where should we draw a line in the sand regarding what is fiction and what is real?

Superstitions polarise opinion as to whether their inclusion in sporting itineraries adds tangible value to how athletes perform. Consider the following scenario as humorously conveyed by former Welsh International footballer Dean Saunders on *Sky Sports*: *Goals on Sunday* regarding his time spent at Newcastle United FC coaching iconic striker Shola Ameobi. Shola was affectionately known on Tyneside as 'The Mackem Slayer' in reference to his extraordinary goal scoring record against derby rivals Sunderland AFC.

Here is Dean's account of Shola's post-match interview after scoring two important goals, *"Shola said, 'I would like to thank the Lord for giving me the strength to score two goals today.'"* However, Dean, who was once a prolific striker in his own right was clearly unimpressed and responded by saying, *"All week I've been training with him. So, Monday morning I come in and I said, 'Shola, talk me through your interview after the game.'"*

Shola happily obliged and began recounting his interview word-for-word. Whereupon, a clearly bemused Saunders interrupted proceedings by demanding to know, *"Where was the Lord last week at Wigan when you missed three open goals?"*

Quick-as-a-flash, unbowed and unrepentant, Shola responded with an incredible retort, *"The Lord was looking after our goalkeeper that week."*

It was priceless to witness the look of resignation on Dean's face as he recounted the tale. It also felt surreal to hear Shola assert his fairy tale hypothesis with such authority as though it was a fact. By humorously recounting Shola's tale live on air, Dean at least brought the topic of superstition sharply into focus. Shola's explanation was so absurd that co-presenter Chris Kamara, as he struggled to compose himself during an uncontrollable bout-of-laughter, replied, *"You can't win, can you?"*

Chris had perfectly summed up the culture of superstitious ignorance surrounding sport. Common sentiments such as 'why reinvent the wheel' or 'if it ain't broke don't fix it' are prevalent in sport. Both equally apply to superstition and translate as 'who cares if a superstitious assertion is true if we're already convinced that it works?' This type of thinking constructs superstitious premises having already concluded that they're true.

Superstition has no respect for status and no one is immune from the dogma superstition creates. It's naive to assume that knowledge alone is enough to evade indoctrination since knowledge is merely a subset of belief, while belief is relative to the information we're given or willing or able to receive. For this reason, it feels appropriate to draw this chapter to a close by lauding the insights of every contributor to this thought-provoking compilation of superstitious related stuff.

Almost every contributor, throughout their illustrious career, has walked a veritable tightrope between micromanaging superstitious ideals and performing successfully to full stadiums, packed auditoriums, or to live television audiences. Now that's pressure! So, who couldn't use a little supernatural help?

A tale of awareness

Education should not be preparation for life - education *should be* life. There is a story in Eastern philosophy which tells of the son of a burglar who noticed his father was growing old. The boy asked, *"Father, can you teach me your trade so that when you retire I may carry on the family business?"*

His father did not reply, but later that night took the boy along with him to break into a house. Once inside he opened a large wardrobe and asked his son to find out what lay within. However, as soon as the lad stepped inside, the father slammed and bolted the door behind him, making such a commotion in the process that the whole house was awakened; at which point the father slipped quietly away.

The boy was terrified and angry, but also puzzled as to how to make his escape. Fortunately, an idea flashed into his mind and so he began to make the noise of a

28

cat, whereupon the housekeeper who came to investigate, unbolted the door to let the cat out. Seizing his opportunity, the boy sprang out as the housekeeper gave chase.

Upon running outside and spotting a well by the roadside, the boy threw in a large stone and then hid in the shadows before stealing away, while his pursuer peered into the depths hoping to see the burglar drown. Back home, the boy forgot his anger in his eagerness to retell the incredible story, but instead his father simply remarked, *"Why tell me the tale, you are here and that is enough. You have learned the trade."*

This metaphorical tale reaffirms that education should not be preparation for life - education *should be* life. The boy's father was aware that a thousand words could not empower his son to the same extent as the learning gained by experiencing the danger, thrill, and excitement of events for himself. The father knew there was talking and then there was 'being', and that 'being' is a personal revelation which he must experience on his own.

Imagine the thoughts which flowed through the boy's mind from inside the dark and dingy wardrobe. Questions such as 'why did my dad leave me?' and 'what now?' followed by thoughts of fear, anger, retribution, self-preservation, and self-doubt. Quickly, however, as reality began to hit home, he became less mindful of unnecessary mental clutter and instead rapidly readjusted his thoughts to focus on the immediate tasks at hand.

In a brief moment of deep contemplation, the boy added another skill to his quest for survival. It was the skill of 'mindlessness' whereby he ceased being mindful of things with no relevance to the task at hand. Instead, he embraced a new state of 'being', perhaps best described as having 'no mind' (mindlessness). It was from within this new form of stateless thinking that he dismissed any thoughts which were surplus to his immediate well-being and could finally focus on the most lucid factor of all, which was executing his escape.

If we retrace the boy's escape from the initial point where he used his cunning to trick the housekeeper into believing he had drowned, to the outpouring of elation when telling his dad of his escapade, then it's easy to miss amid all the chaos, that the boy had discovered the sole purpose of life is not to be dead – which is quite an epiphany.

To experience the sensation of not being dead, try being alive, feeling alert, and acting as though every moment is exhilarating and intoxicating since sport mirrors our lives in microcosm. Hence, our approach towards life influences our approach towards competitive sport. So grab what lessons we can from the son of the burglar who expanded his talent and scope for spontaneity by pushing boundaries and taking risks.

Despite mounting pressure, the boy could not rely on divine intervention by an invisible friend, or on a lucky rabbit's foot or four-leafed clover bailing him out of his predicament. No external agent was necessary, nor was advice from his dad. All it took was the confidence to trust his own initiative to engineer his escape. Living life is not only a journey of self-discovery, but also a profound mystery which we won't edge any closer to unravelling by adding greater mysteries based solely on faith.

My objective when compiling this information is to challenge each reader to seek to believe as many true things as possible and as few things which are false. In conclusion, when appraising superstitions of whichever ilk, keep in mind that extraordinary claims require extraordinary evidence and that each claim should demonstrably exist independent of belief.

Beliefs manifest in our brain and not in the heart, which is a common misconception based on sentimentality. Irrespective of sincerity, the heart is not a 'reasoning' object, but an organ designed to pump blood. Common sentiments, therefore, such as 'my heart tells me so' are rendered obsolete once sentimentality is eliminated from the equation, since the heart has never been scientifically proven to possess supernatural powers capable of influencing how we feel and think.

There is nothing profound about competing at sport; so why add superstitious ideals? Why add anything at all? Why do athletes search for something profound before feeling able to compete? Let's follow the evidence for superstitious compliance as compiled from the insights of sporting elite to determine what superstition may hold in store for us. And where better to start than to question if we can be spontaneous and superstitious at the exact same time since both exist in direct conflict?

Throughout his ordeal, the burglar's son discovered words are superfluous to 'being' since words do not have meanings, merely usages, as do common metaphors such as 'why reinvent the wheel?' Yet, the fear of transitioning is what keeps athletes locked into superstition on an ever-revolving loop, to such an extent that escaping from faith becomes a gamble similar to rolling a dice or spinning a wheel.

"Faith has to do with things that are not seen, and hope with things that are not at hand."

- Saint Thomas Aquinas, Priest

What are Superstitions?

"A psychologist would always say you should control the controllable, but you're not in control of the weather, you're not in control of the opposition, you're not in control of the audience, or the crowd, or the event. That's all beyond you."

- Sir Matthew Pinsent, Olympic Rower

During an episode of ITV's popular series *I'm a Celebrity...Get Me Out of Here!* I once had the misfortune to witness a contestant reluctantly chewing on a kangaroo's 'bits'. Part of the jungle challenge was to swallow the offending delicacy in order to win food for her hungry team. As the torturous entertainment began to unfold, I was struck by a startling observation when the contestant was asked by a curious host to describe the taste of the kangaroo's nether regions.

With face painfully contorted and feeling nauseous, the contestant replied, *"It tastes like chicken."* Yet, it did not taste like chicken, it tasted like kangaroo, but I recalled having already heard a similar response to various other delicacies, such as frog's legs and snails. The chicken phenomenon of Western appeal is symptomatic of trying to describe the indescribable, with no benchmark or context with which to compare. A common tendency appears to exist whereby, once we experience unfamiliar tastes, our default position is chicken.

It seems we'd rather say *something* than admit to not knowing since not knowing induces a sense of powerlessness due to things which exist beyond our control. We are creatures of context but defined by non-contextual ideas, and we possess an uncanny eagerness to base our beliefs on what something *isn't* as opposed to what it *is*. If there is one major flaw in human psychology, it's a collective reluctance to accept that there are things which exist that we simply don't know.

Superstitious manifestations are non-contextual since we can't say that they work and we don't know what they are. Try to hone any athlete's understanding of how superstitions work and they probably won't know, or challenge them to stop activating superstition and they probably won't, or worse still, can't. Who could have foreseen such a correlation between superstition and the taste of a kangaroo's bits, yet, explanations for each cause a common conundrum of trying to describe the indescribable while our imagination dines on unimaginable cuisine. Anyone for chicken?

Omenology

Bookmakers and punters thrive and despair in equal measure at the random effects of superstitions and omens deciding the outcome of competitive sport. So, both parties conspire to elicit prior knowledge of sporting patterns, cycles, and trends before setting the value of betting odds or deciding what value to place on each punt. Most striking, however, is how each conspires to attribute value to the supernatural nature of superstitious beliefs, but are superstitions ever fully warranted or just pie-in-the-sky?

Consider the following commentary from the 2014 World Cup final, as the match between footballing giants Argentina and Germany entered extra time. Commentator Gary Lineker shared a rather innocuous and seemingly random observation as he quipped, *"Perhaps a good omen for Argentina is that the last two World Cup finals which went to extra time were won by teams playing in blue or dark blue; if you believe any of that sort of nonsense."*

Gary sounded dismissive of the curious statistic, but given his role was simply to read the statistics in a so-called democracy of free-thinkers, he was under no obligation to believe the statistics himself. Yet the throwaway manner of this statistical pattern failed to take stock of its psychological impact on an audience of millions in a betting culture where such information is often taken as gospel, thereby influencing potential betting sequences and trends.

A live broadcast of this magnitude does not have such statistics coincidentally at hand; they fulfil a specific purpose. Otherwise, if they were truly irrelevant and nonsensical, then why mention them at all? So did he use the statistic as a convenient means to fill valuable airtime and keep viewers amused during any lulls? To impressionable viewers who picked up on Gary's statistic, it may seem like a valuable piece of insider intel and may even carry additional weight because it was Gary Lineker providing the facts.

Gamblers often look to signs and omens to determine their next calculable punt, so did Gary's stacked statistic inadvertently act as a deciding factor in terms of the value gamblers were willing to stake on their next punt? In other words, to a gambler, might Gary's words have seemed almost prophetic, as though a sign from the gods? Such statistics to a gambler are often viewed as equivalent to a dead cert and may tip the balance in favour of betting the shirt off their back.

The human brain searches diligently for patterns and trends and is a sucker for context since context makes us believe we control our own minds. When events unfolded, however, Argentina (playing in blue) lost to Germany at the final hurdle, much to the delight of bookmakers and tipsters alike. They had titillated the thoughts of willing punters with speculative innuendo of finances aplenty by releasing statistics highlighting that the last two World Cup finals which went to extra time were won by teams playing in blue or dark blue.

The ambiguity escalated even further when Gary conveyed how, up to that point, no European side had ever managed to lift the World Cup on South American soil. To pathological gamblers, statistics such as these provide confirmation-bias that safe bets do actually exist. Yet in terms of what actually transpired during the match, in the space of thirty pulsating minutes of extra-time, two long-standing myths were forever quashed at no obvious cost to Lineker.

Gary appeared to dismiss the legend-and-lore of both superstitions, and on both occasions was proved correct. Yet, who counted the cost to hapless punters or to countless gamblers with betting addictions who felt compelled to place a bet based on Gary's statistical innuendo? Who measures the impact on punters who staked more than just their reputation on the belief that fate and probability would intervene on their behalf, thanks to Gary's longstanding statistical gems?

It's not only punters who embrace superstitious kidology to increase their sporting odds. Consider the following article which appeared on the *talkSPORT* radio website in reference to a Danish football player who at the time was a recent arrival at Tottenham Hotspur FC. It told of the reluctance of Christian Eriksen to vacate the London hotel where he was temporarily situated as he believed it may curse his excellent start at his new club. Christian remarked, *"It has been a good first week. I am still living in a hotel, so perhaps I should stay in the hotel."*

Superstitions can be likened to the properties of a magnet, insomuch as they pull us in the direction of our beliefs; whereas omens and premonitions help fill the void between that which is conceivable and that which is possible, since many athletes believe that something is needed to plug the gap. They believe that superstitions have powers which can affect their ambitions and goals, irrespective of whether they can be demonstrated to work or not.

Omens and premonitions merely hint at the nature of impending fortune, to signal an upturn in sporting outcomes or raise awareness of an impending threat and performance decline. Superstitions exist in the space between appearance and reality, as was duly noted by playwright Oscar Wilde, who once famously said of superstition, *"I can stand brute force, but brute reason is quite unbearable. There is something unfair about its use. It is hitting below the intellect."*

Under your spell

Consider the following tabloid article by journalist Paul Jiggins which reported on Togo International footballer, Emmanuel Adebayor, who at the time was playing for Tottenham Hotspur FC. The story recounts how Emmanuel pleaded with boss Mauricio Pochettino to be allowed to return home to Africa immediately for personal reasons, though the club initially declined to reveal what those reasons were.

Paul reported that Emmanuel's plea came a matter of days after he'd claimed that his mother had placed a black magic curse on his head. Boss Pochettino explained Emmanuel's absence from a European cup match in Turkey by saying, *"Ade is in his country on a personal matter to fix something."* Yet, Mauricio's story was further exacerbated in a *Mirror* tabloid report by Gareth Roberts who elaborated even further by stating, *"The misfiring forward ramps up [the] family feud with claims [that] his mother used juju to stop him hitting the back of the net."*

The story further intensified in superstitious essence when Emmanuel's brother Kola reportedly told *The Sun on Sunday* that *"Emmanuel has been brainwashed by Muslim Alfas – [these are] spiritual men who prophesise when he scores and why he is not playing well. They have convinced him [that] his sister and mother put juju curses on him."* Note how often superstitious beliefs depict shades of fabrication, truth, mystery, obscurity, and shadow from which it becomes difficult to derive any form of sense.

The aforementioned traits when combined form the two most prominent factors in every contingency of competitive sport: 'shades of love' and 'shades of fear'. Every human action originates from one trait or the other, yet even love and fear pale in significance to the greatest smokescreen of all, which is the hidden power of 'shades'. Every superstition is tinged by its own unique shade of fabrication and truth, which leads athletes to become economical with the truth, irrespective of any facts.

Consider the plight of Emmanuel being publicly ridiculed by both Tottenham fans and media alike for a series of under par performances. Yet the circumstance of his fear further served to highlight the hidden impact of the encroaching shadow which lurks perilously behind the scenes of competitive sport. Who among us can remotely imagine Emmanuel's emotions at that particular time, or the practical impact on his psychology of an alleged curse hanging over his head?

Who can truly envisage being born into a culture laced with juju magic, superstitions, spells, suspicion, trepidation, anxiety, and fear? Perhaps we already belong to such a culture, given the superstitions of every religion and culture remain fully dependent on the mercy of whichever shades of belief tip the balance in our favour or to our detriment at any given period in time.

> *"To become a religion, it is only necessary for a superstition to enslave a philosophy."*
>
> - William Ralph Inge, Professor of Divinity

Who among us believes that our superstitious fears differ from the fears of Emmanuel Adebayor, or in terms of authenticity, that our beliefs are more credible or less ambiguous than his? Yet surely the threat of a biblical hell creates a similar sense of trepidation, despite no proof of concept to justify subjecting our overriding psychology to such abject fear.

How consistent are we regarding the authenticity of omens, prophecies, or of juju being prevalent in Western sport? Is it any less practical to blame juju for Adebayor's performances than it is to blame a long-standing curse for County Mayo losing the All-Ireland GAA final to Dublin in 2016? Consider the following humorous comment by pundit Peter Canavan: *"It's the curse of Mayo. Isn't that what they say?"* This referred to the ongoing 'Curse of 51', which is renowned within Mayo as having damned their entire county football squad to failure since 1951.

The year 1951 incidentally was the last time Mayo won the All Ireland title (Sam McGuire Cup). The story refers to an urban myth of the returning victorious *51* Gaelic football squad who travelled through the village of Foxford in a vibrant mood but neglected to pay due respect to a funeral cortege nearby. Consequently, an enraged local priest cursed the team and the county, saying that for as long as any member of the *51* team remained alive, Mayo would never win another All Ireland title.

In an additional twist, in 2013 a local priest was reported in the *Irish Mirror* as having lifted the supposed hex by offering an official blessing for the entire Mayo squad at the exact spot on the bridge over the River Moy where the curse was imposed. Yet, three years following the blessing, it was still a case of 'as you were,' as once again Dublin overcame Mayo in a pulsating replay to reclaim the All Ireland crown and add weight to the escalating myth of the Mayo Curse.

It is also worth noting that as Dublin lifted the trophy, only two members of the *51* team remained alive. So in retrospect, the London media and Tottenham fans ridiculed and maligned footballer Emmanuel Adebayor for succumbing to the psychology of juju magic, while only a short distance across the Irish Sea, a similar superstitious juju was equally prevalent under the guise of the tale of the Mayo Curse.

In a further twist, Irish TV channel *TG4* commissioned a programme entitled 'Mayo God Help Us' to highlight the curse. This was somewhat ironic since the title implied seeking help from a superstition called God to nullify the superstition known locally as the Mayo Curse, and if that's not circular reasoning then I don't know what is.

Such anomalies are common in sports psychology. Why is it, for instance, that some teams seem predestined to win or lose against certain opponents or at specific venues? Why does the bounce of the ball often seem to favour certain opponents but never us? Or, why do the careers of certain athletes appear constantly blighted by substantial injuries, whereas others get to compete for sustained periods injury free? What powers lie behind such unfair phenomena? Is it karma, juju, coincidence, luck, or mistaken psychology?

Emmanuel's fear of juju occurred in London in 2014. While in Ireland, sports pundits and fans couldn't help but imply that Mayo losing the 2016 All-Ireland final was already predestined due to the ongoing consequence of the Mayo Curse, all because two members of the *51* team were still alive. So irrespective of culture, superstition is still prevalent in the current mindset of sports elite.

The What Chromosome

To help gain a better understanding of what constitutes superstitious belief, we must first seek a better understanding of the 'self', since the concept of 'self' is a fix and a scam. It is a self-induced ploy to prevent us from experiencing the present by interlocking our emotions with feelings of sentimentality and nostalgia which belong in the past. Superstitious belief is merely an extension of the 'self' and a form of mental stagnation which locks us in a state of arrested development from which it is difficult to escape.

A curious hypothesis with three components governs our superstitious thoughts:

1. Minus falsifiable context, we lack true comprehension.
2. Minus true comprehension, we lack awareness.
3. Minus awareness, we feel justified in believing whatever we like.

Competitive sport is a process of 'becoming'. For the majority of their careers, most athletes are one step away from 'being', since superstitious faith locks them into aspirations of 'becoming', despite always being one step away from securing their goals. It also tricks them into channelling less mental energy into dealing with the present, to focus instead on what happens next if they dare venture beyond the constraints of their faith.

In a similar vein, the philosophy of theism stifles critical thinking by averting mental energy towards circular reasoning on a continuous loop. Curiosity is superstition's greatest enemy as it throws a spanner in the works of naively conceding the power of inquiry to external sources, thereby leaving us free to contemplate the idea that talent and personal genius are already intrinsic, independent of faith.

Many athletes and coaches point to the sky to acknowledge gods. The superstition called god, however, cannot seemingly be accessed for sport alone, but comes fully-equipped as a package deal with explicit directives for attaining an 'afterlife' (depending on which brand of god), whereby once again the human gaze must extend beyond the here and the now. Welcome to the world of superstitious tricknology, where the true extent of human value lies somewhere beyond the here and now, and the existence we currently experience is a toilet stop or a halfway house on the road to somewhere else.

It's important to sleep with one eye open as the brain is a hub for 'I am' psychology and for the accumulation of delusional 'I ams'. Some examples of which are "I am the best competitor in this field, so naturally I am expected to win," "I am feeling the pressure," "I am better than that," "I am letting people down," "I am not performing as I should," "I am not good enough," or "I am disappointed with myself." Too many competitors are constrained by thinking too much about what comes 'next', but have forgotten how to experience what's happening 'now'.

The inherent need for athletes to achieve often calls for desperate measures, and nothing is more desperate than superstitious beliefs. Once they become hooked on a superstitious delusion, they lose sight of the gift of unique perspective and stack ritual upon ritual and habit upon habit until stacking rituals and habits forms their new way of being and shapes their new delusionary sense of self.

Superstitious belief is universal, but to gain a clearer understanding of how we currently identify with such beliefs, first we must foster a clearer understanding of how best to identify with ourselves. This can start by acknowledging how supernatural fixations can leave us vulnerable to forgetting that our talents, personal genius, inbuilt spontaneity, and thirst for curiosity are already functional, already operational, and already intact.

Sometimes it's easy to forget that we're already fully functional and fully operational without any need for superstitious beliefs or mysterious fallacies founded in ignorance creeping into the way we think about sport. Many athletes subscribe to unfalsifiable context with a superstitious pretext to keep fear in check. This I refer to as 'un-contextualised being', since 'being' is the primary context required to compete. Even if it were possible to remove all human desire to strive and endeavour, the concept of 'being' would still exist.

Irrespective of whether we are successful or unsuccessful at sport, or in personal relationships or business, the fact remains that we still 'are'. Whether we exist as the product of natural selection, were created by agents beyond current comprehension, or are just brains in a vat, we still 'are'. Just as whether we win or lose, or identify as theists, atheists, agnostics, or simply as humanists, yep you guessed it, we still 'are'! Even direction is merely a bonus since our lives need neither direction nor context in order to continue to exist. So, whether we have direction or not, we still 'are'.

Sports performances are often rudderless and lack context and direction, yet guess what? It turns out, irrespective of how we perform, we still bloody well 'are'. Context is subjective in terms of how we choose to interpret semantics and indeed the world. A starving child, for instance, in most western societies typically equates as a hungry child; whereas a starving child in a third-world environment more typically equates, by way of generic interpretation, as a child close to death.

Oh, and just as a matter of interest, there is no such thing as a Third World. There is only one world and we live in it together, and any suggestion to the contrary is disingenuous, ethically suspect, and a myth. Interpretation influences our actions, and every action sparks a reaction, hence our interpretations determine the nature of our response. To delve into superstitious interpretation in more detail, I asked former England Test cricketer and Captain of Middlesex, Ed Smith, for his initial thoughts on superstitious beliefs. Here is his response:

"Goran Ivanisevic, the Croatian tennis player used to watch the Teletubbies cartoon every day throughout Wimbledon the year that he won. He actually got into a routine of watching kid's television in the morning, and once he got on a winning streak he thought, 'I obviously can't change this winning habit I've got.' So, what happens with superstitions is that people infer a cause or relationship between two random things.

Watching Teletubbies probably didn't help Goran to win his first game. You can be pretty sure it was down to his serving, his ground strokes, and self-belief. But, as soon as he started to think there was a cause or a relationship there, he couldn't give it up and he became attached to it, and that's what happens with superstitions.

You know one of the most superstitious athletes is tennis star Rafael Nadal, who lines up his water bottles next to his chair and makes sure that the labels are facing-out towards the court. He also had a phase where he didn't like to step on the line while he was serving. So he'd kind of tip-toe around the line like it was made of hot coals.

I had a few [superstitions]. I used to line my cricket bats up so I would always have three bats which I wasn't using. I'd make sure they were all in the right order and all that kind of stuff. They had to be facing out towards the dressing room. So bats leaning against the wall and facing outwards and all that kind of crazy stuff."

Listening intently to Ed reminded me of a colleague who once invited me to an art showing at a public gallery where he turned my attention to a specific painting and asked how much I thought it was worth. My first impression of the sprawling mesh of colour was that it had been randomly thrown at the canvas by a two-year-old child.

Perhaps I have no eye for appreciating art, but that soon became irrelevant since before I could reply, my colleague offered his own 'cultured' opinion: "It's not worth the bloody canvas it's painted on," he jibed sarcastically. "But some idiot has just agreed to pay hundreds of pounds in Sterling to own it. Can you believe that?" He then asked, looking somewhat perplexed, "So go on then, what's your evaluation and how much would you pay?"

This time without pause, I replied, "Then hundreds of pounds is its actual worth. It's worth exactly the amount that someone is prepared to pay since that is clearly its value to them."

My colleague shook his head in disgust, as I had failed to share in his sarcasm and artful distaste. Superstitions exist, but only come into being when we afford them enough value (as with the painting) to grow their own set of legs, except this time, instead of exhibiting water colours, we exhibit compliance to a bizarre set of rituals, compulsions, habits, and routines. Superstition thrives in secrecy and shadow, but occasionally we exhibit our superstitions in full view of others, almost by way of a badge of honour.

Why not simply discard our superstitions as soon as we notice a dip in form, or lose a match, or get knocked out in a fight, or beaten in a race? Are we confusing sporting aspirations with sporting beliefs? The more we believe that superstitions add value, the greater our sense of ownership becomes, thereby increasing the difficulty we experience in letting go of our habits once and for all.

Superstitions can't activate on their own. This is wonderfully illustrated by the following quote from Cecily Morgan, *"What you put up with, you end up with."* Very few sentiments are simpler than that. So how do we become the people we truly aspire to be. It isn't scientific, it's by refusing to become defined by our past, and that requires choices. We can choose to cultivate superstitious emotions (self-delusions), or we can choose to let go of the past. Superstitions burden us with past values, so here is a short tale to raise awareness of the importance of unburdening debilitating beliefs:

One day two monks walked through a forest and came upon a stream where a woman was struggling to cross. One monk agreed with the woman to carry her safely to the opposite bank. As the day wore on, the monk who had not carried the woman across, despite saying very little, appeared animated, livid, and visibly-annoyed.

The silence continued for a few miles until, unable to contain his anger any longer, the second monk broke his self-imposed silence and raged, "Our order prevents us from contact with women. I cannot believe you would dare to carry that woman across the stream." He was taken aback, however, when in response he was met by a somewhat surprising smile as the first monk very humbly and meekly replied, "Brother, I put that woman down miles ago. Why are you still carrying her around?"

It is a tale of 'let-go-ness' and self-enlightenment, which begs the following questions: Are we aware of the traits we are carrying around on our backs? Why are superstitious beliefs so increasingly difficult to lay to rest? What percentage of an athlete's sporting mentality is unnecessary mental clutter, serving only to subdue and to prevent them from transitioning beyond the constraints of unfounded supernatural beliefs? How many beliefs which once seemed so important are no longer, in hindsight, remotely meaningful today?

How can we distinguish superstitious beliefs which enhance positive mental stimulus from those which eat away at our mental resilience like a corrosive rust? The moment we feel mentally beholding to a superstitious ideal, we are no longer free of will since both concepts are irreconcilable. So why bother appealing to supernatural stewardship when the total number of times which supernatural causation has been confirmed by scientific peer-review as having physically altered the course of a sporting outcome is nil.

It's important for coaches to establish rapport by opening their mind to recognising that the bizarre eccentricities and quirks so often displayed by their sporting peers seem real to them. How else can they earn the respect of superstitious peers than to recognise the perceived authenticity behind even the most bizarre belief? Only by engaging in open conversations can coaches fully explore the motivational drivers which compel athletes to dispense with rationality in favour of acting out superstitions which have never been evidenced to work.

There's a reason why few athletes seem keen to admit to superstitious quirks. It's to avoid the ridicule and scorn which invariably ensues by deviating from conventional norms, and so it's simply much easier to keep their behaviours suppressed. The key to maintaining a healthy pathology is acknowledging the various addictive traits behind the people we have painstakingly become.

The left hemisphere of the human brain is sequential and pattern-orientated. As such, our everyday thoughts lend to everyday habits to create everyday meaning which clouds our everyday judgements and tests our everyday resolve. Former international cricketing star, Ed Smith, revealed everyday patterns when he spoke of superstitions being akin to *"an inferred cause and relationship between random events"*.

Since I had the pleasure of Ed's attention, I grasped the opportunity to delve further into the superstitions he had amassed during his career in top-flight cricket. In particular, the origins of his beliefs, since only through curiosity can we elicit answers to sports' many intangibles and discover what lies behind the mental anomalies that make us tick. Here is Ed's response:

"That's a really good question, I don't know where my superstitions came from... well actually, some of them came about because I had done them on the morning of my first ever game in first-class cricket, during which I scored a century, so I became attached to them for that reason. [But] whether it was sitting in a particular corner of the dressing room at Cambridge, drinking a can of Lucozade Sport, or reading The Times newspaper - I don't know.

And where did some other ones which came to me later in my career come from? Why did I become attached to touching my Velcro gloves and rubbing my wrists together in a certain way? When did it first happen that you think, that's what made the difference? It's impossible to know. One thing I do know though, it's a lot easier to accumulate superstitions than to dispense with them."

So, what lay behind Ed's cricketing eccentricities? Perhaps the answer lies in the following sentiment by cartoonist Bill Watterson, who humorously suggests, *"If you can't win by reason, go for volume."* Whatever the source of Ed's curious behaviours, his superstitions grew legs by their own volition, thereby taking on a life of their own.

Every superstitious action and subsequent behaviour is merely the past being reframed and repeated on a continuous loop. Consider how prevalent the following 5000-year-old (or older) superstition remains in the 21st century; the one about walking beneath a ladder. It supposedly dates back to ancient Egypt and suggests that a ladder leaning against a wall and forming a triangle represented the trinity of the gods. Yet it still carries the same misapprehensions and impact as it did many thousands of years ago.

We are 21st-century hybrids of an accumulated past. To this end, consider the intuitive impact which accumulative memory has on our brain. An example of which is the common occurrence known as 'energy transmission'. This psychic phenomenon (superstition) seemingly communicates universal energies straight to our brain. All of us have awareness of energy transmission, but may not realise the extent to which we are subliminally aware.

To help refresh your memory, try to visualise purchasing a beautiful house minus any prior knowledge of a horrendous tragedy having recently occurred within its walls. Next, consider whether you would still be as enamoured with the property's beauty and value if all of a sudden you were informed of its terrible history and of the shocking events which recently took place. Would you still be as keen to complete the deal? Or might you fear that its energy will transmit its bad vibes onto you and that somehow you too may catch its negative energy? In retrospect, might you seek to avoid the scenario altogether by telling yourself that it's not worth the risk?

Surely logic suggests that only a fool is unable to separate bricks-and-mortar from human tragedy. Yet we can't rely on our brain for reliability since the brain seeks to replicate information-bias using confirmation-bias to further justify our beliefs. As things stand, the house is still just a bloody house, and although the incident was naturally tragic, rationality suggests that it's not *our* tragedy to bear. Logic dictates that the tragic history should not detract from the resellable value of the property, but there's nothing logical about supernatural beliefs.

Energy transmission is a sobering occurrence, as is the following sentiment: 'If you lie down with dogs, you wake up with fleas'. As sentiments go, this sounds pretty horrendous and definitely something we'd try hard to avoid. Consider our natural apprehension at the very idea of contracting fleas. Ugh! Plus the added furore and social stigma which would invariably ensue if news were to leak of our irritable flea infestation. If we lie down with dogs, we may awaken with fleas. Similarly, if we lie down with beliefs of a supernatural nature, we may awaken to find that our minds are infested with superstitious ideals.

"One can resist the invasion of an army, but one cannot resist the invasion of ideas."

- Victor Hugo, French Poet

Einstein once said, *"It is easier to split an atom than a prejudice."* In hindsight, his surmise highlights a very astute and insightful awareness of human conditioning and is an accurate testimony to our obstinate stubbornness, inflexibility, and belligerence once ideals become firmly affixed in our minds. How many of us can recall when we first became smitten, corrupted, or infected by superstitious prejudice, and what means can we use to consciously tell? Prejudice is a process of forming judgments (information bias and confirmation bias) which affirm our interpretations of truth.

It may be wise to sleep with one eye open since if our guard were to slip, we may catch a prejudice. At which point, as Einstein suggests, it becomes easier to split an atom than to disengage from such an inflexible state of mind. So what compels us to bow to superstitious prejudice? Whose expectations are we trying so desperately to meet, and how often do we consider the psychological toll and impact of other people's demands on us?

Are we simply the pawns of energy transmission, trying desperately to respond to the energies (vibes) inflicted upon us by sporting contemporaries? Who is pulling the strings when it comes to performing, and who is calling the shots when it comes to defining realistic targets and goals? Who gets to decide what constitutes sporting success? Are we in control of our superstitions or does superstition control us? In which case, we acquire our beliefs by proxy at the behest of something external, and that's worse again.

All superstitions require interference from invisible agents which extend beyond us and also beyond the physical world in which we exist. Consider the impact of spending a lifetime feeling indebted to third party agents. Surely it would feel similar to tapping a stranger on the shoulder and asking, *"Excuse me, what do you demand of me today?"* Or worse still, *"How should I be feeling emotionally about how I performed?"* What makes athletes appeal with such regularity to supernatural agents?

Who is calling the shots with regard to which energy we choose to receive or deflect? Is winning our overall objective for sport? If so, for whom or for what are we working our asses off? When did winning take precedence over competing, and why allow superstitions to enter the fray? Perhaps the answer lies in this Tamil proverb: 'Known is a drop. Unknown is an ocean'. Proverbs are renowned adaptations of enlightening words by wise sages and astute seers. Sometimes they occur as innocent truisms of those on the cusp of seemingly experiencing the divine, while on other occasions, proverbs slip unexpectedly from the mouths of fools.

The primary purpose of considering proverbs is to uncover the hidden veil of superstitious ignorance which is cloaking our minds from the spontaneous genius secreted within. But what caused us to take our eyes off the ball and to become less observant, less aware, and perhaps even devoid of caring whether our superstitious beliefs are true or false?

There is nothing profound about superstitions; they occur as a result of taking our eye off the ball. To explain this concept further, consider the following humorous tale from *The Telegraph*. It is a comedic anecdote of slapstick proportions, involving a woman going about her business in an American shopping mall. Unfortunately, she was so preoccupied with texting on her phone that she drifted towards an ornamental fountain, tripped, and then fell headfirst into the water as onlookers watched on aghast.

During the fallout from the curious incident, talk of a lawsuit began to emerge as the woman and representatives of the mall failed to agree on the definitive cause. But what *was* the underlying cause? Was it the woman's complete lack of focus due to being distracted by her phone? Or should the positioning of the fountain see her absolved of any blame, even though it seemed harder to hit than to miss? What caused the woman to take her eye off the ball, and who was most proportionately at fault, the mall, the woman, or the phone?

Superstitious beliefs are every bit as distracting as the woman's mobile proved to be, only this time the visual impairment revolves around being no longer able to envisage how our lives used to look prior to superstition's distracting allure. It is estimated that 90% of an iceberg lies submerged beneath the ocean's surface, just as 90% of our potential to exercise scepticism and curiosity may lie equally submerged beneath the remoteness of superstitious beliefs.

Earlier I referred to a Tamil proverb which stated that 'known is a drop'. Hence a drop of awareness is all that's required to start plotting a course for self-correction so that we may implement preventative action before superstitions are allowed to prevail. It's time to steer our thoughts past energy transmissions in search of unchartered territories where we are no longer reliant on confirmation-bias masquerading as fact. All we need to set sail is the guts to be daring, and the most daring part of human nature is daring to be unique.

Here is yet another Tamil proverb to stem any flow of spontaneity from being sucked into the mire of nostalgic belief: 'Defeat the defeat, before the defeat defeats you'. It is a call to action so that we may reverse every superstition which claims to add value to our competitive state. Very few competitors (if any) are free from belief in superstition, mainly due to the realisation that they all have something to lose. This makes perfect sense if we stop to consider that experiencing defeat means losing something of value, and that we are suffering as a result.

Athletes who are prone to energy transmission transmit energies so powerful, intoxicating, and potent that they create the illusion that they cannot afford to discard their beliefs at any cost, no matter how bizarre. Athletes try to avoid being disrespectful to supernatural ideals, lest they fall victim to calamity, fall prey to catastrophe, attract unnecessary adversity, or invite bad luck into their midst. How many athletes do we know who would be willing to take such a risk and dispense with their current belief systems? Come to think of it, would we?

Who among us is willing to run the risk of antagonising 'the supernatural' in case its feelings get hurt or it decides to take umbrage at such an affront and returns to haunt us out of retribution and spite? Welcome to the world of energy transmission, where every thought is our ally, greatest enemy, most trusted confidant, or untrustworthy foe. Energy transmission is rife in sport because athletes allow vibratory superstitious energy (personal vibes) based on impulse to dictate how they behave.

It is often the athletes who deal best with emotions who excel and become elite. So, perhaps now is the perfect time to consider that superstitious behaviours cause us to stumble (as did the woman into the fountain) while wide awake but with our eyes wide shut. So what does superstition look like in a practical sense? Consider the following example of superstitious conjecture as proudly asserted by Belfast boxer Carl Frampton during the lead up to his much-anticipated rematch with Mexican Leo Santa Cruz.

"Barry is a more religious man than I am and he wanted me to win that [Santa Cruz] fight. That's something Barry does still, and I know this because I've been told. He doesn't tell me, but each time I fight, no matter where I fight in the world, he goes and visits these nuns in Belfast who have been sworn to a vow of silence. They don't speak. They're not allowed to ask anything and he goes and sits with these nuns and he gives them teabags, bread, milk, that sort of stuff.

They aren't allowed to ask for anything but he asks them to pray for me. He doesn't know that I know that, and it shows you that he wants me to win. Nun's praying for a little Protestant boy from Belfast… it just doesn't happen. But it's happening for me and it's a good feeling. It's a really nice feeling."

Carl's revelation was broadcast on *UTV Sport* in January 2017 and detailed the actions of his former manager Barry McGuigan's pre-fight routine. The full quote is available in an article on a website perhaps aptly named *balls.ie*. What a wonderfully gracious and selfless gesture, yet the science behind it suggests that bribing nuns to implore divine intervention to meddle in terrestrial boxing affairs just doesn't stack up.

This is not meant as a negative retort but as a rational assertion, as once superstition enters the fray, the role of devil's advocate is to look beyond sentiment and separate what is 'probable' from what is 'possible'. So welcome back to the world of energy transmission, except this time it's Carl's former manager Barry McGuigan who sought to channel the energy (vibes) of nuns to secure success for his protégé.

Superstitions unearth many wonderful heart-warming stories. McGuigan's faith was unquestionable and his sincerity apparent, but sincerity is no guarantee against being dead wrong. Carl's fight later took place at the MGM Grand Garden Arena in Las Vegas, but despite the sincerity of manager McGuigan, Frampton suffered the first ever defeat of his professional career. No doubt the Nuns efforts were truly admirable, yet sadly their superstitious gesture fell on deaf ears.

What are the odds that every time a McGuigan boxer is due to fight he will repeat the superstition and sit with the nuns? With this in mind, I wish to share an idea that athletes are ensnared in an ongoing conflict between two very exacting types of truth, the *actual* truth and the *awful* truth, and that both truths form overriding precursors to every superstitious action they subsequently perform. If they retrace the origin of every superstitious compulsion, they will find it weighted in favour of an *actual* truth or *awful* truth.

To decode the elusive metaphorical DNA of which all superstitions are comprised, I crafted the following living template as an aid to deciphering truth. I call it *'The Actual Truth vs The Awful Truth Hypothesis'*. The *actual* truth refers to the *clarity of our perceptions,* while the *awful* truth charts the *accuracy of our response. Actual* truth realigns and interprets falsifiable facts using only the evidence available.

The *actual* truth relates solely to the evidence which, if laid out before us, would be tough to ignore, and only comes into play when the facts as presented can be verified scientifically. Once an athlete experiences a traumatic, ecstatic, or melodramatic event, the brain instantly strives to interpret meaning by making sense of whichever facts it can grasp or comprehend amidst whatever chaos ensues.

So where's the catch? Okay here goes. The *actual* truth, although seemingly definitive, does not exist on the strength of its merit alone, since running parallel in our mind whether we like it or not, is the *actual* truth's oldest adversary and sparring partner the *awful* truth. The *actual* truth relates to the clarity of our perceptions, while the *awful* truth relates to the accuracy of our response since each of us is more likely to respond accurately to any given scenario when we have access to quality information supported by facts.

Our behaviour in sport is only as accurate as our overriding beliefs since we cannot escape from the thoughts which go on in our mind until we replace each thought with alternative thoughts. The *actual* truth acts as a mirror and reflects our thoughts according to whichever facts can be scientifically explained, whereas the *awful* truth is comprised of whichever thoughts we believe, irrespective of scientific fact. Therefore, every decision we make in relation to sport is a product of *actual* or *awful* truth.

As an insight into my living template of contrasting truths, feel free to conduct the following social experiment and put both types of truth to the test. Select a few willing participants who happen to smoke and show them a variation of *actual* truths (the clarity of our perception) surrounding the dangers linked with smoking, and really spell it out. Next, highlight the latest medical research and statistical evidence to back up the facts.

This is not a moralistic or judgmental exercise to berate smokers but an opportunity to measure the smoker's 'won't power' against their subsequent 'willpower'. So have each smoker look closely at haunting photographs of the gaunt and forlorn faces of many typical patients undergoing serious treatment in the E.N.T Department (ear, nose, and throat), so they can visualise what may lie in store if they continue to smoke.

If all else fails and we feel we are not making sufficient headway, have them read the 'Cigarettes Can Kill' warning written on every cigarette packet. Then throw in a few extra considerations for good measure such as the high risk of cancer, danger of blocked arteries, asthmatic effects on breathing, risk to their children during pregnancy, bad breath, or subsequent poor health.

A non-smoker's psychology may be inclined to assume that such a shock to the system may lead to a smoking cessation, or at least lead to a process of curbing addiction over a sustained period of time. Yet, how many smokers in such an experiment are likely to stop? How many of *us* would be able to stop or would truly believe that we actually can, or that we possess enough willpower to permanently quit in spite of being addicted to chemical inducements and knowing that quitting may prove the difference between life and death?

Only two truths prevail in competitive sport, the *actual* truth and the *awful* truth, and the topic of superstition is no exception to this rule since all superstitions are predominantly governed by one of these contrasting truths. The most practical aim of sports psychology is learning to believe as many true things as possible and as few things which are demonstrably false.

It is said that what the eye sees disappears in a blink. So, speaking metaphorically, perhaps it's time to acknowledge the act of blinking as integral to reawakening our motivation for transitional change. At which point, the only question left unanswered when superstition meets scepticism is: who blinks first?

The Why Chromosome

"Demons are like obedient dogs. They come out when they are called."

- Remy De Gourmont, Poet

The Scorpion and the Frog:

A scorpion was once stranded at the water's edge and so he called out to a nearby frog to assist him across to the other side. *"Not a chance,"* said the frog. *"Once you're on my back, what is there to prevent you from stinging me and then I'll die."* The scorpion, however, using an entirely plausible argument, explained how it would be to both their detriments if he were to do so since if the frog were to die, then he too would surely drown.

"I guess that makes sense," said the frog, as the scorpion climbed on his back and they began to swim between lily pads to the other side. Suddenly the frog felt a sharp sting on his back and began to experience a warm sensation of paralysis coursing through his veins. In sheer panic, he turned to the scorpion and shrieked, *"you stung me, yet you promised you wouldn't!"*

"I know," said the scorpion with a look of sheer resignation due to realising his fate. *"But I just couldn't stop myself you see, it's in my nature."*

So there it is! If the question is 'why superstition?' then the answer is because it's in our nature. Yet, what's in our nature? What is this peculiarity called superstition, how does it manifest, how did it get there, and how exactly is it defined? Is superstition inherent and, if so, can we be held responsible for the way that we feel, act, think, and behave? Or perhaps we are subject to a strange form of genetic coding filtering through our DNA. What causes a superstitious nature, or is a cause even necessary?

Sport reflects our lives in microcosm. Consider how often athletes espouse wild tub-thumping proclamations of 'I achieved all my success through hard work and endeavour', or claim, 'if you work hard enough you can achieve anything'. Anything! Really, can we? Yet superstitious concepts such as luck, fate, fluke, or happenstance rarely get a mention, or in some circumstances are mentioned too often during athletes' winning addresses as they try their best to attribute a cause.

Many athletes attempt to create the illusion that their luck is somehow inherently down to themselves. Yet, what percentage of credit should an athlete bestow on luck as being the catalyst for their success? Or consequently, how much discredit should they heap upon luck when things go badly awry, or should they just blame themselves?

It took us a lifetime to become who we are. A lifetime of piecing together which images we wish to project onto our peers. Yet, something hereditary predates our optimism regarding our luck. Did we choose our parents prior to birth? Or what say had we in the upbringing of our parents, given their upbringing influenced the quality of whatever nurture they bestowed on us? Parental nurture can create a glass ceiling (unconscious barriers) which we subsequently inherit and often struggle to transition beyond.

On other occasions, the positivity of nurture we received from our parents, guardians, or peers enabled us grow up unafraid of being spontaneous and to be completely aloof to any idea that a glass ceiling ever existed at all. What type of nature or genetics did we gain from our parents? What are their unique skill-sets and talents, and have they been passed on to us?

Are we blessed or cursed by our inherited genetics, and to what extent are we still being influenced by our parents' ambitions, inhibitions, faiths, habits, hopes, and taboos? To what degree do their character traits, eccentricities, or phobias impact how we currently interpret the world? Not to mention the fallout from cultural influences which stems from the country, culture, or religion into which we were born. What say had we in any of that?

We are the embodiment of whichever information we accept and act upon and we need only look to the experiences of former long-suffering Warrington Rugby League forward and Great Britain star, Paul Wood, who shocked the rugby fraternity when his story *My Hell at OCD Struggle* was published in the *Daily Star*.

In the article Paul spoke of his crippling daily battle with OCD and his repeated battle to fight-off constant urges to do things over and over again. One such urge was the on-going need to strap and re-strap his arms upwards of ten times prior to every game before feeling enough at ease to go out and perform. On other occasions, the former Great Britain star felt unable to leave his home for days due to the illness and was reported to say,

"I am not embarrassed to say I have seen psychologists and taken medication. I knew I needed help because I couldn't sort it out on my own and emotionally it was

grinding me down. I remember when I played at Wembley, the week was a bit of a nightmare. I was doing bits of stuff thinking it would help us win the cup but it got to the point where it was taking over my life. You hear about mild forms of it where people might have to have the volume on the TV on an even number or they won't walk on cracks on flags [paving stones].

Little things like that. I have had it since I was a kid [15 or 16 years of age] but it was getting harder to deal with as it was spiralling out of control. How bad can it be? I can stand by a light switch and flick it on and off hundreds of times. I can spend half an hour parking my car in a supermarket car park driving forwards and then reversing time after time until I'm completely happy with its positioning.

If I don't do this then I panic. The only time I felt comfortable was at work, training, or playing because I knew my exact schedule and could control everything I did. I'd be on a high there and an increasing low everywhere else."

Paul further implied that he will always suffer from OCD (Obsessive Compulsive Disorder) but admitted that psychological help taught him how to cope and that the one situation he didn't mind dealing with prior to every game was when *"the physiotherapist goes mad and says I'm costing him a fortune by re-strapping my arms up to ten times. The other lads take the mickey out of me, but I can laugh along with them now about it."*

I tried to imagine Paul's sporting peers attempting to digest his incredible story in total disbelief since, to thousands of supporters and peers, he must have appeared to have the world at his feet. Fans would envy his standing in the sport, respect his tenacity, technique, and physique along with his never-say-die attitude on the pitch, plus the financial rewards which inevitably follow a rugby league star in his prime. Paul must have seemed to his peers like a very fortunate guy, and in most aspects, he was.

Paul's reality was that his debilitating thoughts ran adjacent to his emotions and were therefore close enough in proximity to destabilise his state of mind, this was mirrored by his obsession to repeat the same actions time-and-again. Yet, this behaviour was just the tip of the iceberg as his thoughts spiralled further out of control and grew darker and altogether more sinister by spilling into his life beyond the confines of sport.

The most telling revelation throughout the whole saga was how little mention there was of any rugby having been played since sport paled in significance compared to the state of Paul's mental health. So much for the myth that sport is only a game! In a practical sense, it's extremely unlikely that re-wrapping his bandages for the sixth time had any more bearing on his performance than his first bandage or his tenth.

Logic and reason suggests that the whole affair is somewhat bizarre, yet try telling that to Paul or his long-suffering family. Or imagine the struggle he faced while trying to dislodge such an illogical sequence of behaviour from such a compulsive state of mind. The social stigma attached to these types of compulsions are often demeaning to the well-being of athletes and coaches alike.

Social stigmas inhibit less confident athletes from expressing and sharing whatever mental turmoil they may be experiencing with sceptical peers. This is hardly surprising if we stopped to consider the reaction of our peers if they were to become aware of our superstitions or, if in turn, we were to become aware of theirs. Stigmas act as suppressants and sometimes depressants and attract little empathy and even less sympathy. Yet how do we distinguish between the domain where our mind is immersed in a superstitious reality and the domain of the clinically insane?

Perhaps we should be asking if athletes who are immersed in superstition are safe to be let loose on the streets given that many knowingly talk to invisible gods and worse still, the gods seemingly talk back. They also wear items of clothing inside-out, are convinced that numbers are lucky, and are paranoid about *not* wearing lucky pants. There are many definitions of 'clinically insane'. Two examples highlighted on *law.com* are 'mental illness of such a severe nature that a person cannot distinguish fantasy from reality' and 'subject to uncontrollable impulsive behaviour'.

Doctoral Fellow, Laura Marshall, of healthcare PR states on *Quora.com* that *"no self-respecting psychologist or psychiatrist I know ever uses that term [clinically insane]."* Either way, it appears that a common societal perception of clinically insane is someone non-responsive to rational thought compared to thoughts and behaviour which are generally accepted in a societal sense as being the norm, yet who can categorically define what constitutes 'the norm'.

Let's revisit the terminology which states, 'cannot distinguish between fantasy and reality', 'subject to uncontrollable impulsive behaviour', and 'deemed as being irrational compared to the norm', whatever norm is. Let's be honest, we all know someone like that, and if we don't then it's probably us.

The moment we accept vague and ambiguous terminologies as working templates with regards to what constitutes clinically insane, we automatically implicate and stigmatise athletes who are superstitious or have been diagnosed with OCD. Our corresponding behaviours may not be a danger to others, but any form of addiction can be harmful to us.

Perhaps being clinically insane is more aligned with the following definition, 'insanity is repeating the same mistakes over and over again but expecting different results'. This sounds eerily similar to the behaviour of superstitious athletes who moonwalk backwards onto a pitch before every game but continue to lose. Yet the athlete repeats the exact same behaviour time-after-time, while each time expecting different results. Logic such as this is at best irrational since superstitious athletes are just as prone to fantasy and out of touch with reality as earlier definitions of clinical insanity.

Consider the theist who is thoroughly convinced that the god of their choice is actively pulling strings to ensure they win while simultaneously ignoring their god's inactivity or ineptitude during a losing streak. Yet the theist implores God to intervene, only to be repeatedly let down. It all changes, however, when they muster a win, at which point their mind automatically clicks into confirmation-bias by choosing to ignore every previous occasion when their unstinting faith in a god demonstrably failed.

Superstitions are primarily about risk. We are running the risk of being proved right or being proved wrong. Yet take a glance at a dictionary or thesaurus and it's plain to see that what we *believe* differs significantly from what it means to actually *know* because both words mean entirely separate things. We may *believe* whatever we like, yet still *know* nothing at all. So, do superstitions work for us or against us? According to the clinically insane, the jury's still out.

Prior to the 2014 Scottish Open, and not for the first time, world number one golfer, Rory McIlroy, fell victim to what some media were calling 'Second Day Syndrome'. This involved a disturbing pattern of failing miserably on a Friday after setting the pace the previous day. On one occasion, he followed an opening round of 64 with a disastrous second day score of 78. This left him 51 under-par for his combined first-round scores for 2014, but with a score of 9-over during the same period for his second-round scores. Speaking on the matter he said,

"It's something that has gotten into my head. I may be putting too much pressure on myself to go out on Fridays and back up a good opening score. It seems to be a

recurring problem and one I'd like to stop. I have no problem shooting a low one on Thursday, so there's no reason why I can't do the same the next day. Maybe I just need to pretend it's always a Thursday."

How did it come to this? Or is the answer staring us in the face? Does the problem lie dormant in Rory's nature? After all, it was Rory who first used the term 'recurring'. So, having previously failed to tackle his Friday dilemma head on, did pretending each Friday was now a Thursday give rise to a wonderfully ingenious psychological ploy? Or did his strategy create a danger of further accommodating the recurring symptoms rather than get straight to the crux of the cause?

Rory's golfing genius is beyond question, as reflected in a report by *CNN* of his 2017 commercial deal to endorse *TaylorMade* clubs and balls as part of an alleged 100-million-dollar deal. Having consistently performed so admirably on Thursdays during many tournaments, it was clear that his talent was not the cause of the 2nd day syndrome effect. So, to regain control of his 2nd day demons, he adopted a more mindful approach to honing the talents which he already knew he possessed.

Rory implied that the solution was not tactical, technical, or physical, but psychological. He suggested a process whereby he could mentally jettison his recurring fear of performing poorly on Fridays by visualising each Friday as though it was Thursday, thereby freeing himself from any 2nd day syndrome effect.

The key to Rory's transition was psychological, which is no surprise since effective transitioning always begins in the mind. If there's learning to be gained from his attempts at overcoming adversity, it's that human psychology is no respecter of status, prestige, talent, or rank, as typified by his world standing and elite commercial eminence at that time.

Rory recognised that until he addressed his ongoing 2nd day flaw, he could not escape from the debilitating thoughts that were utmost and predominant in his mind when Fridays came around. The key to his success came by way of adopting fresh perspective in the form of a new unaccustomed approach of consciously replicating Thursday's winning mentality on Fridays. This is exactly what happened just one week later at the 2014 Scottish Open at Hoylake where he was crowned champion at the ripe old age of just 25.

On this momentous occasion, Rory successfully banished the demons he attached to the superstition called 'Freaky Fridays' to attain new levels of consistency throughout four full days of tournament competition. And so, it transpired that overcoming his previously debilitating psychology may have been his greatest achievement of all, because lifting the trophy meant he was no longer trapped in his 'Freaky' cycle, but had kicked it into touch where it belonged.

It is a practical a tale of mental 'tricknology' given Rory tricked his own mind into being convinced that approaching each Friday as though it was Thursday would positively affect how he performed. So eliminating the superstition called 'Freaky Fridays' was not only the catalyst for winning the 2014 Scottish Open Championship, but also a decisive factor in securing his elite status as the number one ranked golfer in the world.

His methodology remains open to conjecture. What is certain, however, is that due to the media coining the phrase 'Freaky Fridays', it became a 'thing' in the public consciousness as though it were real. It also became a thing in Rory's consciousness as pressure mounted to resolve a superstition which now had a name. 'Freaky Fridays' do not exist, at least not in a falsifiable sense. Yet irrespective of logic, he could not escape from the thoughts which went on in his mind until he replaced those thoughts with alternative thoughts.

Sports superstitions of a generic nature, despite not being real, still carry less merit and more chance of ridicule than superstitions related to gods, which are no more factually accurate. Both are equally dismissive of the improbable odds of having ever experienced a supernatural intervention while competing at sport. So why are superstitions of either type so deeply embedded in our psyche? How did they get there in the first place and who or what is to blame or to thank? The answer is unequivocal fear, as fear is deeply enshrined in all aspects of psychology relating to competitive sport.

The human brain is hardwired to internalise fear. Consider the earliest messages conveyed to us from childhood and how each subliminally internalised fear. We were warned that if we didn't do as we're told, didn't eat all our greens, failed to achieve the expected grades, or failed to make our parents proud there would be unpleasant repercussions, and it didn't end there. If we didn't win at sport, performed below par, failed to meet peer expectations, or worse still, failed to meet our own expectations, we would experience more of the same. So, who couldn't use a little superstitious inspiration, irrespective of whether it works or not?

The same threat of repercussions exists if we fail to repent by the grace of a mythical god or bow to the whims of whichever brand of god we choose to align.

Many athletes appeal to divine intervention to increase their odds of sporting success. Yet, all that can be achieved by inserting a god is to appeal to a mystery of extra-terrestrial origin with an apparent liking for terrestrial sport. So let's cut to the chase. The real reason that athletes appeal to superstition is because they think that there's something in it for them.

Superstitious belief is a selfish endeavour which isn't helped by the fact that an on-going litany of damn well *don'ts* continues to prime the human consciousness. Don't walk under a ladder and don't touch a trophy before it's been won because it's bad luck. Let's face it, we are living confirmation of other people's damn well *don'ts* which have been foisted upon us since birth, but in many cases remain with us until we die.

Here is a revelation of life-altering proportions to counteract superstitious fear. It's that athletes who carry superstitions do not fear the unknown, and here's why. They cannot fear what they do not know or have yet to experience; what they're actually afraid of is losing what is known. The one reliable aspect of human nature is that no two interpretations are ever the same. Disagreement is prevalent within the nature of terrorists, patriots, and saints alike; all of whom make compelling arguments to being humanists by nature, by asserting *their* philosophy over the philosophy of someone else.

Interpretation is subjective, and superstitious interpretation is no exception. So next time we profess that a superstitious behaviour is 'in my nature', perhaps we should first ask 'what's in my nature' and 'what are the physical elements of a superstitious nature?' Why seek to add value to the superstitious aura which surrounds human nature before first learning how to value ourselves?

There is no current mechanism to measure superstition. This suggests we are flying by the seat of our pants, but don't take my word for it. I asked former Northern Ireland football manager, Brian Hamilton, to provide an example of a bizarre superstition he had witnessed in professional sport. He replied with a curious tale of a former Ipswich Town FC colleague whose name I won't reveal, but his superstition consisted of swathing dollops of Vaseline onto different parts of his body, using cotton buds to apply it to his legs, arms, and back, and that was his ritual before every game.

"He just had to do it. He also had to slap it on other players' backs. So even if the players all had their shirts on, some would have to lift them up again so he could slap a cotton bud of Vaseline onto their back and then take it back off again. It was

just a feel-good factor for him. Something he felt he had to do."

As I shared that rather surreal moment with Brian, I couldn't help but construct a mental image of the same guy playing football for Manchester City FC, as eventually he went on to do, while wondering if perhaps this preposterous action is the secret sauce which prevents so many current amateur footballers from joining football's elite? Yet all joking aside, as Brian clearly recalled, the guy simply had to do it and at no point did his belief appear optional.

Where did such a superstition originate? How did it emerge with such complexity and how was it received at the time by his teammates, particularly by those who were seeing it in practice for the very first time? What repercussions did he envisage if he did not spread the joys of his Vaseline swab amongst his bemused peers? Oh, and just for good measure, how might *you* have reacted had he requested to wipe his swab on you?

There is a saying, although it's not very pleasant, that if we lie down with dogs we may wake up with fleas. Similarly, if we lie down with ideas, we may contract ideals, and no concept is more idealistic than the optimism or pessimism that accompanies superstitious belief. Any thoughts which we cannot abandon, discard, cast aside, or wilfully reject will accompany us forever, unless or until we replace that thought with an alternative thought. To attempt to transition beyond superstitious ideals can be challenging yet equally stimulating; but as we're about to find out, it's much easier said than done.

Consider the Eastern tale of the gambler who confessed to a wise Sage, *"I was caught cheating at cards yesterday. So, my partners beat me up and threw me out of the upstairs window. What do you propose I do now?"*

The wise Sage looked straight through the gambler with a sharp penetrating glance before adding, *"If I were you, from now on I would play on the ground floor."*

His disciples were horrified at his nonchalant response. *"Why didn't you tell him to stop gambling?"* they demanded.

"Because I knew he wouldn't."

Yet how could he know? Was he a prophet or clairvoyant? The Sage instinctively knew that gambling consumed a large part of the nature of the hapless man. Indeed, such was his nature and propensity to gamble, that the Sage was aware that the best he could do was try to preserve the man's life. Similarly, by what means do athletes attempt to preserve nature's precious gift of spontaneity against a backdrop of superstitious ideology and dogma?

Why are sports superstitions considered worthy of ridicule, while advocates for gods lobby for laws to protect against ridicule, despite gods being superstitious ideals? Why are superstitions which relate solely to sport still widely regarded as common taboos, as if they are never to be spoken of in public lest we give the impression we are losing the plot? Is fear of stigma the reason so many weird and bizarre forms of behaviour go largely unnoticed among our sporting peers?

In order to conceal superstitious behaviour, many athletes opt for avoidance since avoidance is a language in which all of us are well versed and can easily relate. Avoidance is primarily a form of denial and the more eloquent we become in our use of denial, the easier it becomes to avoid facing up to the absurdity of superstitious beliefs. As a result, the human brain becomes adept at nit-picking, unpicking, and rejecting philosophies which it deems as surplus to conventional norms.

Few athletes are comfortable with memorising a loss since losing spins them into a mental quandary and they feel that their world has come to an abrupt end. Superstitions seem adept at tapping into a sixth kind of sense, which as yet can't be measured and therefore cannot be demonstrated to exist. Yet thoughts of omens and prophecy still tie their emotions to how they perform. This applies to us all, and a generic example is the emotional vibes we tend to experience while visiting hospitals, which so often feel negative despite only visiting and despite knowing we possess near perfect health.

The idea of emotional vibes is common. Many sense these vibes while walking past a graveyard after dark, just as staring into deep water has left many transfixed in a motionless state of tranquillity. Athletes also claim to have experienced vibes while standing on a podium for their national anthem or when entering an arena prior to a major event.

Every new experience provides further opportunities for an athlete's brain to formulate new memories (behavioural, procedural, and societal memories). But if the data collected is predominantly focused on recalling experiences of failure, then thinking only of ways to fail and of what might go wrong are the thoughts most predominant in their mind.

Avoidance is a subset of superstitious belief. This is clear from the behaviour of athletes who won't speak of success before it has been earned, and is best illustrated by common superstitious sentiments such as 'I don't want to jinx my chances', as if thinking about winning prior to an event means it won't happen. Many athletes opt out of lifting or touching silverware prior to having won it outright. Their belief is prophetic as if touching the prize means they won't get the luck.

Many athletes believe it is disrespectful to the supernatural realm to display over-confidence; they don't want to be seen to be taunting destiny or sticking two fingers up at karma. Yet, what is more absurd than an athlete believing that 'daring to dream' could be supernaturally misconstrued as an invitation to bad luck? It's as if being presumptuous has magical powers which spark supernatural repercussions and cause a downturn in performance, all because they had the audacity to visualise winning before they had actually won.

Imagination is integral to self-progression. Imagine the impact and long-term effect of being too scared to dream. Do we know how that looks, how it feels, or what form it takes in the context of allowing superstition to wield influence over the decisions we make about sport? Perhaps looking inside the mind of one of football's former elite may enlighten us, and the process begins by questioning whether thoughts of superstitious prophecy, conspiracy, and intrigue still wield practical influence over 21st century minds?

Who among us, for instance, *does not* wish to believe that we are in sole control of our superstitious trepidations, anxieties, and fears? Yet are we in control of our superstitions or are superstitions controlling us? Consider the launch of iconic footballer Roy Keane's revealing biography entitled *The Second Half*. His startling exposé granted unfettered insight into the inner workings of his complex mind as he lifted the lid on a successful but often turbulent career.

Scratch just beneath the surface of Roy's written account and it appears that superstition was the main determining factor in a major decision during a crucial juncture of his ebbing career. In a startling admission to the footballing world, Roy announced his retirement from professional football while still playing for his boyhood heroes Celtic FC, despite having only completed 6 months of an 18-month contract deal.

Following his announcement, Roy reportedly received the generous offer of a dream ticket to move to the magnificent Bernabéu Stadium and play for Spanish giants Real Madrid. It was an impromptu offer which presented an amazing opportunity to prolong his career among football's elite. Despite much deliberation, however, Roy turned down the offer, but what he did next revealed the extent to which a superstitious predetermination was allowed to distort his sense of reasoning rationale.

"I should have appreciated Real's offer more. I took a negative approach. The weather and training might have given me another lease on life, another two years of playing as much as anything else. It was fear that decided me; fear of the unknown."

Roy's most startling revelation was not declining the offer from Real Madrid, although that alone is quite startling. It was the reason he gave for turning them down, *"It was fear that decided me; fear of the unknown."* His reluctance to take the plunge suggests a convergence of superstitious ambiguity and his fear of what the unknown may have held in store for him had he taken the risk.

Roy's reputation as a fierce talisman of sporting leadership and aggression made it difficult for readers to visualise him possessing any fear at all, such was the domineering persona which he cultivated over many years. Yet without knowing with any degree of certainty what may lie in wait for him in Spain, he opted to stick with what he already knew. He seemed unaware, however, that he did not fear the unknown, but instead was afraid of losing what was already known.

"Nothing is more frightening than a fear you cannot name."

- Cornelia Funke, Author

Perhaps the oldest human dilemma known to exist is that we generally fear what we don't understand. Roy turned down a lucrative offer from Real Madrid due to fear of relinquishing control of what he already knew. His apprehension outranked his motivation to experience pastures anew (pastures unknown). It reminded me of the following quote by politician Stephen. C. Hogan, *"I don't fear the unknown. I fear what I do know is all that's left."*

Imagine if, in the context of sport, all that we currently know is all that is left. Or if all we have achieved to date is the absolute zenith of our known potential, after which the only way appears to be downhill. Does this concept seem frightening enough to buy into superstitions of theism (the belief in a god or gods), or into superstitious rituals which border on the bizarre? Superstitions are solely reliant on faith, while faith as a concept tells us nothing at all. So is it possible to counter a superstition? The answer is yes, and all that's required is to ask the following question, 'Do I care if the things I believe are true?'

Superstitions have no explanatory powers and are not a reliable pathway to truth, yet human ingenuity has already devised an imaginative means to manoeuvre that which is currently unknown into the realm of that which is claimed to be known. The methodology is childishly straightforward, we simply give names to our fear since names personalise, sanitise, and nullify how we cope with psychological threats.

Lending names to our fear can trick us into feeling more at ease with ourselves. Names do not change our fear's content, they do, however alter its context by allowing us to fulfil the primeval human need of feeling a sense of ownership and control over fear itself. Roy Keane's prevailing reason for declining an offer from Real Madrid was due to his fear of the unknown. But this can also be interpreted as Roy having concerns about his future luck.

Many athletes imply that a lack of success, subsequent failure, or sudden loss of form is linked with bad luck, or that a triumphant success is linked with good luck. But how many variations of luck exist? How can anyone tell if luck swayed a performance, let alone a decision, if they cannot produce falsifiable evidence of luck being an actual thing? For how long is it viable for an athlete to seek solace in scapegoating luck? Is luck merely a tool to avoid personal culpability or to craftily evade the gaze and scrutiny of their peers when they fail?

Superstitious athletes tend to mould their unfounded presumptions around whatever makes them feel comfortable and whatever fits with their artificial belief systems and specific sporting needs. This is a much simpler task and far gentler experience than displaying the courage, ego-strength, and emotional resilience necessary to prevent superstition from overriding their psychology once and for all. We live in a space between appearance and reality, where the best magic is not designed to trick us but to entice us into believing that we have power-of-attorney over things unknown.

Can an athlete perform beyond their limitations if their potential to do so was not already intrinsic from the start? Consider how often prominent sports commentators refer to the subhuman or superhuman efforts of athletes but fail to acknowledge that humans are capable of extraordinary feats. After all, either the performance of an athlete is of human extraction or it is not. They also frequently refer to scarcely believable concepts such as Sod's Law, Second Season Syndrome, and the Commentators Curse, thereby suggesting that something supernatural is stirring from beyond our physical realm.

What makes any athlete or coach begin to assume that a jinx, hex, godlike agent, supernatural law, or curse exists in the first place, or if they do exist, why would they give a toss for their sports aspirations? These are all unfalsifiable propositions, so until there is falsifiable evidence to chart the biological or chemical elements of which a sporting jinx or a lucky break is composed, then we are left with no means to measure their impact in the observable world. This makes it impossible to explain superstitions as being anything other than the offshoots of an imaginative state of mind.

Why do athletes rarely choose to celebrate good fortune with the same veneration as they wilfully bestow on bad fortune? Which feeling tends to stick with them longest? Is it the exhilarating feeling of winning or the lingering sense of deflation of losing? Why do the negatives in sport tend to outrank the positives? The illusion of luck is a double-edged sword since even at best it is merely sporadic. Indeed, many interviewees who helped to compile this information considered luck to be little more than aspirational, momentary, fleeting, and brief.

Most interviewees had low expectations (if any at all) that any upturn in fortune would last very long, while others admitted to having chased the elusive winning feeling for so long that when it finally arrived they could no longer remember how best to enjoy it or how to react. Superstitions and luck are indistinguishable, and few observations are more bizarre than to watch an athlete achieve personal glory, but then dedicate all credit to superstitious constructs, be it gods, lucky omens, bizarre rituals, or luck; all while disproportionately attributing little-or-no credit to themselves.

The most curious aspect of superstition is when athletes ignore the obvious discrepancy whereby, when events go pear-shaped, as they invariably do, the superstition which just moments earlier milked all the credit is now deemed undeserving of any blame. It's all very odd, since what kind of reasoning heaps praise on superstitions when things go their way, but exempts superstitions from blame when things don't go to plan? It is simply irrational.

Very rarely do athletes publicly announce before an event that their superstitions will guarantee success, nor do they instigate post-superstitious investigations to measure the effectiveness of superstition following events. Superstitions are manifestations of hope, while hope is perhaps best summed up by comedian Rich

Hall who surmised, *"Hope is right below wishful thinking and right above performing a rain dance,"* and yet all superstitions are variations of hope. So why are superstitions of theism not held to a similar account as those of a purely sporting nature, despite neither type guaranteeing success?

Even coaching philosophies of blood, sweat, repetition, and tears do not guarantee success. How many athletes line up on a grid, enter into the blocks, step onto a pitch, or climb into a ring with a stonewall guarantee of knowing in advance that they are going to win, despite competing in luck's ominous shadow? Even cheating requires an element of fortune since the timing of deceit often has to be perfect.

It's time to reappraise the true potency of superstitions about lucky talismans and gods, and stop treating them as though they were separate since both are 'otherworldly' in terms of design, but the designers aren't 'otherworldly', the designers are us. Many athletes afford superstitious fantasy the best of both worlds while instinctively knowing that this is a privilege they cannot even bestow on themselves. So when an athlete's superstition fails to materialise, what stops them from tipping their delusion out with the bathwater, secure in the knowledge it didn't work and that they'd be foolish to repeat it anytime soon?

To eliminate superstition from sports preparation requires the delicate skill of practicing selfishness, as selfishness is both necessary and healthy if personal genius is to thrive and evolve. How can we learn to appreciate others until we first re-engage with our inherent birthright by apportioning credit and then learning to appreciate ourselves? Selfishness is not living as we see fit, the true art of selfishness is expecting others to live their lives as we see fit. But who taught us that self-praise was a form of conceit, or convinced us of the ridiculous theistic fallacy that we are 'born sick' and commanded to be well and that the only life-saving serum is to partake of whatever cultural snake oil is on offer from theism's pantheon of invisible friends?

Consider the following tale of a medal. A mother once struggled to get her son to come home before sunset, so she told him that the road leading to their house was haunted by ghosts who came out after dark. By the time the boy grew up, he was so afraid of ghosts that he refused to run errands at night. So his mother gave him a medal and told him that it possessed special powers to protect him from ghosts. This short tale is a metaphor for heightening awareness of the boy's vulnerability to mental conditioning.

Bad religion (the type to which superstitions aspire) tricked the boy into placing his faith in a medal, while good religion would empower him with enough credible insight to recognise that malevolent ghosts are not proven to exist at all. This would help to disperse any lingering fears and encourage the boy to regain confidence based purely on the strength of falsifiable facts. It is only a tale but are you or I really so different? Perhaps we can also recall the scale of reckless abandon which our parents or peers chose to falsely project onto us?

Who can recall being told sinister tales of wailing banshees and bogeymen? These tales were designed to supplant thoughts of free will and spontaneity with thoughts of compliance, subservience, and obedience. These thoughts create overriding fears which continue to resonate and linger deep in our subconscious to this very day. The tale of the medal bears a striking resemblance to how superstitious conditioning has become prevalent in sport. How often do coaches see fit to appraise the type of religion (superstition) they ascribe to aspiring athletes or do athletes appraise the type of religion (superstition) they ascribe to themselves?

In our experience of sport, how comfortable are athletes in expressing their reliance on superstition to their coach due to the stigma which accompanies any form of supernatural belief? Or perhaps it is *us* spreading bad religion, but how can we tell? It has often been said that 'children should be taught what *is* and not what should *be*'. This theory has certain plausibility if its purpose is to expose the type of myths which surround dubious superstitious practices and weave their way through and around children's fragile minds.

Consider as an example the festive superstition affectionately known as Christmas, only to discover as a child that the whole Santa vibe was contrived under false premise. Or worse still, as we become parents, we then inflict the same falsehoods upon the psychology of our children as was perpetrated on us. To buy into the superstition called Santa Clause requires a deliberate process of falsifying a lie, which has transcended the fabric of social consciousness to form part of our festive DNA.

This isn't an attempt to usurp poor old Santa. Yet the superstition called Santa continues to act as the poster boy and marketing tool of a domestic virus of epidemic proportions, but which comes with a catch. It seems Santa has an overriding attribute which bears the same hallmark as many theistic gods, whereby in order to be deemed worthy of reward, we must first learn to behave in a subservient manner in accordance with cultural convention, while wholeheartedly trusting the validity of the information we are being given by the carriers who are closest to us as kids.

No one was better positioned to disperse such a bombardment of loaded sentiments into our thoughts than our parents, guardians, and peers. The downside, however, is that it was only a matter of time before we were confronted by practical truth. Not only did we discover that our first impressions of Santa turned out to be false, but we also found out that we were being lied to by those closest to us since birth.

This is not an attempt to turn the world on its head, and if you're under six years of age please look away now. It is merely a suggestion that once we peddle a myth using emotional content and by fabricating conformational-bias to perpetuate the lie, the resulting effect is bad religion and the promise of reward is our medal of choice. However, the real learning only occurs when the day of reckoning finally arrives and the myth is exposed for the deceit (superstition) that it is.

From that moment onwards, the confidence and trust of each child regarding anything deemed mystical or magical is understandably tainted and irreversibly impaired by their new-found sense of scepticism and active mistrust. The kid is now thinking, 'Hey, if Santa's not real, what else are they lying to me about?' Yet their sense of mistrust does not end there.

"I stopped believing in Santa Claus when I was six. Mother took me to see him in a department store and he asked for my autograph."

- Shirley Temple, Actress

Due to bad religion, in a superstitious sense, that kid became armed with a newfound sense of scepticism and self-preservation to protect against any future misappropriation of implicit trust. This may seem comical or surreal, yet it requires sleight-of-hand to facilitate such a wide-scale deceit. The difficulty, however, is that such deceit is capable of denting that kid's future confidence, particularly in terms of feeling unable to trust their closest confidants ever again, and yet trust is exactly the characteristic which coaches, guardians, and mentors strive diligently to secure.

The Santa superstition implants lasting doubt in developing minds where doubt did not previously exist. It elicits fear which was not previously prevalent, while causing disappointment and perhaps even hostility where previously there was only optimism and hope. No matter how we choose to perceive it, our performance at sport is subject to the sway and overall influence of our social constructs and domestic environments, along with our talent and genetics.

The human brain strives to contextualise sense from nonsense by way of 'figuring out', 'getting the gist', 'making sense of', and 'catching the drift'. From a neurological perspective, the frontal cortex of the brain uses similar processes to establish reasoning and to corroborate meaning. This, in league with the limbic system, creates emotional responses by way of a vortex of neural pathways. Phew! It all sounds so incredibly complex. Yet this merely suggests that definitions of meaning are easily altered once we allow emotion to outmanoeuvre reasonability and rationale. It also suggests that superstitions leave us prone to the mercy of fluctuating states.

"If the facts don't fit the theory, change the facts."

- Albert Einstein

Superstitious beliefs about a rabbit's foot, lucky pants, gods, or dear old Santa Claus have one thing in common, none are prepared to let an absence of facts stand in the way of a damn good story, despite their long-term effects on an athlete's psychology. To introduce some context, try to imagine the child with the previous festive conundrum as a young adult and aspiring athlete, but still caught in a quandary of self-doubt while pondering whether to truly believe that they can jump that final hurdle, go that extra mile, or get up off the canvas one more time.

The difficulty faced by the hapless athlete is that, despite their coach offering reassurance by asserting that now is their moment of destiny, reassurance and trust may have come just a little too late as they are already primed with a distrusting nature dating back to their festive disbelief. Many athletes I interviewed seemed to be at peace when conveying the nature of their superstitious beliefs, while others seemed less at ease or felt ill-at-ease when asked to expand on the origins of what they believed and why.

To eradicate a belief should be straightforward, or so one might think. But how much thought is given to how well a child is able to cope with the mental turbulence and sense of deflation caused by destroying their heartfelt belief in the all-action hero called Santa Claus? Is finding out about Santa the signature moment when a flame is extinguished and the magic dies, or where the realisation finally hits home that trust is expendable and can be erased in the blink of an eye? Does that child's relationship with reality evaporate once trust is broken, until all that is left is a lack of belief? And, once belief is destroyed, can it ever be fully restored?

Who measured the ongoing relationship between the child's psychology and their adult mentality to determine whether the experience left them carrying the remnants of distrust around their neck? Can an innocuous superstition such as Santa legitimise the child enlisting the companionship of superstitious faith as their new-found confidant and surrogate friend? And irrespective of whether they succumbed to the cult of a mythical Santa, to the optimism of wearing lucky boots, or to the magic bestowed on an imaginary apple which gave birth to original sin, does the residue of superstition stay with them for life?

"Faith has to do with things that are not seen, and hope with things that are not at hand."

- Saint Thomas Aquinas, Priest

We don't need to look far to find clues which augment superstition's audacious reasoning ethos since the evidence lies scattered throughout the tempestuous mindsets of the world's most competitive sporting elite. An example of which lay cunningly secreted in the verbal deliberations of Manchester United manager, José Mourinho (formerly of Chelsea FC), and it was while he was still at Chelsea that his revelation came to light. He was reported in the *Evening Standard* as carrying two sentimental possessions which he prizes above all others and takes with him everywhere.

"One of them is a laminated photo of my children. That's love. The other is a crucifix. It's not a question of superstition but of faith, because one day if I forget them, I won't stop winning because of it."

José's balanced appraisal provides wonderful insight into the mind of one of Europe's most enduring football managers whose assessment displayed an admirable form of superstitious awareness and an aptitude for rationality and reasoning, which is an impressive feat in itself. At the time he was subject to the unforgiving spotlight of the media gaze, yet José took it all in his stride and proceeded to coolly and rationally achieve what so many of his peers still cannot, which is to separate subjective emotion from the objective impracticality of superstitious belief.

José explicitly expressed that his sporting endeavours would not self-implode if for some reason he forgot his crucifix of faith. This was a clear indicator that he continued to anticipate success, irrespective of whether he had his crucifix or not.

By way of a caveat, however, perhaps José may wish to review whether a chink had inadvertently appeared in his armour following the comment, *"The other is a crucifix. It's not a superstition,"* as any premeditated pattern of carrying a crucifix into the red-hot atmosphere of a sporting arena is a superstition in every sense of the word. The crucifix is a symbolic token of religion which further cements his relationship with faith, therefore the significance of his crucifix rests solely on the value he chooses to place on his symbol of faith.

The value athletes place on superstition is purely subjective and lacks proof of concept. Few athletes seem willing to believe that they are unreasonable, but let's put their reasonability to the test with a few simple questions. Why do athletes subscribe to superstitions in sport? Is it because when faced with anxiety, trepidation, and fear, they regress towards childhood by clinging to their superstitious beliefs just as they clung to their teddies as kids. What we can say with some clarity is that superstitious beliefs act as athletes' comforter of choice to counteract their anxiety and fear.

The reason I asked the question earlier as to why the scorpion stung the frog was to highlight that stinging is part of a scorpion's reasoning, just as superstitions form part of an athlete's reasoning. But how reasonable are superstitious beliefs? Perhaps the poet G. K. Chesterton already knew the answer when he surmised that *"Reason is itself a matter of faith. It is an act of faith to assert that our thoughts have any relation to reality at all"*.

Fact or Stacked

"It pays to keep an open mind, but not so open your brains fall out."

- Carl Sagan, Astronomer

Consider September 2013 in Glasgow, as WBO World Boxing Lightweight Champion Ricky Burns, controversially retained his Championship belt against Mexican Raymundo Beltran in a contest which, to the astonishment of many observers, was adjudged to have been a draw. Many winced at the dubious decision and wondered if there'd been a mistake given the violent nature of the mauling handed out to Ricky, who was knocked to the canvas in the eighth round.

In a further twist, during a post-fight interview with *Sky Sports,* Ricky's promoter cast serious doubt on whether Ricky would ever be fit to return to the ring. His fears escalated during the interview when Ricky was diagnosed as having sustained a broken jaw. To impartial boxing fans and neutral observers who witnessed the beatdown for themselves, there could only be one justifiable outcome, which sadly for Ricky was a loss. Yet incredibly, the contest was adjudged as a draw, which even caused the partisan Glasgow crowd in attendance to draw a short intake of breath.

Many reeled at the judges' odd decision, since a draw was enough for the bloodied but typically unbowed champion to retain his belt. At this point, however, a boxing commentator was heard to say, *"Sometimes I don't really like this business."* This was somewhat ironic, as once the furore subsided and things eventually calmed down, an understandably emotional Raymundo was asked, *"Can you think of a reason why the judges didn't give it to you?"*

"Politics," Raymundo replied instantly. *"You know it's always the same thing but they've got some plans. There's money involved and it's business. So when they have the chance and the opportunity to protect their own investment, they do it."*

Following Raymundo's post-fight interview, Ricky's promoter, who was still clearly concerned, added, *"Ricky's career now hangs in the balance. He requires a titanium plate in his jaw. So of course it's a major operation since a jaw is an integral part of a boxer's makeup. We just don't know how he's going to recover."* In retrospect, the good news for Ricky, his family, and his fans is that he did eventually return to the ring.

Raymundo cited politics as his undoing, and professional opinions such as, *"Sometimes I don't really like this business,"* at least partially substantiate his exasperated claim. Situations like these are not uncommon. Many dubious decisions cast doubt on the integrity of sport and cause athletes to question whether, irrespective of how well they perform, all their efforts are ultimately in vain. Not because of intrinsic and measurable factors, but due to external factors such as fate, karma, coincidence, luck, and even Sod's Law.

"I have, thanks to my travels, added to my stock all the superstitions of other countries. I know them all now and in any critical moment of my life, they all rise up in armed legions for or against me."

- Sarah Bernhardt, Actress

Many athletes believe they merely exist as pawns in an elaborate game of life. Wow, profound or what! Yet, what if Raymundo's assertions were indeed correct and events (or the judges) really did conspire against him? Did he discover, perhaps not for the first time, that results are often a matter of conjecture and that within every critically-defining moment, fortune and providence either work in our favour or rise up against us to bite us in the ass?

Sometimes all we can do as mere bystanders is watch as fate takes its curious toll. We can, however, question if it's wise or unwise to remain optimistic that beliefs of supernatural extraction can influence terrestrial sporting results. Is it wise or unwise to act on the presumption that the decks are already stacked, either for or us or against us, irrespective of the quality of how we perform?

Consider the initial predicament of former rugby league player Paul Woods, of feeling afraid to leave his home due to suffering the effects of OCD and the banter and ridicule which, by his own admission, he endured at the hands of his peers. All because he availed of mind-coaching to acquire mental stimulus in a bid to nullify the effects of living and coping with OCD.

Paul was deemed as compulsive to the point of a disorder, yet in times of adversity, even the most practical diagnosis becomes obsolete once we are convinced that our luck is already stacked. Sport is awash with supposed experts and gurus full of condescending hypotheses and big ideas. Yet responsibility rests with coaches and mentors to enable athletes experiencing trauma, anxiety, or stress to feel acknowledged on a personal level by gaining an authentic understanding of whatever belief is causing distress.

Sport suffers from largely ineffectual psychological terminologies and authoritative truths. Yet many self-professed experts and gurus in the field of sports psychology fail to divulge that the true extent of their expertise lies solely in mastering terminologies. It's an oversight which allows them to carve out lucrative careers based on the power of terminologies alone. Many athletes who appeal to authority to eliminate anxiety end up suspending their scepticism to instead take experts and gurus at their word.

The loaded nature of 'go-to' diagnoses such as 'conditions' or 'disorders' makes it difficult to identify two experts or gurus who can explicitly agree on a correct diagnosis. Consequently, athletes are being grossly over-diagnosed as having strains of disorders or vague conditions which require medication and drugs to correct, while being discouraged from seeking solace in the place where answers to their anxieties are most likely to be found, which is between their ears.

Many athletes appear inextricably bound by a strange twist of irony whereby they over-subscribe to experts of terminology who rather brazenly presume to know more about them than they claim to know about themselves? Yet, personal empathy begins and ends with our own interpretation of truth, and each truth has its own accompanying state which is fluctuating and transitory, insomuch as states oscillate and continuously alter. In other words, the states we experience ebb and flow.

No one can stay angry, depressed, fearful, happy, frustrated, animated, compulsive, obsessive, dismissive, or even competitive for 100% of the time. We simply cannot physically or mentally maintain it, no matter how hard we try. Neither is it within the intended remit of human nature to exist in a perpetual state of experiencing only fixed emotions for 100% of the time, irrespective of whatever emotion is predominant.

As justification for such a surmise, consider what happens to our emotional state when we are no longer awake and no longer aware. Do we experience subconscious states of depression, self-deprecation, exasperation, or over-competitiveness for 100% of the time that we are asleep, or are we simply asleep? The point is that, irrespective of whether we're awake or asleep, the brain remains in a continuous state of flux. In other words, we can escape from the grip of superstitious states since no state can demonstrably exist without fluctuation for 24 hours straight.

"I know that you believe you understand what you think I said, but I'm not sure you realise that what you heard is not what I meant!"

- Unknown

No one has the capacity to state categorically whether any form of intelligent supernatural agent will intercede on their behalf during times of sporting need. Just as no one has a true understanding of God, since God is a concept, primarily a mystery, and an unfalsifiable superstitious construct on which even theists cannot agree.

What causes an athlete to concede to bizarre compulsions, such as former footballer David Beckham's reported need to symmetrically align cans of soft drinks in his fridge? Or caused former rugby league star Paul Woods to re-wrap his hands with protective bandages up to ten times before every match? Psychology isn't clear cut. It requires an ongoing process of 'figuring things out'.

We can begin the process with a simple question. Are we in control of our psychology, or is psychology controlling us? It may be wise to suspend our verdict until after having considered my eye-opening conversation with former professional footballer, Gary Haveron, which halted my optimism in its tracks. At the time, Gary was plying his trade in the semi-professional ranks of Irish League football with Ballymena United FC, when I made the mistake of asking if he had any superstitious beliefs.

Gary's face lit up instantly as he broke into a knowing smile while nodding his head simultaneously in-sync with mine, as if to jointly acknowledge that we had just opened up a real can of worms. It was at this point that the popular saying 'be careful what you wish for' sprang into my mind. So buckle up, here goes.

Gary began by acknowledging his need to always be the last player out of the dressing room and last onto the pitch before every game. He was vice-captain at the time, so I asked what would happen if he was promoted to captain (which shortly afterwards he was) and had to lead his team out from the front?

"I've had to do it. It's strange, and although it's a big honour to lead out my team, there's always something in the back of my head saying, I want to come out of this dressing room last."

Have you ever led the team out from the front and they have won?

"Yes I've led them out quite a few times this year and we've won."

Have you ever come out last and your team have lost?

"Aw yeah, I've done that also."

So on reflection, how lucky has it been for you coming out last?

"I know it's ridiculous. It's a ridiculous thing I've got into the habit of doing, but I still have to be last out of the dressing room. I mean I'll even check to see if everyone's out of the toilets. I'll go around knocking on the doors to ask if everyone is out of the cubicles. I know it's funny and that, but it's just the kind of routine I've gotten into.

With some of the boys it's turned into a wee bit of a standing joke, and you gather up new ones too. It seems ridiculous, but I eat the exact same things every Saturday. I love tea, but I won't drink a cup of tea on a Saturday. That's not too bad of course but once I get to the ground, it goes on to a whole new level.

Whatever number jersey I'm wearing, I have to rub the back of that jersey the same number of times. Our jerseys are always hung-up facing forward so that the sponsor's name is facing us. But I always turn it back-to-front, so that its number is facing me; and I always get a rub on both of my calves even when I don't need it."

Phew! Let's take a breather. Oh no, we're off again.

"Sometimes the manager wants me out warming up, but I feel I need to have this done as part of my routine. I won't put my boots on until the very last minute. I also wear a white vest that I've had since I was fifteen. In fact, it's hardly even white anymore, but more of a grey.

I wear it for the first half, and then change it to a blue one for the second half come rain, hail, or shine. I don't put my shirt on until I leave the dressing room, and it's got to the stage now where if I don't do those things, either something's going to go wrong, or it's just not going to happen for me on the day."

As far as you can remember, where did all this begin?

"I think the one coming out of the dressing room last came from one time I was playing for Northern Ireland under 16's against Sweden. I just remember it being

one of my best ever games. I had scored my first goal for Northern Ireland and I just happened to come out of the dressing room last that day, and so I think I kept it from there."

What percentage of focus is lost by not having your vests or not getting to come out last?

"It would play on my mind a wee bit. I know it's a silly routine I've gotten into, but it's more out of habit than anything else. It's true that the manager looks at me sometimes as if I'm a bit of a psycho or something, but it's got to the stage now where everyone pretty much expects me to do it. As for my percentage of focus, it wouldn't be a massive percent. Probably about 5% - 10% which I suppose is enough; but I know if I've covered all the bases, then I've left nothing to chance."

Could subconsciously losing 5% - 10% of focus affect or impact your game?

"Normally because I've prepared so meticulously, I don't have to panic, but obviously I still have to go out and perform."

So if it isn't an issue, why make it one?

"I can't explain it, but when I'm wearing my stuff I just feel that little bit better, and it's only a very small little bit. My white vest is grey now and it's falling to bits, and its tatty looking but I just feel, who cares it's mine and part of my armour I suppose. Oh, and by the way, I wear cycling shorts too, and if I don't have them on that affects me also."

It sounds almost as if all this stuff has become part of you?

"I think it has done, but I always take as much stuff with me as I can because I like to leave as little to chance as possible. I mean, if I don't mark my man correctly and he scores, I know it had nothing to do with my superstitions; but I just feel better with my routine."

Despite all your meticulous preparation, is it all just another form of clutter?

"Away from football I can be really untidy, but when it comes to my football stuff it's crazy. You'd nearly think I had OCD or something. My mum's always saying to me, 'I wish you took as much care of everything else.' I'd rather have it and not need it than be thinking about it, not have it and be panicking. Sometimes I do go out and play bad and think to myself, 'what the hell am I carrying all this junk *around for?' but I just have to have it."*

Is the junk in your bag, or in your head?

"It's exactly the kind of stuff I think I need now. It's like my armour."

When did you start stroking your jerseys?

"I don't even know where that came from. I didn't used to do it. I mean, I wore number thirty-seven earlier in England. So I would have been there stroking all day. Thirty-seven is my lucky number. It seems strange because my house number is thirty-seven and when I moved to England I was automatically given number thirty-seven as a squad number as well.

When I moved to Bolton FC, I kept the number thirty-seven and when I moved back home to Lisburn Distillery they used squad numbers, so I changed mine to read thirty-seven. That's the number that follows me all over the place. Like I would turn around somewhere and see the number thirty-seven. Just you wait and see."

Oh, oh! Now I'm being implicated in Gary's charade.

"I guarantee the next time you're sitting watching a film, I bet you the number thirty-seven will come up. It's a number that flashes up for me a lot and it's my lucky number."

What if I suggested that other numbers also flash in front of your eyes, but you're so conditioned to see thirty-seven that you've become blind to thirty-six or thirty-eight?

"I always find if I'm driving past petrol stations, I'll look up and see if my number is there, and I do see it quite a lot. But I suppose if I'm looking for it, I will find it."

Humour me for a moment. Try to visualise being out on the pitch and surrounded by free-running team-mates, each with clear minds and feeling all loose, flexible and relaxed, and there's you in among them, carrying around all that stuff. Can you imagine how it might feel *not* having to carry around all that clutter, from a mental and physical perspective?

"I just feel more compact with my stuff, because I know I'd feel it around me and sense it. I just feel better."

How can you tell for certain if you feel better with it when you can't ever

remember being without it?

"That's a great question and I know this has no real significance, but I just feel when I have it on, that I'm more mentally ready to go. I'm more tuned-in once I have it on. I stop thinking about everything else altogether and then I'm more mentally tuned-in before the game. So, I don't think it holds much significance or bearing on the actual game, whether I have it on or not. But for me, I just feel so much better prepared. It's almost more that I 'like' having it now. More than I need it probably."

What if I were to suggest that you get rid of it? How might that feel?

"I don't think I could!"

If you feel that you can't, might your behaviour be detrimental to your team? Indeed, minus your 'comforters', it may appear in the eyes of others that their vice-captain appears ill at ease with himself?

"It's certainly possible, but my routines only take a small amount of my time, although they're always in my head."

If you say you're a team player, then why spend so much time on yourself? Might you consider alternating your habits, routines, rituals, and beliefs, at least partially, by redirecting your time and energy towards some other area which may be of more use to your team? Perhaps a more inclusive activity which allows you to interact with the rest of the lads?

"Replacing my routines. Um! I suppose I could spend more time and attention helping my squad a bit more, because they are a very young squad, but I won't give them up. I just feel that I need them."

Whoa there! I suggested that we call a halt to proceedings before any further rituals came to light. My conversation with Gary reminded me of the age-old adage, 'once logic fails, opt for volume', and of yet another which states, 'if the only tool at our disposal is a hammer, then the answer is likely to be nails'. In so much as, if the facts at our disposal are distorted, then our thoughts are corrupted and our actions are likely to be flawed. It is circular reasoning.

Gary's superstitions somehow managed to sprout a set of legs and morph into obsessive and meticulous compulsions, leaving him either teetering on the edge of contentedness or on the edge of madness, having seemingly lost the plot. Which one is more likely, you must decide for yourself?

Superstitions such as Gary's are not uncommon, but they validate the wisdom of cosmologist Carl Sagan's quote, *"It pays to keep an open mind, but not so open your brains fall out."* Gary's comparison of superstition making him feel as though he's wearing armour was mirrored by the actions of incumbent Kazakhstan WBC and IBF World Boxing Champion, Gennady Golovkin, otherwise known as 'Triple G'.

During his pre-fight preparation to face IBF World title holder, Kell Brook, Gennady listened with interest as Kell told the world's media how Gennady's former opponents were terrified by his reputation and therefore beaten before stepping into the ring. Statistically, up to that point, Gennady had beaten 32 out of 35 opponents inside the distance and was widely regarded as, pound for pound, the most fearsome boxer in the world.

Gennady's reputation presented a dichotomy, whereby during the lead-up to the fight he was thoroughly charming, disarming, personable, and all smiles. Many questioned how such a mild-mannered champion could transform into one of the most feared fighters on the planet at the sound of a bell. What triggers such a vicious alter-ego to take hold of his body and possesses his otherwise placid mind as he heads off to war? Fortunately, the answer was forthcoming from Gennady's trainer during an interview prior to the fight.

"The change starts when we get to the arena," said trainer Abel Sanchez. *"It is like he is putting his armour on. He is putting his sword in its sleeve and he is ready to go to work. You notice it most when he steps through the ropes. He goes from Gennady to GGG."*

Just for the record, the non-smiling man-o-war, GGG, ruthlessly dismantled and then stopped Kell Brook in the fifth round, leaving him with a damaged eye-socket in a brutal mismatch which caused his trainer to throw in the towel to save him from further harm. So perhaps footballer Gary Haveron wasn't delusional and there really is something tangible to this man-o-war stuff after all.

Superstition and Mental Health

Superstitious belief leaves us vulnerable to thoughts of *losing out* on things we consider as personal and meaningful, by not thinking or acting in a certain (ritualistic) way. Few athletes are schooled in dealing with grievances or experiencing loss. Particularly regarding the mental resilience required to cope with *losing out* or *missing out* on fixed aspirations and goals, or with having their dreams snatched away from before their very eyes, until all that is left is to grieve for dented egos and shattered hopes.

Sports superstitions are shrouded in mystery since no one appears able to verify (in falsifiable terms) whether random, supernatural correlations even exist. Gary's irrationality suggested a fear of *losing out* or *missing out* on things he considered meaningful, such as winning and playing well. It's as if he was anticipating negative consequences for not wearing his superstitious stuff, and what's worse is he's not alone.

The following scenario is a practical example of the impact which superstitious compulsions can exert on our state of mental health. It is a wonderfully self-effacing excerpt written in *The Observer* by former Liverpool FC and England goalkeeper David James, entitled 'If you thought trainspotters were weird... try footballers'.

"Trainspotters, stalkers, autograph hunters and elite sports stars. They're all linked by the same single-minded, obsessive drive. What separates us? Not much. In sport we use the term 'dedication', rather than obsession, but it's a fine line. Trainspotters and stalkers might be seen as socially inept and a bit sweaty, but how normal is kicking a ball 1,000 times a day?

Elitism, by its very definition, is not normal. David Beckham is the perfect example. When he first came to train with England, some of the other players used to think he was showing off hitting all those balls after training. I had a hunch that he was an obsessive then, and that was before hearing him come out about his Obsessive-Compulsive Disorder and the Pepsi cans needing to face the same way in his fridge door.

Often it's the biggest stars who are the most reluctant to come off the training field - Beckham, Steven Gerrard, Frank Lampard, Wayne Rooney - those who live the game 24/7. And it's not just football. Look at Jonny Wilkinson. His obsessive kicking practice won England the Rugby World Cup. When it comes to training, he didn't even take Christmas Day off.

The root philosophy of sport attracts obsessives. 'You're only as good as your last performance,' they say, which can only mess with your head. There were times when I told myself I was only as good as my last kick. But then people do seem to think goalkeepers in particular have a screw loose. When I told other kids I wanted to be a goalie, they said: 'You're mad.' Goalkeepers are seen as eccentric, solitary and insular. Like the trainspotter at the end of the platform, marking down numbers: there are other people around you, but you're in your own world, concerned only with your own activity.

For me, it was always about statistics. At Liverpool I obsessed over Phil Neal's appearances record - he missed one game in eight years. With Peter Schmeichel, or so the story goes, he insisted on parrying 100 shots before each game. Any player who failed to place the ball in the right place would get an earful. With goalkeepers, the game stops when the ball is in their hands. With dead-ball specialists such as Beckham or Lampard, the game stops when they put the ball on the floor. It's all about control. You strike the ball as you have done thousands of times in training - and it ends up in the same place. You expect it to, there is satisfaction in achieving it, but it's no surprise.

Psychology in football is still poo-pooed, but it is interesting. The best teams have a combination of psychological makeups - your obsessives in the back line, and one or two in midfield, who increase your chances of winning through their hard work and repeated practice. Then you have the flair players who display flashes of genius, of brilliance and unpredictability, who could almost be dubbed 'bipolar'. The 'bipolar' sets the game alight, unsettles the opposition, but you can't rely on him to win games.

Perhaps some of the most gifted players of all suffered a medical condition similar to bipolar disorder, their on-and-off-the-field activities marked by soaring highs and crushing lows. Managers still like to think they know what's best for their team and there's a stigma attached to psychology. In football, you're not supposed to put your hand up and ask for help with your mental health. The symptoms show themselves in various ways. Everyone is happy to talk about superstition in football, but superstition is easy to confuse with obsession.

Many footballers have an obsessive routine that goes way beyond normal. Mine used to begin the Friday night before a game and continue right through to the full-time whistle the following day. It was a ritual so complex it could fill a page. It was made up of things like going into the urinals, waiting until they were empty and spitting on the wall, or not speaking to anyone. I saw it as preparation - mental machinery. Every ritual represented a cog in the machine and at the end of it came the performance.

The performance had to justify the process. That was the pressure. I was in this mad little world where as long as I did everything in the right order then anything could be achieved. When you hear some of the stories you start thinking 'maybe the trainspotters are the healthiest obsessives out there'. And if being the best means being obsessive, how healthy is it to be a top sportsperson? Because once you retire from the game, satisfying that obsession elsewhere is hard."

In retrospect, perhaps David's behaviour is not as weird as it first appears since the effects of superstitions and OCDs do not differ so greatly from fear of a common household spider or fear of the dark. The *actual* truth is the common household spider carries no imminent threat to anyone at all. The *awful* truth is, despite being only half the size of a small fingernail, many fully-grown adults still flee in inconsolable terror at the slightest glimpse.

Reason clearly suggests that it's ridiculous to fear such an ineffectual threat, whereby a small and harmless creature can cause such a disturbing adult response. Just as reason cannot fathom what caused David James to behave so bizarrely with no demonstrable proof that his superstitions had worked for him in the past. Was it reasonable behaviour for Gary Haveron to feel vexed and perplexed at the prospect of competing, without his vast array of peculiar and unnecessary rituals and routines?

Welcome to the world of *actual* truth versus *awful* truth, where one small harmless spider can create an unreasonable and reactionary state of terror among otherwise rational and reasonable adults. Indeed, in terms of pure theatre, you couldn't make it up.

Superstitious logic is flawed since all thoughts are corrupted, even where their essence appears to ring true. One superstitious hypothesis is that of an astral time-traveller, spanning the millennia and transcending the ages before laying to rest in our fragile minds. Yet, all we know for certain is that athletes are susceptible to the idea of cosmic, divine, or celestial interventions which hail from somewhere 'out there in the ether' to influence the outcome of terrestrial sport.

Athletes in competitive situations are prone to draw on dual-personalities. One example is failing to apply the same level of scepticism to superstitious rituals as they do to other aspects of their lives. A further example is brilliantly captured in *The Times* by former England cricketer and writer, Ed Smith, who wrote a fascinating article entitled 'The Two Faces of Rafael Nadal'. This was an attempt to unravel the exceptional duplicity which lies behind the 'twin personalities' of which Nadal is apparently comprised.

Ed describes Nadal as one of the world's *"most admirable and least enviable of Champions,"* and then starts to compare the 'two' Nadal's. On one hand, he alludes to Nadal as tennis' great pugilist, who does not walk out onto the tennis court but runs; as if entering the battlefield and signalling to his opponents that he's prepared to slug it out from the first point to the very last. While in contrast, here is Ed's summation of the 'other' Nadal. *"Nadal's motivation remains a mystery. It's as if his competitive qualities somehow crept into his character, without his even knowing how."*

Ed further increased the Nadal mystery by asking, *"How was such a steely champion ever grafted onto such an unconfident man?"* He then crafted this wonderfully precise synopsis of a mercurial phenomenon which belies every athlete competing at sport, *"It is not uncommon for elite athletes to be two different people. One person on the pitch and another in real life, but the disconnect between the two Nadal's is exceptional."*

Ed highlighted the contradictions which lay within the split personality of the enigma known as Nadal. He then drew our focus towards the distinctive powers of a curious anomaly called the 'Sporting Disconnect'. Such a disconnect not only affected elite athlete Nadal, but also appeared evident in the behavioural duplicity of the *two* Gary Haverons and in *both* Gennady Golovkins, each of whom, upon switching to superstitious mode, conveyed split personalities similar to Nadal.

I initially interviewed only one Gary Haveron, that is until he began to visualise his superstitious alter-ego, at which point there was most definitely two. His superstitious beliefs appear to have crept into his persona unannounced, and such character traits are not uncommon, as every athlete is two or more separate strains of his or herself.

One Gary appeared adamant, unwavering, and unyielding when reinforcing his intention to stick with his rituals and routines. His duplicity was at its most obvious, however, when he conducted large swathes of our interview in an unapologetic state, while simultaneously displaying hints of laddish discomfort at behaving in ways which he readily accepted were bordering on the surreal.

"When I was suffering with the drugs and the drink, I thought, 'Legend? I'm no legend. I'm an arse.'"

- Ricky Hatton, Boxer

Consider the Universal Law of Cause and Effect (often referred to as *Causation*), which encompasses the principle that nothing in the universe happens by chance. As such, everything we experience has a correlating *cause* which predates its *effect*. Every human endeavour derives from one or the other dual characteristic: *love* or *fear,* and aligns with three primary factors which affect us all:

- Our sincere beliefs *(The Hook)*
- The origins of our beliefs *(The Line)*
- The value we attribute to our beliefs *(The Sinker)*

These three factors have a prominent bearing on forming the behaviours which accompany our beliefs. Speaking metaphorically, I refer to this trilogy of strategic convergence as the manifestation of 'Thinking DNA', and as a practical blueprint of how athletes internalise meaning by devising mental truisms based on assumptions which evolve into superstitious beliefs. To explain how it works it may help to consider the sensory nature of a real-life scenario, and no one is more real in terms of wearing their heart on their sleeve than former World Boxing Champion, Ricky Hatton.

"He's a superstar but he had normal friends. So you can imagine how much he had to tear himself down just to be normal. He had to destroy himself to be normal. He's not meant to be normal but he wants to be normal [but] he's a superstar. He's got forty thousand people screaming his name, but he's got to tear himself down or else his friends won't accept him."

- Mike Tyson, Boxer

Let's begin with a question. Who gets to dictate the 'terms and conditions' of insanity? I refer to the same type of insanity of which former World Heavyweight Champion Mike Tyson candidly speaks, in not-so-glowing terms, regarding his friend Ricky Hatton. Mike was speaking to presenter Clare Balding in a frank and honest interview in Paris, during which Ricky (who also participated in the interview) chose to publicly allude to his failings at a human level and to bravely admit:

"I wanted the fans to be proud of me. I wanted people to like me. I would say to my Dad, I'm going out tonight, I've got to meet the lads. I've not seen them for three weeks and they'll think I've gotten above my station. I always wanted to remain normal. That's how I used to think. Crazy! When I got beat by [Floyd] Mayweather the first thing I thought was, look at all these people who have paid money, that I've just let down. I felt like a fraud."

Ricky began to lean heavily on the idea of publicly tearing down his previous 'self' in an attempt to meet the expectations of others. He wanted to appear as *normal* to his friends, be at peace with himself, and feel comfortable in his own skin. He talked of destroying any aspect of 'self' which could ostracise his childhood friends or lead boxing fans to believe that the iconic legend he had become was consumed by the trappings of superstar status and could no longer be considered the 'salt of the earth'.

As the interview unfolded, what began to emerge was his apparent need and perhaps even addiction to experiencing applause and public acclaim. Ricky revealed vulnerabilities and insecurities which are common traits among elite athletes. Even the trappings of superstardom couldn't prevent Ricky from overvaluing other people's applause, unaware as he was that the trait of sincerity is not necessarily a virtue and gives no guarantee against being dead wrong.

Ricky built his emotions around the belief that being happy required the approval of others; others with unrealistically high expectations of what *their* superstar represented to them. Yet, few understood the incessant psychological demands he faced when trying to accommodate *both* Ricky Hattons, as how could anyone other than Ricky comprehend that?

Who was pulling the strings to Ricky's emotions during the turbulent period after being devastatingly knocked out by former WBC and WBO World Champion, Manny Pacquiao? Following the defeat, Ricky graphically described unrelenting thoughts and persistent feelings of having disappointed his adoring public who followed him in droves around the world. He then admitted to falling into what he described in the *Daily Mail* as 'a very bad place'?

Who or what had control of Ricky's psychology, and what did Mike Tyson mean by *"He's not meant to be normal"*? The answer, in typical Tyson fashion, cuts straight to the chase. He referred to the unrealistic expectations being placed on Ricky by boxing associates, enthusiasts, friends, and colleagues, along with various limpets, leeches, and self-styled experts. Each of whom, in their own unique capacity, qualify as hangers-on, and none of which, irrespective of intent, understood how it felt to be Ricky Hatton when his world fell apart.

Each could only imagine the pressures endured by Ricky throughout his career and were totally aloof to his greatest dichotomy, which was balancing the fact that the 'Ricky of old' had transitioned and evolved to align with his superstar status, fortune, and fame. Yet, despite his best efforts to be seen as a regular guy, Ricky's lifestyle and profile as an elite professional boxer made it virtually impossible for him to remain the 'same old Ricky' which his friends and associates had grown to revere and adore.

My earlier characterisation of the 'two' Ricky Hattons referred to his wonderful interview in Paris, where a reflective Ricky shared an extraordinarily brave and honest assessment of much darker times when the pale-and-subdued Ricky consumed the happy-go-lucky, bubbly, and vibrant Ricky who the boxing public had grown to love.

"The difficulties we face with life-changing events are that they affect us for life."

- Unknown

It takes mental resilience to wilfully disrupt our current thinking affairs. Particularly once we consider that most athletes' drug-of-choice is applause. Yet ego is a key motivational driver which, if left unguarded, can enslave psychology within a need to experience public acclaim. As Ricky's legend began to rise in stature, an intrinsic demise began to occur to offset the demands of superstardom against the demands of remaining a regular guy.

Seemingly key to Ricky's stated woes was one major character flaw which the following tale of philosophical folklore may better help to explain:

"We listen," said the Zen Master to his disciple, *"not to discover, but to find something which confirms how we already think; and we argue, not to find truth, but to vindicate our current thinking."*

He then spoke of a curious King who, when passing through a small town, saw repeated indications of amazing marksmanship in every direction he looked. On trees and barns and even the on fences were bullet sized circles of chalk, and in the exact dead centre of each circle was a bullet. The King was astonished and asked to meet this extraordinary marksman in person but was even more astounded when it turned out to be a ten-year-old child. *"This is incredible,"* said the King. *"How in the world did you manage it?"*

"Easy as pie," was the reply. *"I shoot first and then draw the circles later."*

"So you see," said the Zen Master, *"first we draw our conclusions and only then do we build our premise around them to ensure that they fit. Isn't that how we manage to hold on to our religions, superstitious ideologies, and barefaced*

beliefs?"

The sheer simplicity of this humorous tale is extremely pertinent to the beliefs which encircle us when competing at sport. An example is former world boxing champion, Ricky Hatton, who appeared to conclude he was some kind of fraud unless he continued to win and adhere and comply with the unrealistic demands of expectant peers.

"Almost anything is easier to get into than out of."

- Allen's Law

If we follow the path of Allen's Law as a gentle steer towards personal enlightenment, we may find ourselves teetering on the brink of becoming codebreakers in our own right. Allen's Law empowers us with the necessary skills to crack the long-standing riddle of how best to transition beyond superstitious beliefs. It begins with an understanding that getting into superstitious mindsets is easier than getting out.

There is nothing complex about Allen's law. Superstitious philosophies fool us into believing that experiences grounded in emotion are the result of intuitive states of mind, which is why superstitions feel instinctive and impulsive. Getting into a frame of mind is easy, while negotiating a way out is altogether more difficult.

"Everything we hear is an opinion, not a fact. Everything we see is a perspective, not the truth."

- Marcus Aurelius, Roman Emperor

How often do athletes stop to consider whether their perceptions of winning and losing are over-rehearsed? Ricky for instance, spiralled into the grip of depression as a result of feeling he had let down his supporters, simply because he didn't win. Yet why do athletes claim to 'get into the winning or losing habit', when neither winning or losing are actual habits? Nor is either trait verifiably beholding to superstitious patterns, sequences, and trends.

Superstitions are sequences we activate to gain leverage when seeking favourable odds, often motivated by the belief that each sequence has helped us to taste success on prior occasions. Yet superstitions are fairy tales and lack authenticity until they are subjected to the rigour of repeated testing in a controlled environment to prove that they work.

Losing and winning are not habits. We may have some semblance of control of our personal habits, but we cannot control what our opponents do, or how they think, act, or behave, or the weather or the decisions of referees. Therefore habits are equally contingent on external factors beyond our control. Superstitious ideologies such as fate and luck go one step further by advocating for external factors which are not proven to exist.

Superstitious beliefs represent an intuitive 'sense' or 'feeling' of something mysterious working to our detriment or acting on our behalf. Our sincerity ties us to superstition, but sincerity isn't a virtue nor a guarantee against being dead wrong. It's not wise to discard scepticism and curiosity since, what if up until now we've been getting it wrong? What if our superstitious compulsions are not easing our performance worries at all, but instead are increasing our sporting anxieties?

What if superstition fuels fear and trepidation to such an extent (as aptly demonstrated by footballer Gary Haveron) that many athletes experience a sinking feeling when unable to execute their bizarre routines. Does this sound familiar? Athletes are susceptible to gut-feelings. The superstition called luck is an example, whereby in the minds of many athletes, their gut-feelings are telling them prior to competing that things will either go right or wrong.

Many habits are neural, viral, and cultural, while others are optional and conveniently convey the illusion of offering mental relief. Superstitious compliance is an optional habit. To explain this concept further, consider how, by actively internalising superstition, our reflexes become every bit as predictable as crying when we peel an onion, or as triggering our gag reflex when pushing our fingers down our throat.

Superstitious athletes are predictably prone to confirmation bias, where they spin and decipher conclusions in any manner they see fit. Superstitious bias bears a striking resemblance to the earlier tale of the child shooting bullets into a barn, whereby the King prematurely drew false conclusions to fit with his ill-conceived beliefs. The King drew his conclusions solely from ignorance, just as superstitious athletes draw ill-conceived conclusions that supernatural agents influence sport.

"You are the embodiment of the information you choose to accept and act upon. To change your circumstances you need to change your actions and subsequent thinking."

- Adlin Sinclair, Author

Once we learn to accept an extraordinary premise with no supporting evidence, our thoughts become vulnerable to third-party interference due to the unwarranted value we place on faith. One definition of faith is gullibility, since despite being sincere, faith tells us nothing at all. Who can claim expertise on superstition or luck, or demonstrate the intervention of a god to a sceptic, or prove that miracles are caused by thinking agents or even exist?

Every competitor displays a dual personality: the *instinctual* personality and the *expert* personality. The *instinctual* refers to the childlike performer - full of natural vigour, spontaneity, impulse, curiosity, intuition, and still somewhat oblivious to superstitious compulsions, obsessions, fear, guilt, and luck. The *expert*, in contrast, draws repeated strength and relief from superstitious sentiment, which is formed in the depths of imagination and entails the belief in a supernatural realm.

The mental disconnect between athletes and their superstitious states is common, as was wonderfully demonstrated by the curious insights of footballer Gary Haveron and the connection between his superstitious delusions and his pursuit of a definitive sporting edge. Gary did not allow the absence of demonstrable facts to stand in the way of his comfortable delusions.

Superstition in sport is nothing new. Many competitors wrestle with the dichotomy of whether supernatural ideals should be allowed to outrank demonstrable facts in a selfish bid to experience mental relief. An example of which is the following dichotomy which came to light prior to the 2015 Rugby World Cup finals, when England 2003 World Cup winner Jonny Wilkinson was asked during an interview what advice he passed onto the current squad:

"I just said, you're desperate for that momentum to kick in, but it's your job to do it. It's your job to start it, and that's the unknown of rugby. That's why you wake up on Saturday morning feeling that horrible feeling, or Friday night before you go to bed. It's because of the unknown. You know you've done all you can, but you just want someone to come back from the future and say, look it goes fine, don't worry about it. But you don't get that. You've got to trigger that yourself."

Many athletes embrace superstitious faith as a means of controlling the unknown, since fear of the unknown resonates in the mind of every competitor. Even Jonny Wilkinson recognised the dichotomy by wanting to see into the future to know everything was going to be okay, but had no practical means of doing so. His suggestion, therefore, was for athletes to assume personal responsibility, unlike superstitious athletes who invoke a third party and simply make shit up.

In retrospect, what Jonny failed to mention was if we could channel the future, the news we receive may not be comforting, but disappointing, horrific, and less than okay. Sports psychology is rife with terminologies, one of which is 'mental disorder'; but what is a disorder? It refers to a disproportionate sense of order, which can be argued is a common trait among every human alive, since to adhere to a disproportionate sense of order is as natural as breathing.

Why choose to be disproportionately selective by apportioning stigma to generic superstitions, but fail to apportion similar stigma to superstitions relating to deities, apparitions, ghosts, and interfering-entities called gods? A disorder implies a dis-alignment of focus, whereas a realignment of focus helps to re-establish order, and once order is mentally restored, disorder dissipates of its own accord.

Former England goalkeeper David James was acutely aware of the need for balance, as indicated when he surmised, *"Once you hear some of the stories you start thinking, 'perhaps the train spotters are the healthiest obsessives out there,'"* and in retrospect, he wasn't wrong. Ask a superstitious athlete to refrain from crossing their heart out of sheer habit, or from rubbing their rosaries prior to sport, or from calling on invisible and omnipresent friends to swing results in their favour, and it's highly probable that they will feel awkward and agitated and find that they can't.

Try asking an athlete to stem the urge to moonwalk backwards onto the pitch, or to stop stroking the number on their jersey a specific amount of times and see if they can. But what about us? How successful are we at transitioning habits? Could we stop drinking tea or coffee, or eating chocolate, or do without our mobile phones for a day, or not carry frustration throughout the weekend as a result of our team losing at sport? Oh, and can we stop that funny thing we do with our hands?

"Getting rid of a delusion makes us wiser than getting hold of a truth."

- Ludwig Borne, Satirist

Human nature is such that, more often than not, once all is said and done, a lot more has been said than has actually been done. David James wrote that fabulous piece in 2006, but since then, how much has changed to redress the mental instabilities, anomalies, stigmas, fears, phobias, so-called conditions, and mental disorders which still feature prominently throughout every contingency of sport.

When did superstitions first emerge as integral components of sports psychology, and what stops the concept of sports superstition from becoming redundant in the 21st century? Sadly, that wonderful piece by David James is as relevant today as it was when first written. This confronts us with two burning questions: where does the power lie within superstitious belief, and what is our understanding of power?

Power is easily broken down and dispersed into two comprehensible truths: *'willpower'* and *'won't power'*. Earlier, we read how former professional footballer Gary Haveron's state of will was outflanked by his overt addiction to *'won't power'*, as the sheer volume of superstitions he had amassed began to stack up against him, to such an extent that when ask if he was *willing* to give them up, his response was he *can't*, or more likely *won't*.

It is easy to tell when our minds are in trouble. It begins the first moment we are no longer aware if we control our superstitions or if superstitions control us. Part of conventional Western philosophy is to obey the directive of 'never answer a question with another question', whereas the Eastern equivalent is to question everything. The generic pursuit of awareness, however, begins by endeavouring to believe as many true things as possible, while suspending belief about the unknown until evidence renders those beliefs as true or false.

Values of Superstition

"The past is for learning from and letting go. You can't revisit it. It vanishes."

- Adele Parks, Author

I once shared the good fortune of participating in a UEFA football coaching course in Belfast with former Liverpool, Blackburn, and England International footballer David Thompson (son of Phil). This unique experience afforded me an up-close and personal opportunity to garner his thoughts on superstitious beliefs. Being the character he is, however, he wasn't shy about sharing an opinion or two, but although his response was immediate and scathing, it also made me smile.

First came the scorn. *"I always put my socks on before my boots,"* David mocked in self-gratifying hysterics before adding, *"I effing love laughing at my own jokes."* Yet, just as I felt I was getting nowhere and feeling that he had made enough of a fool of me, he finally began to contemplate superstition with a little more purpose, and his opinion was key since he'd been surrounded by top-level footballers his whole life and footballing career. So I listened intently to his rationale:

"I think when you're talking about superstitions; some players have got to have done the [exact] same things. It's a procedure. It's like a routine, like military precision, just to keep getting their minds tuned-in to get ready to play. I think for some people it's like OCD. I've seen a lot of footballers with the OCD-type thing, with their touches and certain stuff they have to do."

I welcomed David's scepticism. It was honest and typical of many athletes' instinctive reaction to such an unconventional, weird, odd, neurotic, eccentric, unnerving, paranoiac, and perhaps even uncomfortable topic when considering the impact of superstitious belief on competitive sport. When confronted by superstition, he gravitated straight to the rather predictable tactic for human avoidance, he 'laughed it off'.

David joked and made fun of superstition, and by doing so he turned any semblance of awkwardness into light-hearted banter and a bit of craic. His initial response was typical of many athletes who mask their debilitating beliefs behind laughter. Yet, for many competitors, such as Rugby player Paul Wood or goalkeeper David James who were caught in the vice-like grip of obsessive compulsions, superstition is no laughing matter at all.

Next I interviewed Josh Wagner, former Canadian international football goalkeeper and a wonderful ambassador for his Christian faith. I asked him to share his superstitious experiences during a speaking engagement at Falkirk FC, where I enquired as to whether he had witnessed any strange forms of behaviour or eccentric quirks while in the presence of teammates during pre-match preparation. He very graciously replied:

"A player I played with at Yeovil town, before he would go out onto the pitch if he was starting a game, would always make himself puke before he went out. Yeah [it was] just very weird, but he said he needed to do it all the time while he was playing at a higher level. It just helped him with the nervousness of the overall day and then he'd make himself puke before he went on, and that would help him to relax and ease into the game."

Charming eh? I pursued Josh's revelation by asking whether he'd detected any noticeable change in the player, perhaps like a much greater sense of calm, after having thrown up?

"You know what? I usually tried not to be around for it, as it's not a very nice sound emanating from the bathroom. But I think definitely there was a difference in him once he started a game from when he came on as a sub, because he didn't have the time or the privacy to do what he needed to do [puke] and [because of that] I think he seemed a bit more agitated or something."

I was keen to explore this thread in more detail to find out at which conscious level superstitious conditioning existed in younger age groups, and whether younger perspectives could place a numerical value on superstitious belief. To this end, I had a conversation with Simon, a young hockey player who at the time played for Mossley Hockey Club in Northern Ireland. Simon had previously represented his province of Ulster at U16 and U18 levels, so I asked if he used superstitions to prepare to compete.

"Superstitions, yeah I do. I don't change my socks throughout the season. I have to wear my red ones underneath the Mossley ones in every game. If I was to change that then perhaps I'd have a bad game, and I think mentally it would affect me also. So throughout the whole season I'd wear the same socks, but next season I'll have a different pair of socks, and then I'll wear them throughout the whole season. If I didn't, it would be on my mind and it would affect my performance because I'd have something else on my mind and so I wouldn't be 100% fully focused on what I'm meant to be doing."

I tried to coerce Simon towards reasonable logic. So, I asked for five specific reasons as to why he might lose any given hockey match on any given day.

"Not having my usual routine on a Saturday, not having a proper sleep the night before, lying in on a Saturday morning, not drinking enough water to be hydrated, and not getting the right food."

I ask if he could give five practical situations which may adversely affect his performance on the pitch once the match had begun?

"Lack of preparation, not having a good warm-up or stretching enough, missing out on my sprints before a match to get my heart rate up and to get me going, not having a practice period to get used to stick-and-ball, and perhaps an inferiority complex."

Next I felt it was time to explore the technical and tactical aspects of his game. I wanted to know if he had a bad game, where perhaps his shooting was consistently off target or his positioning or passing out-of-sorts, did his socks have a role to play in that?

"No, not technically but mentally. To me it just rests my mind knowing I have the right socks on."

Notice how quickly he switched any talk of the technical and tactical aspects back to the mental. So I opted instead for a different approach, by redirecting his thoughts back to exploring *causes* and by asking if he'd ever lost a hockey match while wearing his so called 'lucky' socks?

"Yeah but that was probably down to performance or perhaps it just wasn't meant to be our day as a team, but individually I felt more comfortable wearing those socks. In fact, we lost three matches this season and also drew a couple as the season went right down to the wire."

Finally I had something concrete to build on. So I asked if the dropped points ultimately cost them the league?

"Yeah, I think they could've done."

Ah! Now we're getting somewhere. So I seized the moment to reflect on his admission of losing while wearing his lucky socks. Only now, armed with concrete facts, I asked Simon if he still thought those socks were lucky, given that he lost while they were still on his feet?

But refusing to budge even an inch, Simon casually replied, *"Not very lucky I suppose, but it's just a mental thing that rests my mind on a Saturday."*

Dammit! So now, aghast and perplexed, I found myself pointing out that while wearing his lucky socks, his league form had dipped when it mattered most, sometimes his performances were way below par, and he finished the league winning nothing at all. So feeling somewhat smug, I asked if he would finally admit that his lucky socks weren't so lucky after all?

"It sort of puts things into perspective I suppose; but when all is said and done, it's my routine and I'll never change because I've done it ever since I was 15 years of age."

Okay, so last throw of the dice. With my earlier smugness turning to despondency, I challenged him to consider what might be the outcome if he chose to embrace an alternative focus during the lead up to every match. Perhaps something technical that may add a measurable attribute to his game?

"Hmm, I think it would work. If I could find something else then I wouldn't be so focused on my socks."

So finally, while pouring myself a drink in the last-chance saloon, I sought to determine whether it's possible to measure the impact of a superstitious belief. So I asked Simon to offer an honest appraisal in the form of a definitive number which best represented the actual percentage of mental impact he felt likely to experience if he forgot his lucky socks?

"Personally I have to be 100% focused on the hockey match, and if I didn't have them on then 5% of my mind would be on my socks."

So finally, from beneath the mental blockade, I began to unearth the underlying *causes* of Simon's restrictive belief. *"My routine"* he called it, having first internalised and then attributed 5% of his focus to wearing those lucky red socks. So not only had they morphed into an integral part of his core being, but he also believed with utmost sincerity that a red pair of socks could affect his luck.

Simon's sock superstition had well and truly stuck, and it's easy to tell because he called it *"my routine"*. He presented his socks as an active placebo to alleviate any likelihood of experiencing bad luck, but once he accepted ownership of his illusion, he validated its meaning, whereupon it grew a set of legs and sprang to life. His behaviour is typical of many superstitious compulsions and habits insomuch as, to the untrained-eye, they appear relatively harmless, innocuous, inoffensive, innocent, and safe.

Simon's memory tricked him into adding emotional value in the form of sincerity, which then took on specific numerical value (5% of focus) right before my very eyes. And so instead of negating any niggling doubts which may on occasion have crept into his mind as to whether he is losing the plot, he reinforced the longevity of his delusion using two simple words (*"my routine"*) to justify thinking and acting the way that he did. The degree of sincerity which Simon placed on wearing his lucky red socks shone through like a beacon during our interview, despite sincerity being no guarantee against being dead wrong.

Superstitious belief is the 'god of the gaps' and exists in the void between appearance and reality where imagination runs rife and scepticism is rendered obsolete. All it took to hook Simon on superstition was a placebo effect which caused him to ascribe mathematical value to a superstition which, due to his team's win-loss ratio, was proven to be fundamentally flawed.

Simon magically pulled 5% of focus from nowhere, with no scientific process undertaken to measure the cost of discarding his socks. Instead he plucked his assertion out of thin air, minus the bells-and-whistles and subsequent fanfare which would accompany being able to produce a formula to validate his superstitious belief.

Simon's solid refusal to change his opinion or amend his behaviour any time soon was due to not being able to remember having acted any differently since he was fifteen. The historical nature of his belief was hard-wired into his brain to such an extent that it felt as though it was a part of him, as if part of his skin and integral to his success. Yet, the only reason his superstition felt real was that he wished for it to be so; in fact, so normal was his dependency on wearing those socks that he could no longer fathom what the all fuss was about.

Simon based his belief on circular reasoning due to feeling compelled to repeat his routine every time a match came around. He only praised the benefits of superstition when he won, but was quick to dismiss superstition's culpability when results failed to go his way. This raised many questions such as whether there is validity to superstitious values and what practical purpose is served by pulling unfalsifiable constructs out of thin air?

Simon's habit is real because he *thinks* it's real, and because he *thinks* it's real he then *feels* it's real. Yet, when asked to explain the origin of such obstinate tomfoolery, his mind drew a blank and he couldn't recall. As justification, all he could say was, *"I've been doing it since I was fifteen,"* as if starting at such a tender age was vindication for maintaining a habit with enough power to affect his performance on the pitch.

Where is the evidence that superstition added 5% of magical value to increase his focus to a potential 105% or decrease his concentration levels to 95%? Simon's superstition left him less mindful of the most lucid factor of all which, lest we forget, is the actual competing. It reminds me of a quote I once heard by an athlete who, during a moment of deep reflection, said: *"I kiss my necklace before every race to remind my mind that I'm ready to run."* Isn't that the real reason for instigating rituals, to reacquaint our memory with comforting rhythms so that we feel comfortable and mentally at ease enough to compete?

An athlete has no need to repeatedly remind themselves of how to run since muscle memory reminds their leg joints to move and rotate, irrespective of whether they kiss a lucky necklace, wear lucky red socks, or pray for divine intervention. Once the thoughts of an athlete tumble into the groove of a beat, rhythm, habit, pattern, or trend, it becomes increasingly difficult to escape from the vibe each sequence creates.

Simon fell into the psychological groove of believing that his lucky socks possessed supernatural powers which affected his luck, but what percentage of numerical value did he unconsciously attach to the idea of luck and how did he determine that luck was a thing? Since why bother subscribing to superstitious values without first accepting the existence of luck? No one to date has demonstrably deciphered luck, which means only a liar, imbecile, or fool believes they have cracked its elusive code.

Luck is superstition and cannot be accurately pinpointed as an intelligent agent with the capacity to interact with terrestrial sport. Yet Simon's 5% of historical intrinsic value, when combined with the tender age of 15, implied a relationship of such personal value that as far as he was concerned, no lucky socks meant no win, and he wasn't prepared to take the risk.

The time has arrived to draw attention to some of sport's most avoided questions such as, does subscribing to superstitious beliefs mean we're gradually losing touch with reality? By what means can we measure luck? And where is the tipping point whereby a bizarre superstition is considered normal?

The term 'normal' is perhaps the greatest behavioural misrepresentation ever to grace the collective mindset of mankind since human behaviour is primarily subjective. But don't take my word for it. Consider how best to describe your own superstitious faith. Is it a cautious faith, mindless faith, hopeful faith, guarded faith, or just pie-in-the-sky? Or does faith's distinct lack of proof create the necessity to pull mysterious rabbits out of illusionary hats?

Once faith enters the equation, how can we differentiate between misplaced sincerity, questionable integrity, intellectual dishonesty, and gullibility? Consider as an example the underlying innuendo behind the following quote by former Chelsea manager, José Mourinho, referring to his team's need to experience an extended run of good fortune following a string of poor results.

"Only mother nature can do it. They need luck. They need to feel luck. They need to arrive at half-time winning 2-0 or 3-0. They need to fly without pressure, to play and to feel that everything is going in their favour. Not to feel this pressure, this panic, this negativity against unlucky mistakes."

Many viewed José's words as an honest appraisal of how it feels to be stranded on the wrong side of luck. Others viewed his response as a typical rant, which at least spared poor old luck from facing culpability for the bulk of his woes. Yet, more astute observers were of the opinion that luck was merely a scapegoat and that the answers José sought to his losing dilemma lay much closer to home. Football is a game of varied opinion, and Mourinho is rarely short of one of those. So let the inquisition begin as to whether highlighting luck as a major contributing factor was by accident or by design.

Was José trying to avoid taking personal responsibility for Chelsea's extended run of poor results by deliberately implicating luck? Was it merely a ruse to secure luck as a scapegoat or a genuine plea to providence and fate to ride to his aid as his knight in shining armour during his managerial hour of need? Did he simply tout luck as a well-rehearsed cliché or was it the first thing which sprang to his mind?

From where did such a poor run of luck originate, how did it get there, and how could José tell if what his team had experienced was the result of luck? Might they have been better occupied seeking practical solutions to address practical problems such as how best to defend, improve concentration levels, and be more prolific in front of goal? Instead, José succumbed to supernatural hearsay, which is the perfect example of why every athlete and sports commentator should be asking whether luck is a practical matter, a supernatural matter, or doesn't matter at all?

The crux of José's woes was predominately human. Or was that his plan all along? Did he choose to cite luck as being the culprit because it not only sounds plausible but cannot be disproved? In the end, it's up to us, the impartial observers, to determine how much blame should be levied on José or redirected to luck? Let's begin by questioning whether it's plausible to place a numerical value on the impact of luck or to claim beyond all shadow of a doubt that luck can intervene in terrestrial sport, either to our detriment or on our behalf.

It's important to question what kind of hybrid we really are. What makes us act and behave the way we do? What causes us to fail or succeed in equal measure (often spectacularly), or inspires us to rise or subsequently fall? What makes us do something amazing but then something ridiculous?

Is the key to performance open-ended given Simon's lucky socks bore no technical, tactical, or social bearing on how he performed. Yet he saw fit to afford a pair of socks parity with other components of sport which are not supernatural in essence, but instead can be calculated, catalogued, and benchmarked with relative ease. These components include his strike-success ratio, physical conditioning, pass-completion ratio, and flawless commitment to the cause of his team. The only glaring incalculable component of Simon's performance was a potential loss of 5% focus due to his superstitious belief.

Former professional footballer David Thompson earlier alluded to the OCD-style military precision which remains in-situ in the sporting mentality of many players, irrespective of whether those rituals produce the desired effect. There is a saying, 'the bullet which kills you is the one you never see coming'. To apply this metaphorically, we may be wise to sleep with one eye open to stay alert to the smoking-gun that is superstitious belief.

To transition beyond superstitious ideals requires opening our minds to scepticism while ensuring the door to supernatural susceptibility remains firmly shut. Superstitious beliefs, in essence, are fractal, as are clouds in the sky as they accumulate mass before subdividing into smaller clouds. The concept of fractal in this particular context is surprisingly easy to understand and can open our minds to the cyclical nature of superstitious beliefs.

The branches of trees are also fractal, growing as they do to accumulate mass before subdividing into patterns of ever-decreasing frameworks on a continuous loop. Rivers are also fractal, by continuing to flow as part of a larger moving mass before subdividing into streams, estuaries, brooks, and pools within endless cycles of calm and tranquillity or torrents of turbulence and rage.

In order to explore nature's anecdotal link with sports psychology, it's first worth pointing out that superstitions are also of a fractal nature, whereby their natural tendency is to accumulate mass and increase in myth and legend before subdividing into endless mental frameworks of ritual and farce. The way nature divides and then subdivides the branches of trees does not reduce the trees in stature, as supported by the magnitude of a hundred-year-old oak with its roots so firmly embedded into the ground, it would require an incredible effort to shift.

The same applies to the magnitude of superstitious beliefs. Can you spot the similarities between the fractal nature (the spread) of the branches of trees and the way superstitious innuendo spreads into sub-superstitious beliefs? Maybe you can or maybe you can't, since looking does not always guarantee seeing. Just as looking at the true value of sports psychology does not guarantee seeing that psychology is not just an academic vocation. Psychology is life, and when the brain ceases to function, life also ceases to function, and so we die along with our superstitious beliefs.

In an earlier quote, Sir Francis Bacon alluded to confirmation bias. This characteristic is evident in athletes who see superstition as a sure-fire hit when it works in their favour but ignore the misses when they fall flat on their face. Hockey player Simon stubbornly refuted the idea that his lucky red socks weren't lucky at all, and basked in the comforting glow of confirmation bias. He eulogised his socks as being lucky when results and performances went his way but chose to turn a blind-eye to their ineffectiveness when the tables turned and performances dipped.

Superstitions undermine spontaneity, and minus spontaneity we are lost to an amazing concept which I call drunken consciousness. The best example of this is a roller coaster ride which leaves us lightheaded and shocks our thoughts out of mental mediocrity, leaving us no choice but to be fully present, alive, alert, and feeling somewhat intoxicated by the absolute thrill and exhilaration of experiencing spontaneous but shaken beliefs.

"I'm not sure I always feel like I'm in the seat. Sometimes I'm only holding on by one hand and flying out behind the roller coaster. I don't know anybody who doesn't feel that way"

- David Morse, Actor

Sports superstitions are personal vices, as is the belief in a god, the need for applause, or the feeling of winning. Even losing has vice-like qualities, since the risk and apprehension which accompanies losing can prove as addictive as the risk and anticipation of trying to win. Superstition is no less of a vice than smoking cigarettes, the frequent urge to check our mobile phones, biting our fingernails, or needing our daily fix of caffeine in coffee or tea.

If we can't give it up or detach from it mentally, then in all probability, the damn thing is a vice. Every culture, religion, and sport is a vice, given each is comprised of its own unique folklore, myths, and traditions, or laden with customs and conventions, most of which predate *us*, the hapless competitors, who buy into each culture and then fall into line.

"Memory believes before knowing remembers."

- William Faulkner, Writer

What is the practical impact of superstitious belief? Consider the following bizarre series of events as illustrated on the *talkSPORT* radio website regarding midfielder Malvin Kamara who at the time was a football player at Stafford Rangers FC. Malvin manfully explained his vice-like compulsion for watching the film *Willy Wonka and the Chocolate Factory* prior to competing. *"I have to watch it before every game as it gets me in the right mood. It's been my favourite film since I was little. It calms my nerves and gives me luck."*

Malvin isn't alone with superstition. *The Independent* reported how goalkeeper Shea Given carried a vial of holy water onto the pitch to be placed in the back of his goal. I found this claim interesting due to the fact that when I interviewed Shea to enquire about superstitions, he made no mention of this ritual at all. He did mention crossing himself before walking onto the pitch but was unsure as to whether this constituted superstition. The report then described how Shea's predecessor for the Republic of Ireland goalkeeping position, Packie Bonner, carried a piece of clay from County Donegal onto the pitch in his glove bag.

Next consider former Leicester City manager, Claudio Ranieri, who prior to winning the English football Premier League in 2016/17, was told by a reporter, *"It's 8 hours and 10 minutes since you conceded a Premier League goal. That's extraordinary isn't it?"*

Claudio seemed visibly unsettled by the statistic and so replied, *"Why you remember me this? I'm not superstitious but you don't tell me this."* Yet Claudio's deeply animated protest suggests that he *is* superstitious after all, otherwise he would've just thanked the reporter and smiled. He seemed concerned that by daring to dream he may inadvertently insult some supernatural thinking agent, thereby making it angry and intent on exacting revenge.

Superstitions are rooted in nostalgia, and nostalgia steers athletes towards irrational beliefs. So much so, that there is a high probability that Malvin saw nothing bizarre in the compulsive nature of how he behaved. His habit highlighted how easily an athlete's focus can be offset by a myriad of oddities, weird irregularities, peculiarities, and twists, each of which has their own incisive bearing on how athletes prepare to compete.

The nature of Malvin's superstition meant its impact was calculable. It starts with an awareness that the Willy Wonka film runs for 90 minutes, which when multiplied by 46 league fixtures, gives a total of 4140 minutes or 69 hours of watching the same film for the same duration prior to every game.

Assuming the details of his superstition are accurate, the sheer volume of spontaneity lost to nostalgia meant this was quality time he could never recapture with family or friends or use to experience something new but of equal value. Malvin's tale may seem humorous at first glance, but closer scrutiny reveals damning repercussions when faced with the prospect of appraising nostalgia. But what did Malvin achieve by using nostalgia as a template for success which could not have been achieved just as efficiently had Willy Wonka failed to exist? Furthermore, what is nostalgia?

"The Greek word for 'return' is nostos. Algos means 'suffering'. So nostalgia is the suffering caused by an unappeased yearning to return."

- Milan Kundera, Writer

The upshot of nostalgia is that athletes are burdened by sentiment and obsessed by a yearning to return, but a return to where? To which previous nostalgic scenario do superstitious athletes seek to return? There is a wonderful quote concerning nostalgia by humourist Will Rogers which states, *"Things ain't what they used to be and probably never was."* So, what drives us to only see the parts of our past which we choose to remember with fond nostalgia?

The superstitious mind is immersed in nostalgia. So, I offer a challenge to access the left hemisphere of the brain and reset all current logic back to zero, to a time when nostalgia wasn't even a word. Very few active champions are afforded the luxury of wallowing in nostalgia, but are preoccupied with the ongoing search to discover the next competitive edge. In contrast, superstitious beliefs are steeped in nostalgia and therefore, by default, so is every athlete who facilitates a superstitious belief.

Consider the dramatic turn of events recorded in the book of Genesis in the King James Bible. The story recounts how Lot, the nephew of Abraham, while fleeing from the impending destruction of Sodom and Gomorrah, pleaded with his absconding wife not to turn around and look back at the encroaching calamity, but to keep moving forward with great haste while focusing solely on the road ahead. Sadly, Lot's wife needed one last glance at the unfolding events. One final glimpse at nostalgia, whereby she was turned into a pillar of salt.

The cult of nostalgia is potent and has the potential to increase an athlete's mental resilience to compete or to turn spontaneity into something inanimate like a pillar of salt. It's important to sleep with one eye open since, despite nostalgia's comforting public persona as a harmless sentiment, it seems that deeply secreted within its warmth lurks the inanimate characteristics of quicksand, quietly drawing us back to our accumulated past before sinking us mercilessly into sentimentality.

Nostalgia clearly influenced hockey player Simon who partly justified his superstition about socks by claiming he'd acted that way since he was 15. Similarly, Malvin's bizarre game preparations were due to feeling nostalgic about replicating emotions he'd experienced while watching Willy Wonka as a child. Superstitious beliefs evoke thoughts of nostalgia by looking back with affection on the warm fuzzy pretence that we maintain ownership over things which are clearly external to us.

Nostalgia is adept at bamboozling athletes into believing that superstitions have worked for them in the past and can do so again. It encourages athletes to look back in fondness at times when the planets appeared to perfectly align by creating a sense that if they're serious about winning, they must retain their superstitions at any cost.

What's luck got to do with it?

"Genetically I'm quite fortunate."

- Carl Froch, Boxer

While speaking on *talkSPORT* radio, Olympic Gold medallist Denise Lewis was asked what advantage she believed competing on home soil had played in Team GB's record medal haul at the London 2012 Olympics and how many medals did she think were won as a result? *"Many. Almost all,"* was her reply. What an emphatic stroke of good fortune for Team GB & NI athletes, if Denise's off-the-cuff assessment is to be believed.

Given Denise's candid observation, what percentage of merit should be credited to the unrivalled brilliance of Team GB athletes? Or in contrast, what percentage of merit should be credited to luck? Is it even possible to tell if the home nation's athletes were lucky or unlucky, given no one has ever been able to categorically define or decipher luck?

If we take a stroll or a quiet meander through the inner sanctums of our mind to conjure a sense of what the word 'superstition' conveys, we may experience intrigue and curiosity, and the same, I contend, applies to luck. Both superstition and luck are intertwined, equally ambiguous, unfalsifiable, and currently impossible to untangle. Both also present zero evidence to the contrary, just as no explanations appear forthcoming as to why either trait is allowed to gain traction within any athlete's frame of mind.

Little meaningful thought is given to the supernatural origins of luck, as to how, why, or when it is able to manifest in the first place, or appear permanently endowed with the freedom to act as a physical extension of us with no means of redress. That is until we happen to lose, at which point all bets are off. So what makes luck such a force for good or evil for many competitors engaged in sport? And who can deny that the reason superstition exists in the first place is that athletes believe it affects their luck.

Some athletes believe luck has a major bearing on sports performance based on the talents they feel they've been blessed with or denied, or due to the genetic potential or limitations duly inherited from birth. Others see luck as a prophetic supernatural thinking agent, which either conspires to work in their favour or to bring them back down to earth with a bump.

Very few competitors, at some point or other, have not fallen foul to believing they exist at the mercy of a strange and as yet unknown phenomenon called luck. So, why then is the topic of luck so rarely discussed in any meaningful capacity, as being an integral learning component of sports education or coaching itineraries? Why is coaching in sport more attuned to the idea of advocating hard work at the gym or track?

Why do conventional sporting directives display such an unbalanced penchant for advocating reward for dedication to training, or for seeking to improve tactically or technically, rather than to unlearn the debilitating impact and effects of luck? Why is coaching 'emotion' undervalued and why are these questions so rarely asked? What makes us afraid of discussing the practicalities of luck?

"How do you become the fastest man in the world? It depends on your raw material. How you're assembled. How you're built."

- Michael Johnson, Sprinter and BBC Commentary

A huge blow was dealt to coaching emphasis being placed on brute force and ignorance, following the men's 100-metre final at the London 2012 Olympic Games. This transpired when Usain Bolt, the greatest sprinter in history announced to the world that his Jamaican teammate and incumbent World Champion Yohan Blake possessed a far more committed attitude towards training than he. *"Yohan trains harder than me, but I know I've got a talent."*

Bolt, for the record, was speaking after having just beaten the entire field, including Blake, with a time of 9.65 seconds to retain Olympic gold and set a new Olympic record. Now that really is impossible to ignore. So, why is sport's overall focus for coaching development so often attuned towards blood, sweat and tears, and less attuned towards better comprehending the impact of rogue elements with seemingly limitless powers to affect how athletes perform on any given day?

Bolt's honest appraisal of Blake's contrasting attitude to training sparked a need to debate the importance of genetics, regarding what percentage of inherent genetics, in the context of winning or losing, can be attributed to luck? Or, why not broaden the conversation to question why athletes appeal to luck to navigate their way through sport's most critical and defining moments, given luck doesn't appear to operate within the jurisdiction of human control.

Luck is a superstition which, if it is to be believed, shapes the destiny of every sports performance and subsequent result; as does applying brute force, ignorance, blood, sweat, and tears. Athletes, however, are rarely consistent when it comes to paying luck its fair dues following times of great achievement. Preferring instead, as many do, to claim all the credit, as if they did all of the winning by themselves while blaming luck when they lose.

Former England cricketer Ed Smith referred to athletes' aversion to crediting luck, *"as if in some kind of meritocracy,"* whereby all merit for winning belongs to the athlete, while no grace, respect, or appreciation is credited to the mercy of luck. But is it wise to bite the hand that feeds us, given the same hand can just as easily take everything away? We are under no obligation to *like* luck, nor may we find ourselves *favoured* by luck. However not liking luck does not give us licence to ignore that, in the minds of many athletes, luck is a thinking agent and therefore a 'thing'.

Many sports protagonists take luck for granted, as a result of being historically blinded to the idea of luck existing purely as a selfish trait to be summoned at their beck and call. Consider the following public boast by former WBA and WBO World Heavyweight Boxing Champion Tyson Fury during a press conference in Manchester prior to his July 2016 rematch with former champion Wladimir Klitschko.

"I don't live an athlete's lifestyle. You couldn't call me an athlete. I hate every second of training. I hate boxing, but I'm just too good at it and I'm making too much money. [There's] easy money to be made. I don't take boxing seriously as you can tell. I really am a joke, aren't I? But can I fight? Yes!"

In the end, the rematch never happened. The overriding message, however, as conveyed by Tyson's verbal tirade, bears many hallmarks of Usain Bolt's earlier assertion about Yohan Blake's superior attitude towards training. Yet, Tyson went a step further by seemingly revealing that he had fallen out of love with his sport and perhaps inadvertently with himself.

The immediate shock of Tyson's verbal shenanigans almost dwarfed the issue of luck. Particularly when he very publicly lifted his shirt to reveal poor physical conditioning and to describe himself as a 'fat man', presumably to discredit Klitschko by drawing attention to his inability to beat a boxer so completely out of shape.

Tyson took full advantage of the public platform by ridiculing himself. Yet irrespective of physical conditioning, his 'lucky' genetics means he stands 6 feet 9 inches tall [2.06m] with an 85 inch [216 cm] reach. This makes him an extremely dangerous opponent, as was evident when he rather majestically brought an end to Klitschko's eleven-year winning streak.

In hindsight, there can be little dispute that Tyson's height and reach came in very handy to overcome his formidable adversary who himself stood at a whopping 6 feet 6½ inches tall [199cm] with an 81 inch [206 cm] reach of his own. Tyson's size advantage leads to questions such as, what percentage of winning was solely due to being physically bigger than his opponent as a result of genetics and luck? Tyson did not choose to be bigger than Klitschko. He just inherently is.

Consider the following traditional Persian saying, 'Go and wake-up your luck'. Yet perhaps the real challenge facing many competitors is to reawaken their minds to luck since luck travels with them, lies ahead of them, and also lurks behind as a shadowy-companion. Irrespective of race, creed, or denomination, there is simply no escaping from luck as no matter which direction we turn, luck exercises a psychological pre-eminence which inflicts a stranglehold on the collective mindset of competitive sport.

It's time to open our eyes and mind to luck. To this end, I will share a story of self-introspection which began as I contemplated the enigma commonly referred to as luck. During the aftermath of a demoralising footballing defeat, I recall being sat alongside teammates with head bowed in the changing room trying hard to avoid sharing eye contact with our manager who was clearly unamused.

As I listened intently, it soon became clear that the manager was struggling to make sense of the offending debacle he had just witnessed. I also sensed there was more going on than him just being disappointed by the defeat, and this was promptly confirmed by his post-match analysis, whereby, still caught in the emotion of the moment, he raged:

"We hit the woodwork twice, and that referee was effin' shocking. Even the wind changed bloody direction in their favour near half-time, and we should've had a penalty. We just didn't get the rub of the green today lads, but heads-up, it's nobody's fault. We just didn't get the luck."

His response caused me to contemplate and question the gist of what he had said, with regard to what it all actually meant. To my teammates, his discrepancy went unnoticed, but as I travelled home I began to recall his pre-match team-talk in much greater detail, where he spoke about tactical and technical requirements. He also spoke tirelessly of maintaining concentration, discipline, endeavour, comradery, and team ethics. In truth, he pretty much covered all the bases and touched on everything except for luck.

Bizarrely, never once did the manager mention luck, not even once, and yet in defeat, he saw fit to ignore any talk of all previous footballing attributes in favour of blaming 'bad luck'. So let's explore athletes' attitude to luck in more detail.

Within sporting circles, the term 'legend' is frequently overused to describe talented and professional, yet at best, relatively ordinary performers. A true legend, however, is extraordinary. So, in order to do justice to the topic of luck, and to ascertain where the credit for a successful sporting career should lie, I defer to two 'proper' legends of Irish and Northern Irish sport.

The first is Gaelic football star Peter Canavan, who is a two-time All-Ireland Champion, six-time All-Star, winner of four Provincial titles and an International Rules series participant. I asked him what percentage of his fantastic career he attributed to luck. This was his response:

"It's not something I would buy into. You make your own luck by being there and by looking for openings. The example I would use is a ball coming off the post, and you being the first to react and to get there. If you don't anticipate these things to happen, then the ball will not come your way. So on a lot of occasions, I think you have to persist, and you have to make your own luck and things have a way of working out. So, I wouldn't like to attribute any success I have had to luck."

I then asked a similar question of Dame Mary Peters, who is a former Olympic Gold Medallist in the Pentathlon, representing Great Britain and Northern Ireland at the 1972 Munich Olympics. I specifically enquired as to what percentage of her success she attributed to luck. This was her initial response:

"Very little, a very small margin. I wasn't a talented athlete. I worked hard at it and trained for all the skills that I required. It was years and years and years of work. It's just that little element of luck that could have made the difference between being first and second; and boy I would've hated being second."

This caused me to smile, as despite her genuine politeness, the glint in her eye momentarily confronted me with the same sense of steely resolve that drove her to achieve Olympic Gold. *"I would've hated being second,"* she said, and I could tell she bloody well meant it. Yet, the speed by which both sporting legends initially declined to refer to luck cast a glaring oversight into the mix.

Luck was viewed initially by both parties as the poor relation to physical endeavour, skill, determination, opportunism, and graft; but what of luck itself? Are athletes in danger of misinterpreting correlations of two or more random events as being luck, or is luck beyond mortal consideration? Many athletes view superstitions as a viable pathway to favourable outcomes and also as a means to create or influence luck.

Who or what should be credited when Peter Canavan combined his anticipatory and reactionary skills with resolve and persistence, and the ball broke in his favour by rebounding off the post at the perfect angle to score? Or who or what was to blame if the ball shot off at a different angle than he anticipated and so the chance was lost and his efforts in vain? Was it luck, chance, probability, or coincidence?

I decided to revisit Dame Mary's initial response, to draw out in more detail her considered reaction to being asked if luck played any part in her rise to prominence and glorious career. *"Oh very much. Being in the right place at the right time, and particularly the people I met that helped and supported me and put me on the road to success along the way. Even on the night of my final two events in Munich, everything went right for me and I'm sure a lot of that was down to luck."*

A clear dichotomy appeared to exist between the value Dame Mary seemed willing to place on the role played by luck, and her diametrically opposing values or seeming unwillingness to view luck as the cause or part of the cause of her resounding success. Yet luck's mysterious aura contributed massively to Dame Mary's career, as the planets aligned by her own frank admission, *"On the night of my final two events in Munich, everything went right for me."* It was an honest response which caused me to ponder whether Dame Mary's losing opponents shared in her new-found respect for luck.

How feasible is it for Dame Mary to discount the positive impact of luck? Consider the fascinating tale she happily recounted, whereby she spoke of her dad's eagerness for both her and her brother to participate in sport. So much so, that as a surprise for her sixteenth birthday, she became the proud recipient of a ton of industrial sand to practice the high-jump in a field nearby.

Not to be outdone on her seventeenth birthday, Dame Mary was lovingly gifted a load of cement from which her dad built a shot circle to enable her to practice the shot-put. Within a matter of weeks, she had broken the Northern Ireland record. She then explained how the shot she trained with always weighed light, so her dad set off to the local foundry to have a proper shot made, and, partly as a result, Dame Mary went on to break the Commonwealth record.

"The laws of genetics apply, even if we refuse to learn them."

- Alison Plowden, Historian

What an incredible piece of good fortune to have a dad so committed and enthusiastic towards her progression in athletics, and to grow up in a household with a shared love and appreciation for sport, but what of her genetics? Dame Mary initially implied that she wasn't particularly talented and yet, inadvertently, there was talent in abundance as-and-when required.

What value did Dame Mary attribute to lucky genetics? There is an argument to be made that she had advantageous genetics since *something* equipped her with the capacity to gain an added two-stone of weight. *Something* also equipped her to squat and bench-press weights which she described as quite exorbitant for a young woman at the time. As such, it's at least worthy of consideration as to whether all women and men possess a genetic potential and physical capacity similar to Dame Mary; and the answer is no.

Why are so many athletes reluctant to accept that luck impacts every contingency of sport, and that they are not at risk of losing face in front of their peers by paying luck the dues it deserves? To imply that luck played an integral role in their success need not be internalised as condescending, patronising, or derogative in any way, shape, or form. Acknowledging luck need not detract from anyone's gut-wrenching efforts or sacrificial endeavours, nor does it denigrate any prior accomplishments, nor lessen the feeling of success.

Acknowledging luck does not diminish a work ethic or detract from a long-term sporting legacy since each of the aforementioned still applies. It requires the illusion of personal ego to trick us into believing that luck somehow detracts from a personal legacy. Yet irrespective of ego, every successful sports performance owes a belated debt of gratitude to luck, just as Dame Mary experienced tremendous luck and extremely good fortune throughout her incredible career.

Dame Mary was the beneficiary of a committed dad and favourable genetics, plus the people she met along the way who, by her own admission, set her on the path to success. She also acknowledged how various components just fell into place during her final two events in Munich. Looking back, she has so much to be proud of, and the British and Irish public are proud of her. She acknowledged many things throughout her career for which she is thankful, but at the forefront of her gratitude should be luck; the true definition of which we shall explore later.

As for Peter Canavan, he is widely regarded as one of Ireland's finest and most talented Gaelic football players of the modern era. His luck lay within his audacious talents, plus his ability to motivate teammates through his unerring gift for staying calm in the tightest of situations, and being able to change or affect the course of any game. Due to his wonderful kicking ability, Peter quickly became the go-to player who opposition players would try to knock out of his stride.

His nickname was 'Peter the Great', but many simply referred to him as a 'natural' who was destined for greatness; but is such an assertion entirely accurate, or even plausible? Was Peter truly 'destined' for greatness, or is such an assertion a slight on his legacy, having grafted so hard to establish the incredible landmarks he achieved? Is labelling Peter a 'natural' the greatest compliment any athlete can be paid? What percentage of Peter's success was due to natural talent or, in contrast, what percentage was due to luck?

The point being, there are thousands of aspiring kids and adults within Gaelic sport, equally as enthusiastic as Peter, and prepared to work just as hard. Most, however, for various reasons, will fail to achieve the same levels of unprecedented success. Perhaps their limited natural talent or genetics will prevent them from becoming elite. Perhaps they won't get the breaks, or perhaps the fallout from conflicting cultures in Northern Ireland means many children and adults may never have opportunities to participate in Gaelic sport.

For many Protestant sporting enthusiasts, to participate in Gaelic sport in Northern Ireland means traditionally adhering to a plethora of religiously oriented, unwritten rules. One of which is bowing to peer pressure to not participate in the sport of a diametrically opposing culture, irrespective of whether the player possesses the talent, skill, genetics, enthusiasm, and resolve to participate in Gaelic sport.

The point being, there are many potentially gifted Gaelic footballers who, due to the constraints of a religious divide, lose the opportunity to fully experience the full array of Gaelic sports. This trait is not specific to Northern Ireland. The same sense of division exists within many communities worldwide, whereby a lack of opportunities to share in various sporting disciplines is already decided by luck of the draw, in terms of the genetics, family, environment, culture, or religion into which we are born.

Every sporting performance is enhanced or impinged by the luck of genetics, due to probability and chance. That's because luck is merely a subset of probability and chance. None of us got to choose our biological parents, or the genetics we inherited by way of conception, or our country of origin or birth. Nor did we actively choose to exist in a world full of supernatural connotations such as superstitions, divinity, fate, or fluke.

The field of sports psychology faces a dichotomy of whether to concentrate the bulk of its focus on scientifically methodological aspects of sports performance which are easier defined, or to unpack philosophical sporting anomalies masquerading as omens, prophecy, superstitions, and luck. Where is the proof that luck is a thing, and what percentage of current coaching itineraries is spent questioning the practical implications of believing that luck has intelligence and the faculties to purposefully influence the outcomes of sport?

Every athlete or coach, at some time or other, has hinted, insinuated, or blamed unfortunate results and circumstances on luck, or has 'thanked their lucky stars' when results went in their favour. However, no one has produced repeatable and falsifiable examples of luck, yet it wields real influence on how athletes act, react, respond, and behave when competing at sport.

Many athletes act hypocritically by denying luck any credit while they are winning, but when things go wrong they look for a scapegoat, and what better than luck? They are quick to document how hard they work at honing talent and flair, or cultivating their image, or crafting their careers. Yet, minus the proper nurture, genetics, talent, opportunities, or breaks, could Peter Canavan or Dame Mary Peters have accomplished dreams which most of their peers could only hope to achieve?

Both sporting icons benefited from extremely good fortune throughout the course of their careers, as does every successful athlete who sprints on a track, plays on a pitch, races a bike, swims in a pool, fights in a ring, or stands on a podium to receive a medal or lift a cup. So why did both initially appear to harbour snobbery towards luck? Was luck viewed as a slight on their ego or a stain on their legacy? Why does a dichotomy surround luck?

It's time to put an end to the prevailing air of resentment and hostility so often associated with praising luck. Or at least to suspend intellectual dishonesty which causes us to believe, without falsifiable evidence, that sports superstitions wield supernatural powers to increase our luck, or that superstitions called gods can connect us by way of a make-believe hotline to the great ear in the sky. Theism doesn't allow its lack of falsifiable evidence to stand in the way of a damn good story, and so advocates for a worldview based on the suspension of human intellect and violation of known natural laws.

Scepticism, however, empowers us to question whether superstitious belief is the 'god of the gaps'. So I offer a challenge. Try not to envisage the role which luck plays in every practical sporting contingency as a professional insult or as threatening to our legacy or iconic status, irrespective of whether we perform at grassroots or elite. Concepts such as graft, psychology, and luck can coexist hand-in-hand throughout sport, particularly since luck is an illusionary subset of probability and chance.

It's the job of a sceptic to question why athletes feel compelled to defer to faith through the power of prayer, which is yet another form of superstitious belief. Moreover, why do athletes feel psychologically driven to reframe the 'unknowingness' of luck as a physical concept which can be overridden by rituals and routines, as if somehow repetitiveness and subservience offers the athlete greater control of future events?

If luck really can be overridden by blood, sweat and tears, generic superstitions, god assertions, and prayer, then why is luck deemed culpable when performances dip or athletes have been outmanoeuvred and outplayed? Is it simply much kinder to the sporting ego to downgrade the success of an opponent to luck?

"People always call it luck when you've acted more sensibly than they have."

- Anne Tyler, Novelist

If luck cannot be seen, defined, or deciphered, can it truly be said to exist, or is luck merely an afterthought which only comes into being when we become tongue tied or bamboozled by things which defy explanation, or which we cannot grasp or comprehend? Perhaps this sense of 'unknowingness' is what compels us to fabricate names for things we don't understand. So far on our planet, the current number of verified and falsifiable superstitious interventions in sport stands at a paltry zero, nil, and none.

If we have no way to measure a superstitious claim to confirm that a supernatural agent caused a specific event to occur, then we are faced with two simple choices. Either continue in ignorance or admit that the only plausible answer is to say we simply don't know. The superstition called ego is bound by the misconception that all unexplained things require an explanation, and as such, *everything* should be known as *something*. It's the illusion of ego which often compels us to explain away mysteries as luck.

Luck splits opinion 50/50. Some athletes praise luck irrespective of the outcome, even when it's undeserving of any praise at all. Others excommunicate luck from receiving acclaim when things are going well, but blame luck the moment things start to go wrong. It's time luck got to plead the Fifth Amendment while it attempts to compile its own defence, as it should be presumed innocent until proven otherwise.

Superstitious competitors should be made aware of luck's heart-wrenching plea to be granted leniency due to diminished responsibility. Poor old luck, always blamed and yet so rarely credited. So the next time we seek a convenient scapegoat to account for our failure to perform, please ensure luck is unanimously acquitted, and that we instead take its place in the dock.

"I busted a mirror and got seven years bad luck, but my lawyer thinks he can get me five."

- Steven Wright, Comedian

In order to validate luck with impartiality, we must pay luck its dues when we win. Otherwise, luck is rendered invalid as an excuse when performances dip, since citing luck as a one-sided assertion is not only unscrupulous but intellectually dishonest and logically inept. Once we take the decision to cite luck as a mitigating circumstance in defence of an under-par performance, we are no longer at liberty to dismiss it as an option when performances once again start to soar.

Irrespective of whether we are for or against luck, there is no escaping its shadowy enigma. So let's begin a petition to clear luck's reputation while conducting ourselves in a dignified and pragmatic manner since no one to date has scientifically harnessed luck, just as no one to date has scientifically harnessed God. So please, I appeal to you all; give luck a break and cut it some slack.

Ultimately luck is a superstition, but what is the point of superstitions and why bother complying with them at all? The answer is simple! Many athletes believe superstitions affect their luck, just as acolytes of religions believe deities and gods affect their luck. Superstitious belief qualifies as an *'ism',* whilst superstition itself is the god of the gaps. To adhere to superstition is *Superstitionism,* just as belief in a god is *theism.* Both *'isms'* are equally ambiguous symptoms of faith.

So what is faith? Faith in a superstitious sense is gullibility and also an excuse to believe anything we like. Faith acts as a precursor to hope, which is a variant of luck, yet neither hope nor luck can provide any guarantee against being dead wrong. Irrespective of the degree of absurdity, is there anything we can't believe from a standpoint of faith? Luck, for example, cannot be defined but is an uncharted, unfalsifiable, and inexplicable unknown, yet many athletes rely on its mercy before feeling confident enough to compete.

No one can scientifically decipher luck. What is apparent, however, is the frequency by which luck freely enters and exits many athletes' psychology, seemingly at will. Luck adopts the guise of a crafty chameleon and if I were to dedicate a book to luck's memory, it would be entitled *The Changing Faces of Luck,* since no one knows where they stand in its presence.

Earlier, I drew attention to luck favouring Usain Bolt's genetics over Yohan Blake's relentless dedication to training. Luck has many faces, however, as was apparent during one memorable occasion in 2011 in Daegu, South Korea, where the tables were turned in favour of Blake who, against all the odds, finally became the 100m sprint champion of the world.

From Bolt's perspective, the reasons were entirely practical, while from Blake's perspective, what followed was perhaps the luckiest sequence of events in the world. In full dramatic effect, as a global audience looked on aghast, Bolt was disqualified for a second false start, having previously been warned. Pretty lucky for Blake, eh! Or was it the result of probability and chance?

Genetics has greatly impacted the careers and the sprinting styles of both athletes. Bolt, being the taller sprinter, had to work harder at getting out of the blocks quickly to stay close to Blake over the first few metres; particularly during shorter races such as 60-metre and 100-metre sprints to remain in contention against a much smaller and sharper athlete. Bolt's advantageous genetics, such as his longer stride, only start to kick in after approximately 20 metres.

It was an open secret in the world of athletics that when Blake applied pressure right from the off, a good start from the blocks by Bolt was imperative, and Bolt's disqualification suggests he understood this disadvantage only too well. It appeared to weigh heavily on his mind and act as a chief contributing factor for overshooting the starting gun in his over-eagerness to get off to a flying start.

Sprinters refer to this tactic as 'going on the B of the bang', and employ it as a ruse to outfox the starting gun by attempting to pre-empt hitting their stride precisely as the gun goes off. It is an anticipatory skill which requires optimum focus and timing if they are to bluff their reactionary times as adjudicated electronically at the start of each race.

In the grand scheme of things, Usain Bolt seems a phenomenon of luck who is genetically crafted for fast-paced sprinting and possesses the crème de la crème of all possible surnames to be the fastest human on earth. Imagine instead if his surname was 'Snooze'. Usain Bolt was a marketer's dream with a surname to match. How lucky was that?

Or what about us; how many of us have endeavoured to coach, nurture, or practice honing luck as a practical component of competitive sport? Surely this is a plausible proposition given so many competitors use superstitions as preparation to compete and also as an exit strategy when they lose. So, why isn't 'comprehending the effects of luck' being coached as a part of competitive sport, and even if it was, where would we begin and what would we say?

How might it be practical to introduce luck into coaching sessions, and how might we specifically tailor a style and a format for deconstructing the superstition called luck? For example, do we possess enough ego strength to overlook the types of personal bias which persist in us all as a result of our prior experiences with luck? And might those same experiences lessen our ability to share and interact impartially and open-mindedly with our peers?

So let's personalise luck. How conscious are you of the message you involuntarily transmit to others when the topic of luck raises its head in a public domain? How balanced is your portrayal of luck during conversations about sport? Are you able to discuss luck in a meaningful way with your sporting contemporaries, and what is the proof that the thing you're experiencing is luck?

Luck is sport's most iconic intangible. Other aspects of sport have measurable characteristics such as rigidly structured fitness regimes and innovative, scientific technologies from which we attempt to elicit an advantageous sporting edge. An example of this was the new "revolutionary skin suit" revealed by Team GB's Olympic cyclists on the eve of the 2016 Rio Olympic Games. The skin suit comprised of a special drag-resistant material designed to make cyclists an astonishing 7% faster on the track.

The *Mail Online Sport* reported this technology as having the potential to shave more than 3 seconds from a 4km team pursuit. If Team GB were prepared to explore every conceivable contingency so meticulously to achieve success, then what prevents superstitious athletes from following suit by exploring new and innovative avenues of mental resilience in a bid to stay one step ahead of the game.

Let's begin by debunking the supernatural where possible, since nothing is more innovative than kicking a superstitious belief to the curb, thereby accepting full responsibility for how we perform. Stop confusing chance and probability with the superstitious paradox called luck. Many athletes are quick to label seemingly improbable outcomes as luck. Yet improbability is mathematical, otherwise the improbable would be the impossible. Hence, more-often-than-not, the thing we call luck is a mere correlation of mathematical chance, probability, and random odds.

If we are serious in our pursuit of procuring an elusive sporting edge, can we truly afford to spurn opportunities to critique the growing influence of luck, given luck is hardwired into our brains as being a tangible living 'thing'? Consider as an example the paranoia luck causes within every dressing room, or the air of confidence coursing through every athlete who experiences a winning streak and feels invincible. Once an athlete believes luck is on their side, the placebo effect eradicates doubt as they become convinced they can do no wrong.

Luck is a flimsy proposition, as irrespective of confidence, all it takes is for events to turn against us before our goodwill quickly disappears and all of a sudden we're back to cursing luck. Who among us at some time or another has not cursed our luck? Yet who or what are we cursing and what good it can do? Do we think someone or something is listening, and if luck does exist, then what is the criteria that makes us believe it is favouring or penalising us?

Many athletes compete in a space between appearance and reality where superstitious belief is god of the gaps. So it's time to pay heed to luck's hidden implications by re-evaluating our ongoing relationship with luck. Given that superstitions can impact mental well-being, they are at least deserving of a conversation about how best to unpack their potential effect on an athlete's mental health. Furthermore, every time luck is implicated as a convenient scapegoat, closer scrutiny reveals that the cause lay a little closer to home.

The superstition called luck is a supernatural fabrication of probability and chance. Many motivational speakers, athletes, and sports psychologists misinterpret luck. Even luminary Thomas Jefferson, the third US President displayed an ignorance of what constitutes luck by proclaiming, *"I'm a great believer in luck and I find the harder I work, the more I have of it."* In effect, he is referring to probability, speculation, and chance, but provides no evidence of a supernatural intervention having taken place.

Jefferson's quote has transcended politics and made its way into sport. Proof of which can be seen in the following quote by golfing legend Arnold Palmer, *"It's a funny thing. The more I practice the luckier I get."* Sound familiar? Yet, he provides no evidence that working harder or practising repeatedly causes a supernatural intervention to take place. There is no correlation to be made between hard graft and luck beyond probability, since luck has no verifiable prerequisites and hard graft is no exception to the rule.

Does luck play a role in an athlete's fortune? Were Dame Mary Peters and Peter Canavan initially too quick to disassociate from being the beneficiaries of luck? Peter maintained his scepticism throughout the interview while Dame Mary rather thoughtfully performed a U-turn by acknowledging how, during her Olympic Heptathlon final, the stars in the sky appeared to align for her on the night. Similarly, Usain Bolt's 'lucky' fast-twitch fibres (genetics) empowered him with the tools to become the fastest man on earth.

Yohan Blake's lucky break in a World Championship final came when Bolt was disqualified for a second false start. His disqualification sparked a chain of events which led to Blake being crowned champion of the world; a result which, in all probability, would not otherwise have occurred. The topic of luck as a practical assertion should be part of ongoing coaching conversations and viewed as a key psychological component of modern sport.

Consider the practical implications of an athlete beckoning to gods, repeating weird and bizarre rituals, wearing lucky charms, or cursing their luck when things don't go to plan. Superstitions are often debilitating even though luck has no bearing on reality except through faith which is, in effect, the residue of nothing tangible at all. It's time to stop praising and blaming luck, but to open our minds to scepticism and advocate for the spread of critical thinking across a broad spectrum of competitive sport.

There is no better way to wrap up these considerations than to revisit the prophetic words of Tamil wisdom which states, *"It's time to go wake up your luck."* Somehow this sentiment just feels appropriate since it's time to wake up to a world where thoughts of superstitions such as luck, fluke, and karma influence and coerce the decisions we make in competitive sport.

So what's luck got to do with it? The jury is still out as to why in the 21st century, athletes still place more emphasis on luck and less on probability and chance, both of which dovetail perfectly with sports analysis. Instead they turn to luck to paper over the cracks of things which, at face value, they cannot explain. So what is luck? Luck is an attempt to solve a mystery by appealing to an even greater mystery; as are all superstitions including those concerning gods. Superstitious beliefs are primarily cosmetic in a similar sense to applying lipstick to a pig.

"Ego is unnecessary. So skip the 'E' and let it 'Go'."

- Unknown

Lucky Metaphors

"Yeah, I think there were little strokes of luck, and the bounce of the ball you need sometimes to get to where you are, and luckily that went in my favour."

- Gareth Bale, Wales and Real Madrid Footballer

"Wake-up," said the nurse.

"What is it, what's the matter?" asked the startled patient.

"Nothing's the matter," replied the nurse, *"I just forgot to give you your sleeping pills."*

Isn't human nature wonderful if not somewhat peculiar, but also compelling at the same time? The same can be said for every superstitious compulsion that startles our senses with dogma, cultural ideologies, and variations of irrational truths. All of life is a metaphor for something. First, however, we must learn how to embrace life itself if we are to discover what each metaphor implies.

The most wonderful description of the term metaphor is that of a 'colouring in' of language; a typical example of which is the statement *'I'm feeling blue'*. Obviously it's impossible to *feel* the colour blue, as blue is merely a common descriptive attempt to highlight surplus emotions which rarely get to extend beyond the blandness of stating *'I'm feeling sad'*.

Metaphors are intended to exaggerate meaning using deep, impactful language and a creative process of exaggerated truths, each of which is enhanced by poetic licence. In metaphorical context, a generic term such as *'I feel sad'* can expand to become *'I feel I am drowning in a sea of grief'*, despite no one actually drowning and there being no sea. Athletes lean towards metaphors to verbally convey how their emotions are making them feel.

Metaphors add supplementary value to the way athletes think by allowing them to express the inner-depths of emotions which they might otherwise find difficult to share. It is their hope that the gravity of whichever emotions they may be experiencing will transmit to their peers, and in a cognitive sense, will best convey what they smell, taste, hear, feel, or see.

Metaphors don't stand up to rigorous scrutiny or make practical sense, yet they are ever-present in competitive sport. Who, for instance, has encountered a boxer with a chin which is literally 'made out of glass', or how are they meant to win 'hands down' when boxing requires them to fight with their hands up for 100% of the time? Or consider another boxing metaphor, how many pounds or kilos does a 'heavy' defeat actually weigh?

If the 'gloves are off', then why do boxers wear gloves when they fight? Moreover, why is the metaphor 'the gloves are off' just as prominent in non-fisticuff sports such as athletics, rowing, snooker, swimming, and darts? Is it possible to obtain a 'ballpark figure' without a ball or a park? Is there a name for the biological process whereby a teammate begins to 'grow on us'? Is it physically possible to 'wear a smile'? What temperature must an athlete reach before their 'blood begins to boil'? There is little doubt that sport is engulfed by colourful metaphors.

The odd thing about sporting metaphors is that they appear to make perfect sense despite making no bloody sense at all. The human brain is conditioned to adapt to incoherence, an example of which is when two drunks engage in conversation where, despite the slurred speech and incoherence, both seem uncannily able to understand what the other one says. There is a danger with common metaphor, that by taking our eye off the ball we allow incoherence to grow its own set of legs (oops, more metaphors).

Often memory conspires to withhold information which it deems as unpalatable to our well-being by deselecting and syphoning off recollections it associates with experiencing bad luck. Part of memory's functionality is being able to harness the power of suggestion. Yet, how can we tell if our memory is acting impartially? Or what happens when memory is afforded the freedom to self-regulate the types of information it prefers we remember or forget?

When did memory become an honest broker and why trust it to interpret our prior experiences of luck? The power of suggestion is one of human memory's greatest attributes, but also one of its greatest flaws. All memories are corrupted by information bias, an example of which is how athletes are quick to deny luck any credit for a winning performance, yet hypocritically, are quick to credit gods, prayers, and deceased family members for overseeing success from some imaginary vantage point in the sky. The concept of God has no explanatory powers and so is just as reliant on optimism as luck.

Why credit deceased loved ones with having the ability to manipulate sport? One would think that if an afterlife does exist then the deceased already have enough on their plate. Are superstitions and luck convenient means to avoid facing personal responsibility and also a scapegoat on which to hang all the blame when things go wrong? How do we begin to decipher luck? Consider the following assessment of luck from former Sunderland AFC manager Gus Poyet:

"The difference between winning and losing in the [English] Premier League is one of action. Literally, it is one goal, it is one decision, it is one deflected shot, it's a good or bad decision from a referee, and that can make you win two more games. I don't believe in luck in the long term, but I do believe that there are certain moments when you need that change of luck that is going to change the season around."

The thing most fascinating is Gus's random prioritisation of luck. *"I don't believe in luck in the long term,"* he arrogantly conveyed. Yet, what is more conceited (no disrespect intended) than an ego large enough to believe that it can apply physical time constraints to something as ambiguous as luck? Despite his assertion that luck has long and short-term value, he provided no evidence of this being true.

Few athletes are comfortable with luck stealing the credit for their success, yet where are the agreed protocols and ethics which determine how athletes should conduct themselves around luck? Many ignore reason and instead choose to place all their eggs in a superstitious basket in the misguided hope of gaining an edge. Consider how many athletes, coaches, psychologists, and neuroscientists are personally invested in sports-science in search of fresh innovations to extract that elusive 'little bit extra' which may nudge their noses in front.

Luck is the underlying cause of superstitious compliance because athletes believe that superstitions will affect their luck. But where does such a supernatural notion fit into our current understanding of sport? How innovative or restrictive is conceding free will to conventional thinking and how best can we measure the impact of conventional thinking on current attitudes towards sport?

For decades, conventional thinking led us to believe that a man could not sprint a sub-ten-second 100-meter race. Recently it also cast doubt on the ability of Austrian daredevil Felix Baumgartner to descend safely back to earth from the edge of space. Felix eventually achieved this incredible feat after freefalling for 4 minutes and 19 seconds from a height of 128,000 feet. Thanks to science and a blatant disregard for superstitious convention, both feats have since been overcome and their constraining psychological impacts obliterated once and for all.

We cannot push a boundary without first taking some risks, and most risky of all, if we wish to remain at the forefront of cutting-edge sports innovation, is to redefine luck as a superstition. It's time conversations about redefining luck became integral components of all sporting itineraries and future design since it's the collective responsibility of sports educators to embrace fresh perspective regarding the utilisation of luck. Coaching some form of understanding of luck should be just as significant as coaching any other active component of competitive sport.

Redefining luck as a superstition is pioneering, and hey, who knows, it may even be fun. Spontaneity is free from superstitious belief and encourages athletes to act more instinctively and intuitively when trying out new stuff. Do we ever wonder in our quietest moments how things may have turned out if only we'd placed that missed penalty to the left of the goal instead of the right? Might the outcome have been different if only we'd trusted our boxing instincts and threw a flurry of punches instead of holding back? What if we'd called heads instead of tails, batted first instead of fielding, or opted for different racing tyres, golf clubs, or studs?

Where does the crossover begin between making good and bad choices or experiencing good or bad luck? Superstitious beliefs don't exist in a vacuum as often their repercussions remain with us for life. By applying scepticism, however, we can transform our entire coaching philosophy by increasing awareness that luck does not directly influence a win or loss. So, in the interest and pursuit of sporting excellence, it's time to consider what current provisions we incorporate into our coaching philosophies to accommodate conversations about luck.

"Luck's luck, you can't win without it."

- Sir Alex Ferguson, Football Manager

The reason superstitions exist is we believe that their presence will affect our luck while we fear that their absence may impact the quality and nature of how we perform. Hence, the things which we *fear,* we invariably *feel* since fear is a physical manifestation of emotion, and as such, every time we experience negative emotions we simultaneously *feel* our *fear*. Superstitions exist because we fear something good is *not* going to happen or that something bad invariably *will* if we dare to dispense with our customary rituals. Therefore, we feel fear of letting go of our beliefs.

"Many of us crucify ourselves between two thieves. Regret for the past and fear of the future."

- Fulton Oursler, Playwright

When did we first believe that fate, luck, and karma are practical components of competitive sports? Does having the option of blaming luck decrease our ability to accept culpability in a more considered and practical manner, or enhance our efforts to cope with the euphoria of fluctuating success? Loosely translated, luck is an intangible since it possesses no explanatory powers.

Consider the final of the Keirin cycling event in the velodrome at the London 2012 Olympic Games. Here we find Team GB cycling legend Sir Chris Hoy taking centre stage in the wake of a tense and tight affair. He had finally secured his sixth gold medal of an amazing Olympic career to become arguably the most successful British Olympian to date.

During the build-up to the finale, as a worldwide audience looked on with anticipation and hope, we became privy to the brutal nature of his training regime as Chris was asked by a BBC presenter, *"Can you please explain the physical nature of what you do to yourself during one of these sessions?"*

"We call it the lactic acid tolerance session. So basically, while you're working very hard, you produce more lactic which burns and stings in your legs. Then you rest and do it again, then rest and again, and then again. So, every time it's feeling worse and worse before you even start the effort. Obviously your legs just shut down and you almost grind to a halt.

You get off the bike and fall onto the mat next to the bike, and then it gets worse. The sting in your legs and the pain in your legs just keeps getting worse and worse and worse for about five minutes, and you're rolling about the floor in foetal position. Sometimes you are physically sick. You know it's not very pretty, but that's part of the training and part of what you have to do to get to the top."

Undoubtedly, Chris was as well prepared as it was possible to be and needed only to focus on his performance to practically guarantee success, given his painstaking and excruciating preparations, previous experiences at the Sydney, Athens, and Beijing Olympics, and now benefitting from a home crowd in London at 36 years of age. Yet, having successfully negotiated his way unscathed through the heats, he was about to reveal a performance defining edge.

Chris emerged as the only athlete during the heats to wear a specifically designed aerodynamic helmet and explicitly tailored leggings, which afforded his legs the best possible opportunity for recovery between each heat. The innovative technologies formed an integral part of Team GB's speed defining edge. To the untrained eye, such trivial measures may appear of little overall significance, but to Chris, the end justified the means. He believed that the cumulative effects of such technologies aligned with his unparalleled experience would create a marginal edge which would help him to reclaim Olympic gold.

Chris thrived on the added stimulus of knowing that both state-of-the-art pioneering technologies, which he referred to as the 'aggregation of marginal gain', could empower him to steal a definitive march on his rivals by creating an ever-so-slight leading edge. This, in effect, is exactly how things transpired as he was triumphant in winning the final by a mere fraction of a second. But once again he'd won gold, and after the event, who even remembers or cares about times?

"The Keirin is a lottery, and you never take anything for granted."

- Sir Chris Hoy, Cyclist

The most interesting aspect of Chris' post-Olympic-gold-winning interviews was when he quietly mentioned something of tremendous significance which very few in attendance (if any) appeared to notice due to their immediate delight. *"A lot of it is down to tactics and luck,"* remarked Chris. *"A lot of it is down to chance. You can never take anything for granted in this sport."* Wow! So there we have it, straight from the cycling genius' own mouth at the crowning moment of his illustrious career.

Quite incredibly, despite the inevitable rush towards patriotic fervour and inevitable clamour to acknowledge Chris as arguably the UK's greatest ever Olympian, he twice went out of his way to willfully acknowledge the roles played by 'chance' and more significantly by 'luck'. It was luck's greatest ever sporting endorsement, yet it appeared to have fallen on deaf ears.

Compare Chris' experience to the contrasting fortunes of fellow Team GB cyclist, Victoria Pendleton, who took to the track in pursuit of gold in the women's sprint final where she was reunited with her nemesis, Australian Anna Meares in a repeat of the Olympic final in Beijing. During the first of three potential heats, Victoria just about managed to pip Anna over the line in a nerve-jangling sprint of sinew-stretching proportions by what was adjudged to have been a one-thousandth-of-a-second marginal win.

The response was deafening as the home crowd cheered in anticipation of Victoria marking her swansong with Olympic gold, as this was to be her last ever cycling competition. As such, everyone associated with Team GB was willing her to one last great cycling hurrah. As she recovered in the holding area, however, (wearing the same aerodynamic helmet and specially designed leggings worn by Chris) the television cameras picked up on something seemingly untoward. The cycling officials had reviewed Victoria's previous heat on their monitors and agreed to penalise her ride, much to the bemusement of the patriotic crowd.

Victoria was informed that she was to be penalised for veering out of her lane and told her previous win was to be reversed. Despite multiple reviews, action replays, and countless remonstrations by Team GB overlord David Brailsford, it soon became clear to bewildered spectators, that as decisions go, this one appeared harsh. The decision stood, however, and as the pressure intensified on Victoria, she was comprehensively beaten in the following heat in what became her last ever competitive race.

Victoria didn't seem able to recover and appeared beaten before the second heat had even begun. Her motivation and confidence had taken an irreparable knock as she faced up to the possibility of missing out on a golden Olympic swansong. Many argued retrospectively that the decision drained and destroyed her psychologically. In the end, Victoria's Olympic dreams lay in tatters and she was left to ponder what might have been.

Victoria's dilemma further justified Sir Chris Hoy's earlier appraisal of not taking anything for granted within the lottery of competitive cycling, where he appeared to suggest that cyclists compete at the mercy of providence, fate, chance, and luck. Fellow Team GB cyclist, Victoria Pendleton, is likely to share his belief since she must surely have felt that the sporting gods had connived and conspired against her to rain on her parade and that luck had deserted her just when she needed it most.

If the superstition called luck really did negatively impact Victoria's destiny on that rather sad and fateful day, then what possible learning is to be gained from her experience? First, we can acknowledge that a radical shake-up is long overdue regarding how athletes view supernatural phenomena since many continue to believe there are supernatural forces at play with enough power, kudos, and intent to intelligently manipulate the destinies of all who dare to compete at sport.

We should pay more attention to the superstition called luck since it creates the illusion of being a force of nature with a seeming intelligence of its own. Luck is commonly viewed as an independent entity far in advance of any of us, while superstitions are commonly viewed as metaphorical condiments of luck. Hence, in the same way that metaphors exist for the sole purpose of 'colouring in' language, superstitions exist to add 'colouring' to our fears.

Some athletes prefer to claim all the credit for their sporting success in an egotistical self-styled meritocracy, whereby they feel fully justified in ganging up against luck. They should be careful, however, since luck isn't afraid to get its hands dirty unlike athletes who casually hide their sporting failures behind a culture of blame when events fail to go their way. Many fail to own up to a mediocre performance by blaming their misfortune on luck.

The superstition called ego has become adept in the art of avoidance by transferring full responsibility for how we perform onto the shoulders of the superstition called luck. How many athletes do we know who are willing to accept outright blame for producing a mediocre performance? Instead, with little semblance of shame or remorse, they call on a third party by dialling a supernatural toll-free number which redirects all their troubles and woes to luck.

Luck, for its part, appears equally keen to reverse the charges due to the free publicity it receives when athletes brandish its name to convey its importance as an avid game-changer in modern sport. The upshot is simple, we may believe we have wiped our hands of luck, but perhaps luck hasn't quite finished with us. How much time do we spend considering whether the bad luck we experience is a hidden blessing, since who can possibly tell what 'worse luck' our 'bad luck' may be sparing us from?

Consider the following five implications of luck as reported in an article by *changingminds.org*. The first is that we risk hiding our skill when we say, 'we were just lucky'. Consequently, we risk hiding our *lack* of skill when we say, 'we were just unlucky this time'. We also run the risk of flattering others by attributing their failures to bad luck, just as we avoid praising others by attributing their successes to good luck. Fifth and finally, we may be encouraging others to take unnecessary risks by telling them they are lucky, despite having no demonstrable means to tell whether they're lucky or not.

Luck is a superstition and has no explanatory powers which is why it has never been deciphered. The left hemisphere of the human brain is aligned with logic and analytical reasoning, but logic and reasoning according to what? Is it reasonable to assert superstitious logic or is there a need to go back to the drawing board and revisit whatever rationale is driving the logic of superstitious belief?

It's time to openly converse and debate luck and engage in topical discussions regarding the practical implications of incorporating superstitious constructs such as providence, fate, karma, and luck into the fabric of competitive sport.

"I was a little bit lucky, but I wish to always be lucky and score goals for the team."

- Sadio Mane, Liverpool FC

Sadio's quote is from a December 2016 article by David Lynch for *Liverpool FC.com* and refers to the apparent good fortune surrounding Sadio's derby match-winner against rivals Everton FC. The implication was that he tailored his run having already anticipated a potential rebound from a shot by teammate Daniel Sturridge falling directly into his path, which as it happened, was exactly how events transpired. Daniel's shot struck the post and rebounded back into play, directly into the channel in which Sadio was travelling; but was the trajectory of the moving ball a manifestation of luck, probability, or chance?

It was a perfect example of wonderful anticipatory skills being utilised by an elite athlete who was switched on, alert, and thinking on his feet; but what if the ball had instead struck the post and taken an opposite trajectory, meaning Sadio's run had been in vain? What percentage of his success was due to alertness and what percentage was due to luck?

There is a wonderful Zen Buddhist koan (paradoxical riddle) which asks the pertinent question, 'If a tree falls in a forest and no one is around to hear it, does it make a sound?' In the true spirit of Zen Buddhism, I submit the following pertinent questions. By what means can we tell if an experience was luck and where is the proof that luck is a thing? Luck has an inherently endearing quality, almost as though it were a friend since, whether good, bad, or indifferent, all of us share a close affiliation with the idea of luck.

Eureka! We may have just discovered the key to unlocking the metaphorical DNA of luck. Consider the amazing transition which may potentially occur in an athlete's demeanour by learning to embrace the illusion of luck as though it was already a close and valued friend. The following analogy highlights the hidden intimacies which often exist in our complex, yet familiar relationship with luck. Let's face it, at some point every athlete or coach criticises or sucks up to luck because it's viewed as an adversary as well as a friend.

We fall in with friends and we fall out with friends and often we spend more time in the company of friends than we do with our own family. Sometimes we meet friends in the strangest of places or in the oddest of circumstances which we did not anticipate nor envisage, and yet friends just appeared nonetheless.

Sometimes friends pull through for us when least expected; while on other occasions our friends let us down just when we needed friends most. Often during adversity is where our friendship is strongest. Other times it's our friends that create the adversity, so much so that at times we are left to question whether our friends are friendly at all.

There are times when understanding the logic of friends is completely unfathomable, irrespective of how hard we try. Friends can be surprising and sometimes intolerable. We may have friends and not even know it, while sometimes friends pass us by, desert us, or sell us out behind our back. Yet, time-after-time, we make excuses for friends, even when we're aware that it isn't warranted; but our loyalty is not always reciprocated, as sometimes our friends drop us in at the deep end, leaving us up shit creek without a paddle.

Go on admit it! This *has* to be ringing some bells. Yet what if we were to revisit this friendly analogy, except this time exchanging the word 'friend' with the much more evocative word 'luck'? Might we then gain a better understanding of how, too often in sport, sentimentality is allowed to outrank practicality and rationality? One example of which is when athletes cannot separate sentimentality from luck to such a degree that the relationship starts to resemble a marriage, whereby both parties are tied to each other for-better-or-for-worse and till-death-do-they-part.

So backtrack to the previous 'friendly analogy' and give it a go. Simply replace the word 'friend' with the word 'luck', then watch as the essence of the *friendly* metaphor begins its transitional journey towards *lucky* metaphor, thereby highlighting the intimacy and rapport which each of us share with our interpretation of luck. The correlation is startling, since luck is primarily comprised of similar attributes and repercussions to those we associate with an intimate relationship with friends.

Friends are often joined at the hip and inseparable; but, as with the nature of any relationship, there is often one friend who is eminently more assertive and who, as a result, gets to call most of the shots. Once again, this trait is comparable to our ongoing relationship with luck. The only difference being, in the context of sport, that it's not our friends but our luck which is the dominant other, but as with so many tempestuous friendships, our relationship with luck is often skewed.

It's impossible to tell if an athlete has suffered or benefitted at the hands of luck. One thing which is evident, however, is that luck neither suffers nor benefits from us. Instead it is us who are always the beneficiaries or unfortunate recipients of experiencing luck; yet luck as a concept eliminates choice. What choice do we have when we fall foul to a refereeing decision, or suffer defeat as a direct result of inherited genetics, or when a tennis ball strikes the top of the net and falls tamely on the wrong side of the court?

What choice do we have when a teammate scores a spectacular own goal or when an athlete is tripped by an opponent in a long-distance race? Who deliberately chooses to have their vaulting pole snap in half, or to receive a cut from an accidental head butt in the sport of boxing, or to be obstructed as a jockey by a horse with no rider down the final straight? Or, on a positive note, what say has a sprinter who breaks a world record due in part to a wind assisted sprint?

Luck is unquestionably ambiguous, and the best we can do is to pay luck its dues and then open our minds to the dynamic of luck with the same sense of acknowledgement as is befitting of an old and valued friend. Embracing a friend should not constitute dependency any more than embracing superstition should foster a dependency on luck.

Do athletes compete at the mercy of luck or is luck merely chance and probability? Consider the following post-race reaction from former world champion and long-distance freestyle Olympic swimmer, Keri-anne Payne, after having lost at the 2016 Rio Olympics.

"I was hoping for rough, choppy conditions. The race was just not my perfect conditions today unfortunately, as I'm an open water swimmer. I'm a well-rounded swimmer. So gimme waves, gimme rain, gimme anything. But today it was beautiful sunshine, there was no wind and it was really flat. It just totally played into the pool swimmer's hands. The girl that won the race, Sharon Van Rouwendaal, came second at the World Championships last year. So we knew going into this that if it was going to be flat, it was going to be absolutely in her hands."

While documenting her frustration regarding the unhelpfulness of the weather on that potentially historic day, Keri-anne clearly hinted that luck played an integral role in both her and her team's thinking long before the race had even begun. Luck does not get mentioned in coaching itineraries, yet the illusion of luck is perhaps the greatest game-changer in competitive sport.

Athletes are frequently drip-fed the curious line that if they work hard enough they can achieve anything. Wow, 'anything'? Really! While in retrospect, what is altogether more practical is simply trying to do their best at maximising whichever unique tools and resources are at their disposal and whatever genetics they possess, just to see where it takes them and how far they can go. Coaches should refrain from spreading the same old tried-and-untested superstitious diatribes and myths that were so irresponsibly bestowed on them.

Stop spreading the myth that the key to unlocking 'winning' is through blood, sweat, arduous repetition, and tears, with no mention of the impact of favourable genetics, which many athletes attribute to luck. Why are athletes' genetics so rarely discussed in an open and honest manner? Consider the role played by genetics in the case of Keri-anne Payne, who struggled to produce a winning performance during weather conditions which were not conducive to her specific racing skills and physique.

There is a wonderful sentiment which states, 'If the only tool at our disposal is a hammer, then the answer is likely to be nails'. Similarly, if athletes are taught from the very first moment of becoming embroiled in competitive sport that the only answer to losing is blood, sweat, repetition, and tears, then these same characteristics will unconsciously apply every time they lose since they are hardwired to work harder instead of smarter. Sentiments such as these encourage athletes to neglect certain practicalities such as endeavouring to understand that winning and losing are equally dependant on probability and chance.

Who can recall the first time we mistakenly confused chance with luck? Perhaps we're still not aware that this is what we are doing, yet sport mirrors our lives in microcosm and all throughout our lives we use common metaphors to 'colour in' language which is otherwise hard to express. Similarly, many athletes embrace superstitions to 'colour in' any voids that exist in their psychology when attempting to overcome sporting anxiety and fear; the most common of which is the mystery called luck.

If superstitions are real, then there can be no denying that luck is the ultimate game changer for sport, yet when was the last time we tested its legitimacy to determine whether or not we experienced luck? Making assertions about luck is easy, but justifying those assertions isn't so much. This is why we should sleep with one eye open, so that our natural curiosity is not brushed aside by unfalsifiable beliefs with no explanatory powers.

What practical means of redress is on offer to athletes when perspiration doesn't get the job done because supernatural elements are seemingly at play? Yet, no one to date has provided falsifiable evidence of luck having ever made an impact on sport. All athletes have experienced good and bad fortune, but the only reason they oversubscribe to superstitious premonitions, omens, rituals, charms, and prayer is because they believe it affects their luck and that luck will reciprocate their 'friendly' alliance by sending good fortune back their way. Perhaps until then they can hurry the supernatural process along by crossing their fingers, touching wood, and maybe crossing their legs as well.

"Though the race is about the running, the running itself encapsulates the journey, and somewhere along our journey, as with life, we require that little piece of luck along the way."

- Unknown

Luck or Chance, which is it?

"It would definitely, definitely annoy me. It definitely would now. It's happened that something hasn't gone right. I remember when I brought the wrong boots to a game and it was panic stations. Fortunately I was able to get the boots, but definitely it did affect my performance that day. If my routine isn't the same it definitely puts me off my game."

\- Paddy Cunningham, Antrim GAA

Prior to the Ulster GAA final against County Tyrone in 2009, I asked Antrim captain Paddy Cunningham what would happen if, for any reason, he was unable to comply with his superstitious belief? He admitted to feeling predisposed to wearing a specific pair of lucky boots in order to compete at his full potential. Happily, the odds already seemed stacked in his favour as his boots were delivered on time for the game since his family were nearby and sprung to his aid; but what if they hadn't been there to ride to his rescue?

What if Paddy played badly during the game, or horribly skewed a vital kick, or lost concentration at a definitive moment given all of these hinge on unerring focus which he may have lacked as soon as it became apparent that he'd forgotten his lucky boots? Let's apply some poetic licence and visualise the disappointment among Antrim supporters as they streamed out of the ground, each blaming bad fortune and accursed luck for how the outcome could've been different had Paddy not scuffed or misplaced a few kicks.

I asked Paddy to offer some personal insight into the role superstition played in his performances on the pitch. I asked if he could affix an actual figure to the impact superstition played on his overall focus and concentration prior to and during competitive games. Surprisingly, from out of the blue he immediately nailed down his personal value to an incredible 70% of focus. This meant 70% of his focus would be disrupted as a result of failing to wear boots which he deemed as lucky; but where did he pluck that number from? Why settle on 70% and not 7% or 97% since all are equally as likely or unlikely to be accurate given no scientific process ever took place?

Irrespective of Paddy's random assertion, it would not have been wise for his manager to dismiss or discount his reasoning as being merely a number off the top of his head since it carried the potential to impact an estimated 70% of his focus on the pitch. His numerical assertion was hypothetical since there was no way to measure its impact in terms of performance-related outcomes, yet that should've been a priority since Gaelic football is a game of fine margins. Hence, what seems to have escaped the attention of Antrim's passionate supporters during the lead-up to 2009's Ulster Final was the degree of personal value (70% focus) afforded by their captain to wearing a pair of magical boots.

Throughout Paddy's tenure as Antrim captain, the supporters were oblivious to his superstitious trait, as were his unsuspecting management team. It seems none were aware of the underlying factors which could've impaired his competitive mentality prior to or during each game. He also kicked his team's frees (set pieces), which raised further questions as to where blame should lie in the eyes of supporters when he miscued a kick. Scapegoating seems part of human nature, but would the Antrim supporters blame defeat on bad luck, chance, or perceived unprofessionalism? Might they question his talent or mental resilience in high pressure situations or display pragmatism and blame the defeat on a poor kicking performance and nothing else?

What caused Paddy to believe he needed to be rescued by superstition at all? What did he actually know about the origin of whatever luck he attached to those boots? Why was he motivated to affix a 'lucky' moniker and afford himself leeway to believe that a pair of boots could be lucky at all? At what point did his boots seemingly begin to merge into his physical anatomy, as if they were part of his very being? In other words, when did the superstition he possessed end up taking possession of him? Prior to my simple line of inquiry, no one had ever asked him these types of questions. Yet here stood an athlete of County standing, who by his own candid admission felt prone to distraction due to a superstition about boots.

How did he get so far as to captain his county without his coaches identifying the underlying psychology which made him tick? This of course begs the question as to how many *other* athletes, from grassroots to elite, compete in a similar coaching vacuum? Many coaches are convinced that the topic of superstition is not worthy of mention during sports preparation. Yet this doesn't prevent them from spending copious amounts of time and energy blaming bad luck when they happen to lose. They can't have it both ways, however, as every reference to luck is a nod to superstition since no one has necessarily deciphered luck.

I felt compelled to ask Paddy why he didn't lose faith in his superstition when he lost a game or played poorly? Why compartmentalise faith and ignore the ineptitude of his superstition when he lost, only to reinstate its authority when the
134

next game came around? Was it already presumed, from a coaching perspective due to his prominent status as a County footballing star, that his need to be coached in mental resilience was a thing of the past? If so, surely an example to the contrary was feeling unable to focus 100% on the task at hand without the comfort of his so-called lucky boots.

Where is the evidence that his boots were magical, and why did he continue to believe in their miraculous power even when he experienced defeat or his shooting sucked? So in retrospect, why are practical methodologies to unlearn superstitions not prevalent in sport?

"We are what we think. All that we are arises with our thoughts. With our thoughts, we make our world."

- Buddha

Former captain of Antrim GAA, Paddy Cunningham, was resolute and sincere in believing that an inconspicuous pair of boots could elicit a definitive sporting edge. To him those boots *were* the difference between winning and losing, and the perfect placebo in terms of succumbing to irrational beliefs. The *actual* truth is ostensibly clear; at face value those boots possessed no special powers at all! Yet the *awful* truth is that his boots placed his mind at ease and were therefore symbolic of inner-contentment.

Paddy's subjective reasoning lent personal credence to the idea that superstitions decrease the anxiety athletes experience during the intensity of inter-county games. All observable logic suggests he's deluded to attach emotional value to a run-of-the-mill pair of boots. Yet at a personal level, irrespective of evidence to the contrary and despite zero verifiable facts, his reality was such that those really were the luckiest boots in the world. Not the whole world perhaps but most certainly Paddy's.

"The ancient Egyptians considered it good luck to meet a swarm of bees on the road. What they considered bad luck I couldn't say."

- Will Cuppy, Satirist

In the field of psychology, the 'four stages of competence' or 'conscious competence' learning model relates to the psychological states involved in the process of progressing from incompetence to competence regarding a skill. The model was developed by former GTI employee Noel Burch who suggests that no matter what skill we attempt to master, there are four learning stages. It's a practical model with the potential to prove that the things athletes freely attribute to luck are mere products of chance and probability. I therefore present the following sporting scenario in an attempt to disprove that luck has any influence in sport.

I begin with a genuine account of when three colleagues and I were once in a snooker hall in Belfast. All of us were snooker enthusiasts but none of us were particularly good. To maximise the time available, we agreed to partner up and play two against two, which seemed to go well until my partner potted a red ball but then suffered the misfortune of watching the white ball follow the red into the pocket. We all laughed in a jokey sort of manner but our smiles soon disappeared as my partner produced an outburst of profanities, one of which was, *"That always fucking happens to me, I never get any fucking luck."*

Seeing his frustration, I offered a solution which a more competent snooker player once passed onto me. When relaying this story to you, the reader, I intend to draw on Burch's **four stages of competence** model to disprove that luck played any part in my partner's transition from incompetence to competence regarding the skill of potting a ball without the white ball also following into the pocket.

Stage 1. Unconscious incompetence: Initially my snooker partner displayed all the facets of unconscious incompetence. He was not even aware that a method existed to correct his misuse of the skill, nor did he recognise that potting the white ball was due to incompetence. Instead he just cursed and blamed his misfortune on the superstition called luck.

Stage 2. Conscious incompetence: I explained how I used to do the same thing until a snooker player explained that I was striking the white ball too high up, hence its forward momentum carried it into the pocket. So he advised me to strike the white ball lower down. Although my snooker partner listened intently, he remained incompetent regarding the skill since he hadn't as yet had any opportunity to try it for himself. What had changed, however, was that he was now conscious of the technique required to become competent in the skill and also of how to correct it.

Stage 3. Conscious competence: Next he began to practice and demonstrate the skill as he was consciously aware of the correct method, and the more shots he played the more competent he became. He even relapsed at one point when he forgot my advice and potted the white, only this time instead of getting frustrated, he corrected himself while explaining aloud where he'd went wrong. This demonstrated his new-found ability to consciously and competently master the skill.

Stage 4. Unconscious competence: At stage four my partner would have practiced so much that the skill would become second nature. It wasn't possible to reach this stage in one session, yet professional snooker players demonstrate Stage 4 all the time by planning three or four shots ahead. By Stage 4 the bulk of their focus has shifted to strategically positioning the cue ball in preparation for the next shot; they are no longer conscious of trying to avoid potting the white. Watch any professional snooker tournament and, in terms of competence, it's extremely rare to witness a player potting the white.

Initially my partner didn't know the technique to correct the skill of not potting the white. He wasn't even aware that a deficit existed. So how could he fix his dilemma when he wasn't even aware there was something to fix? When I explained the solution, however, he automatically became conscious of the deficit and how to put it right. He still wasn't competent because he hadn't practiced, but once he focused and practiced he quickly became conscious and competent at completing the skill, even to the point where he began correcting himself.

Had he kept on practicing he would have reached a point where not potting the white would become second nature. Yet something incredible *did* occur by the end of Stage 3, whereby similar to Elvis at the height of his popularity, luck had left the building and wasn't coming back. Not only was he conscious and competent at completing the skill, but he now also recognised that his previous shortcoming had everything to do with poor technique and nothing at all to do with luck.

What does anyone actually know about luck other than it's ambiguous? So how should we approach the delicate subject of whether luck is primarily good for us or bad? Let's begin with the following astounding tale of skydiver Anders Helstrup who reportedly leapt from an aeroplane over Hedmark, South East Norway, only to find to his utter astonishment that a meteor from space was hurtling past him towards earth at a staggering 300mph. It was supposedly the first time in recorded history that a meteor was captured on camera (attached to his helmet) during a process known scientifically as 'dark flight', whereby the meteor was still in the process of falling through the air with its light already extinguished.

Some reporters implied that Anders cheated certain death by a matter of metres, thus raising the question as to whether, due to the intervention of karma, kismet, destiny, or fate, survival had been his greatest slice of luck? Others implied he was never in danger at all as it simply wasn't his time to die. Thus, his greatest slice of fortune (and claim to fame) was being the first person to capture and record such an incredibly historic and mind-blowing occurrence while still in the air. Consequently, the overriding question (the mother of all questions) is whether his odds of avoiding a collision had already been predetermined by luck, predestined by fate, or a matter of chance and probability? Which of these seems most likely?

Another story widely-reported at the time told of fellow Norwegian skydiver Idrup Remo, who survived a near-fatal fall as he plummeted to earth with his parachute refusing to open. Yet bizarrely, he managed to safely and commendably negotiate his own crash landing... only to be run over by a car as he landed on a busy street. He was taken to hospital with numerous injuries but survived to tell the tale.

Given that Anders and Idrup were both Norwegian, are we turning a blind eye to a near-fatal conspiracy? Was a shared nationality the actual cause of their joint misfortune and the reason why both came within inches of death? Were they the near-fatal victims of a Norwegian hex or curse? Did they fall prey to a skydiving hoodoo or jinx, or does this conspiratorial hypothesis carry no merit at all because it's simply absurd? Are our brains overworking when processing the potential for such a ridiculous claim to be true, and are we forced to employ poetic licence when lumping these random coincidences together in such a way that they bear all the hallmarks of a Norwegian conspiracy while being devoid of verifiable facts?

The most practical conclusion is recognising that both skydiving incidents were unrelated and unrehearsed. Superstitious mentalities are primed to see traces of conspiracy in pretty much everything, irrespective of how strong the evidence to the contrary may appear. Consequently, the greatest threat facing athletes with superstitious beliefs is that the human brain is a sucker for context, patterns, and trends, even if the behavioural sequence in question is concocted by the athletes themselves. The human brain is awash with mental tricknologies which bamboozle our thoughts into believing that it's okay to be economical with the facts.

Superstitious beliefs don't exist in a vacuum, which is why I deliberately concocted the farcical example of a Norwegian conspiracy in league with two stories which were seemingly true. I wanted to expose the flawed methodology behind superstitious mindsets which seek to correlate ambiguity with cherry picked facts. Anders and Idrup were simply Norwegian skydiving enthusiasts who encountered life-threatening occurrences while tumbling from the sky. Both almost died at the mercy of chance and probability; or perhaps not! Maybe neither were in any danger at all if we believe in superstitions such as luck, destiny, and fate.

All we can tell from the information available is that both skydivers faced unrelated scenarios which, if pieced together in a random fashion, provide some indication as to how easily the brain merges sequences into preposterous yet seemingly credible events. Superstitious belief of whichever ilk means stringing two or more random events together using poetic licence to elicit a fact. That's why no one to date has proven beyond doubt that carrying an element of superstition can increase their luck and enhance their chances of winning at sport.

No superstition to date has proven capable of withstanding peer scientific review in terms of fashioning successful sporting outcomes, swaying fate and luck in a certain direction, boosting our chances of lifting a trophy, protecting us from injury, or preserving our lives as we compete. The latter two of which may have proven useful during the plight of our skydiving friends, one of whom found himself hurtling towards earth faster than anticipated, while the other drifted too close for comfort to a passing meteor hurtling past at 300mph.

Who or what lay behind these extraordinary escapes? Perhaps citing a miracle is overstating the fact since Idrup also had an emergency parachute which decreased his momentum in the nick of time. Anders on the other had was deemed to be lucky not to be struck by the passing intruder in the sky, yet no one mentioned the prospect, even in jest, of the meteor being struck by him, as this would mean it was he who instigated the strike. An article in *Space.com* estimates that thousands of meteors strike the earth every year but most go unnoticed due to their insignificant size and weight or because they land in the ocean.

Falling meteors aren't uncommon, and this fact alone catapults Ander's tale into the realms of probability, coincidence, and chance, far away from suggestions that being struck would be due to karma, fate, or luck. Every time a skydiver hurtles through the air, the possibility arises that something wonderful or frightful may occur. As a result, many believe that their fate lies in the hands of imaginary constructs such as gods who interact with terrestrial sport by way of superstitious rituals such as prayer.

In 2006, a study of Therapeutic Effects of Intercessory Prayer (STEP) found two major results. First, intercessory prayer had no effect on recovery from surgery without complications. Its second finding was that patients who knew they were receiving intercessory prayer fared worse. So prayer has not been demonstrated, in a falsifiable sense, to be effective beyond the rate of chance.

Luck, for its part, is merely a series of presuppositions such as karma, randomness, serendipity, fluke, destiny, and fate. The superstitious beliefs which many athletes hold, reflect how they subjectively interpret both cultural and colloquial semantics. So in order to establish some common ground, let's begin with the understanding that words don't have meanings, merely usages, most of which are subjective and change over time.

The similarities between luck and chance appear obvious when interpreted in congenial terms such as bumping into an old friend where perhaps we might say, *"As luck had it, I bumped into X today,"* or *"As chance would have it, I bumped into Y."* It's difficult to detect whether either scenario refers to an inbuilt sense of happiness or to a sense of resignation, as if the meeting could not be avoided. Consider the following viewpoint on luck through the words of one random interviewee who described luck as *"a strange amount of good things happening."* His implication, while using my analogy, was that the meeting of X and Y was a happy encounter or fell in the region of generally good.

The generic reaction to luck in conventional thinking is, unless we go out of our way to specify a particular experience as being bad, then primarily the experience is perceived as good. A chance meeting, however, depicts something more neutral, as if we are not yet 100% sure as to whether the experience was happy or not. So how can we tell luck and chance apart? It's easy, just ask a gambler since both they and mathematicians view luck and chance as worlds apart. Chance is calculable with a probability factor of how likely or unlikely it is that an event will occur. This gives rise to common phrases such as, 'What were the odds?' or 'What were the chances of that?'

As things currently stand, the superstition called luck is incalculable, mysterious, and immersed in imponderable odds since no one has demonstrably authenticated it as being a 'thing'. Nor has anyone infiltrated, captured, recorded, or exposed luck's mysterious origin at source. Luck is an ideal that displays the characteristics of a cold-hearted renegade who refuses to be bound in any way, shape, or fashion by emotion, convention, or affiliation to logic. Yet luck continues to wield unlimited subliminal control over many athletes and maintains its stranglehold for as long as they concede intellectual integrity to believing in hearsay, mythology, and divine intervention by invisible gods.

For a superstition to manifest in a physical capacity, first a supernatural intervention must demonstrably occur since the very idea of supernatural is a superstition by default. To rely on luck's mercy only sends athletes spiralling even

140

deeper into its debt with no verification that it even exists. Not even the appliance of deep-seated and esoteric human insight has managed to crack luck's mystical facade. So the best any superstitious athlete can do is pay luck its dues and then bow to its mercy in the hope that it's favourable, bountiful, and not too harsh in its deliberation of what they deserve.

It's important to initiate convivial discourse and healthy debate to ask whether luck is a sporting asset or a performance drawback which skews our interpretation of events. It's a complete dereliction of duty towards our spontaneous, creative selves to disregard luck's impact on competitive sport. Instead, it's time to show luck some polite appreciation as if tipping our hats to a worthy adversary since the topic of luck is sport's elephant in the room. When asked, many athletes contested the idea of luck, yet adjusted their behaviour as though it were real. Perhaps we should be struck by just how precarious it all is since we're about to find out that nothing is more complex than our relationship with luck.

I was once told that you don't get to choose your friends, they choose you. In terms of who chooses who, the facts are often ambiguous, just as many relationships which herald success or heartache in sport often prove as ambiguous as luck itself. Consider the story of 25-year-old amateur sport shooter Peter Wilson who won Team GB's third gold medal at the London 2012 Olympic Games. He spoke of his success on *talkSPORT* radio and had many interesting things to say on relationships, randomness, and luck. He was asked for some insight into the difficulties he faced while attempting to raise enough money to sustain himself while competing. Consider his response and then ask yourself if what he experienced was really luck?

"It's a tough place to be when you come back from an Olympic games and you have to scrape and scrounge as much money together as you possibly can to train. That really is a mentally terrible place to be and it was a struggle."

Next Peter alluded to his fortunate relationship with Sheikh Ahmed Al Maktoum who formed part of the ruling royal family of Dubai and, according to Peter, was pivotal to him achieving Olympic gold. So when asked how the unlikely partnership came about he replied:

"They're an amazing family and I can't thank them enough. It was a bit random really. I had the opportunity to talk to him [Ahmed] and that only came about through a coffee and a handshake at his house and only after he had decided to quit. [Earlier] he had held a press conference at the Olympic Games in Beijing and

announced his retirement out of the sport. I was in the right place at the right time to ask him to be my coach. Suddenly, from having nothing, I had everything. I was very lucky, I had an Olympic gold medallist as my coach who I believe is the greatest double trap shot of all time. Ahmed has now coached me for the last four years to win the big one [London 2012]. It's the one that matters and I can't thank him enough.

By any standards that was quite a result. Yet words such as randomness, luck, fluke, fate, and destiny lack any prior sense of meaning in terms of deciphering what caused the scales of fortune to tip in his favour. How was he meant to tell luck's many imponderables apart? Is there a straightforward answer or, in retrospect, did Peter discover to his advantage that deciphering luck's many imponderables is not only unnecessary but also a waste of resources and time since the answer to luck is general aloofness? After all, he'd already implied that the planets had aligned in his favour with no great effort on his part at all.

The fact that Peter grabbed his opportunity because he was in the right place at the right time is a product of chance; luck isn't part of the equation at all. Certainly there were elements of fortuitousness since he could spend a lifetime attempting to replicate such good fortune but never again be the recipient of such a break. The idea of good fortune need not take away from his hard work, endeavour, and skill, nor from his obvious talent. Contrary to the myth that athletes' egos get offended when sharing the spotlight with the idea that they were somehow quite fortunate, it appears fortune, dedication, and talent really can co-exist after all. All it takes is to redefine luck in its proper context, which is the manifestation of probability and chance.

Luck has no explanatory power, hence there is no way to measure its impact on the psychology of athletes who subscribe to bizarre superstitious beliefs. An example of which was brought to my attention one afternoon in The Hague, Netherlands, as I listened intently to Thai boxing instructor Jerry reveal the behaviour of one of his fighters during the build up to every fight:

"I have a fighter and he trains for six weeks before every fight in the shorts he will wear in the fight. During those six weeks he will wear them inside-out, but on the day of the fight he will wear them like normal, I mean the right way around. That is his thing for fight preparation. To him it's like, 'my sweat is in these shorts; I've worked very hard and now I will bring all of that with me into the fight and kick his ass.' That's his thing and he has to do it."

Once again superstition had reared its enigmatic head and caused an athlete to modify their behaviour to gain a definitive edge. The fighter had internalised his superstition to such an extent that ignoring its allure felt like a precursor to losing his skin. Instead he embarked on a peculiar routine, whereby wearing his shorts inside-out was viewed as a precursor to experiencing good fortune, but what was he really hiding in his deified shorts? Did he visualise payback for sacrifices endured during the lead up to the fight? Did he actively visualise the accumulation of sweat as some form of penance?

Did superstition give Jerry's fighter the confidence to make that lonely trek to the ring one more time? Was he harbouring traces of mild schizophrenia by succumbing to superstitious belief, or was wearing his shorts correctly on the day of a fight his way of unleashing suppressed anxiety to bring mental closure to another chapter in his life? Perhaps, in cynical terms, he had lost his mind, or was it merely a question of rhythm and routine to help navigate safely through the adrenalin fuelled emotions of fighting? Did superstition allow him to pace each performance to run like clockwork alongside the pictures he'd built in his brain?

Athletes are primarily creatures of habit who derive comfort from adhering to chronological rhythms, sequential rituals, and consecutive routines. The fighter embraced a superstitious ritual as a chronological means of managing his demons. He trains hard, sweats hard, gets hit hard, and hurts hard during every fight, which is why it's of equal importance that his coach understands the degree of comfort he mentally derives from the sense of rhythm which accompanies his superstitious routine.

"I have CDO. It's like OCD except all the letters are in alphabetical order - as they should be."

- Unknown

Who can legislate for the thoughts in an athlete's mind? Yet it's of vital importance to actively counter the many wild declarations that exist in sport such as, *'with enough faith and belief you can conquer anything.'* At face value this seems such a tantalisingly sentiment, apart from the fact that it isn't true. This was substantiated in the wake of the London 2012 Olympics by numerous Team GB gold-winning athletes who heaped gushing praise on the benefits of competing on home soil. Even former Olympic heptathlon gold medallist, Denise Lewis, mentioned on talkSPORT radio that the number of Team GB medallists may have significantly decreased without the roar of the home crowd cheering them on.

The number of medals gained by Team GB athletes due to home advantage is a matter of conjecture, as is the most frequently overused, inspirational sentiment in sport which is *'with enough faith and belief you can conquer anything'*. This directly conflicts with Denise's implication that, minus considerable home advantage, some athletes may have been lucky to win medals at all. Many sugar-coated sentiments in sport highlight the benefits of faith and belief but conveniently fail to mention the high volume of athletes who, despite an abundance of talent, faith, and self-belief, often find they are powerless to prevent their dreams being snatched away.

The impact of 'self-talk' in competitive sport can prove inspirational but also misleading when it catches us off guard and its impact comes crashing to the fore. An example of this occurred during an interview with former Commonwealth boxing silver medallist Stephen Ward, who graciously agreed to humour me with a soul-searching and even philosophical response to the common winning misnomer that athletes can achieve anything with enough faith and belief:

"You can certainly choose to succeed but you can't choose to be lucky can you? People often talk about the powers of positive thinking and the powers of the universe [Law of Attraction]. They say if you think positively then positive things will come to you and I agree with that 110%, but there have been situations going into a fight where I have planned things out but things just haven't happened for my benefit.

So I've thought about all the 'what ifs'. Sometimes I even think I'm going to win but they [the boxing referees, judges, or selectors] are going to take it off me, and a prime example was just before the Irish Senior Finals where I thought I'm going to win but they're not going to give it to me and it's funny because it panned out exactly that way."

Stephen's intriguing insight regarding the prophetic qualities of self-talk (the language he used to communicate with himself) appeared to insinuate that talent, faith, and belief may not be enough to swing results in his favour if luck or conspiracy decreed it to be so. I next sought to explore his insinuation of universal energies conspiring against him in more detail, by enquiring as to whether (as is often associated with the Universal Law of Attraction) his thoughts really did have the wherewithal to manifest as things. If this widely believed hypothesis (pseudoscience) is true, then Stephen was inadvertently the architect of his own demise from the very first moment his pre-fight psychology fixated on being robbed of the correct result.

I asked whether he'd conceded the fight in his mind before a punch had ever been thrown, thereby initiating the pull of negative energy towards a negative conclusion by default?

"Yeah could be. I definitely agree with that. I was always lucky enough as a child to be told that everyone should have a goal because if you can see it in your head you can always think about it [positive reinforcement by visualisation]; but luck definitely has a big say in things along the way."

Stephen still felt aggrieved by the selectors' decision which he then attributed to bad luck, and if his conspiratorial recollection was correct then it's hard not to empathise. Yet in keeping with his earlier musings about the law of attraction which suggests that negative thoughts attract negative energy and positive thoughts likewise, the question still remains valid as to whether his negative self-talk proved to be the underlying catalyst for his unfortunate demise that particular day? The average career of an athlete or coach is blighted by losing, every bit as much as it is by a win. So what makes athletes place all their eggs in one ambiguous basket full of hearsay, faith, and dependency on the superstition called luck?

Let's test the effectiveness of the power of belief in a little more depth to determine how well the notion of overreliance on faith in supernatural forces actually stacks up. The reason athletes harbour superstitious beliefs in the first place is to improve their luck. Let's compare the account of boxer Stephen Ward with that of ultra-confident Belfast boxer Michael Conlan, who was quick to remind his growing band of admirers that he was destined to win gold while fighting as an amateur for Ireland at the Rio Olympics 2016. However, his dream was abruptly offset when he experienced what he perceived as a shocking indictment on amateur boxing's credibility worldwide.

Michael lost his Olympic bantamweight quarter-final bout in controversial circumstances following a unanimous points decision being awarded to Russian opponent Vladimir Nikitin. Consequently, in one of the most spectacular outbursts ever broadcast live on Ireland's *RTE* Network, he raged, *"They're fucking cheats. That's me! I'll never box for AIBI again. They're cheating bastards, they're paying everybody. I don't give a fuck that I'm cursing on TV. I'm here to win Olympic gold and my dream has been shattered."*

Despite the shock factor which invariably followed his vitriolic tirade, the general tone of his accusations gained traction following the International Boxing Association's decision to send home a number of judges and referees (reportedly six) amid ongoing suspicion of wider corruption following a string of contentious decisions. Irrespective of any truths yet to unfold, the repercussions of Michael's response, which reportedly included flipping-the-bird in the general direction of the referee, continued to gather at pace. Boxer Stephen Ward had spoken earlier of experiencing a similar sense of injustice when he too was robbed of his moment of glory. The only observable difference appeared to be that Michael took no prisoners and left nothing to misinterpretation as he left amateur boxing with a bang.

In retrospect, the same lingering question remains pertinent as to whether both boxers were partially responsible for their undoing due to the negative energy generated by prior beliefs? Both claimed to have visualised the potential for judging skulduggery before a punch was ever thrown. Stephen pulled no punches when admitting to visualising his eventual scenario being played out before it actually occurred, yet visualisations can lead athletes to presuppositional beliefs which create dangerous precedents when competing at sport.

Michael has since embarked on a professional career which began by headlining the St Patrick's Day event at Madison Square Garden in March 2017, yet he may always feel bound by a personal sense of vendetta, as if amateur sport has robbed him of something he can never reclaim. His degree of mistrust may never dissipate, nor may his reticence of raising his hopes in advance of anything boxing related every again. Unfortunately, having since quit amateur boxing, he will always be left with a permanent itch which can never be scratched.

A similar scenario existed for Stephen Ward who struggled to overcome and dismiss what he perceived to be confirmation-bias, where everything he visualised in advance of the senior boxing finals ended up coming true, exactly as he professed. During our conversation, Stephen displayed an understandable air of conspiracy, yet neither of us were any wiser as to the true cause of his loss since asserting conspiracy and feeling hard done by isn't remotely the same as having proof.

Perhaps psychologically it could even be argued that Stephen's initial scepticism of the selection process meant he gave up the ghost before lacing his gloves, almost as if he was getting his excuses in early in case events failed to go his way. Oh, and just for the record, I didn't dare mention this hypothesis to his face. I did ponder on whether his real battle lay in thwarting the threat of intrinsic self-talk (internal monologue) from coercing him into believing he was predestined to fail before throwing a punch. In retrospect, it may have been more productive of Stephen to square up to the conspiratorial self-talk running amok inside his brain.

The challenge facing all athletes is managing self-talk as it pre-empts the way they act and behave. So what future implications might self-talk throw up for both boxers? Might it seek to convince them before upcoming fights that sometimes the odds really are stacked against them, and that split decisions are unlikely to fall their way? Isn't that the exact kind of paranoia which self-talk seeks to instil in the mind of a boxer who has already visualised a conspiracy and is predisposed to experiencing defeat? This leaves boxers vulnerable to falling into the groove of believing that every poor decision which fails to go their way is further clarification of sports déjà vu?

Only time will tell if the psychology of boxers Stephen and Michael has transitioned beyond feeling cheated by events which belong in the past? Much of this surmise is pure conjecture, but since Stephen's prophetic visualisation appeared to come true, it then calls into question whether self-talk furnished his thoughts with a plausible strategy which shifted the focus of underlying blame away from how he actually performed on the night.

"The L in my luck has been displaced by an F."

- Unknown

What does anyone actually know about luck? Is the advantageous or disadvantageous nature of personal genetics a product of luck? Are our genes the result of superstitions such as fate, destiny, and luck or merely the result of probability and chance? What percentage of athletes participate in the sport most suited, compatible, and conducive to their anatomy and genetics? None of us got to choose our inherent genetics, and few of us had any say, choice, input, or viable alternative but to participate in the sport into which we fell or were placed, even if it wasn't best suited to our individual genetics.

Many athletes are indoctrinated by common coaching mantras such as *'with enough faith and belief you can overcome any obstacle'*. Statements such as these are intellectually dishonest and the fact that they happen to sound upbeat and aspirational tells us nothing at all as to whether they're true. So is it true? Can athletes overcome any obstacle that arises in sport by hard work, faith, and belief? What if the obstacle was being limited at birth by slow-twitch fibres? What then are the chances of fulfilling their dream of becoming a sprinting sensation like Usain Bolt? Or why stop there, are we likely to witness a 6'4" (1.93m) and 20 stone jockey winning the Grand National horse race anytime soon because the jockey believes that he or she can? That really would provide interesting viewing and betting odds.

The human ego likes to believe that nothing lies beyond its capability, and that somewhere within us lies the potential to overcome and succeed against any odds.

This flies in the face of nature, genetics, and chance, which force us to concede on a regular basis that there *are* things beyond our control. This is where superstition converges with ego to redefine athletes' previous perceptions about power.

Athletes hate to acknowledge that there are forces beyond their control as this causes a sense of disempowerment. Hence, managing their psychology is integral to competing in terms of benchmarking, motivation, and appraising how they perform, yet somewhere in the chasm between thinking and doing, it turns out they are prone to gathering beliefs.

Consider the mindset of Irish golfer Rory McIlroy as he powered to his first PGA Tour victory in almost 16 months by winning the 2016 Deutsche Bank Championship in Boston USA. Focus in particular on questions regarding the how, where, and why? Rory won the tournament in September, having previously described his putting as pathetic after missing the cut at the PGA Championship just two months earlier. In hindsight, what followed may seem glaringly obvious, but what wasn't so obvious was the action he deemed necessary to rectify his form.

The 'where' factor deemed necessary to rectify Rory's demise meant identifying where his game had gone wrong. The 'why' component is best explained using his own words immediately following his win where he admitted, *"I knew my game was in good shape. I just needed to do something with the putting. I found something."* The 'how' had already transpired a week prior to his win when he took the decision to replace both his putter and putting coach. It was a brave decision and fraught with complexity, but he had successfully identified how to get back to winning ways. Yet even he seemed surprised at how quickly his decision to change personnel and equipment led to a dramatic upturn in form.

Rory's bold proclamation that *"I knew my game was in good shape"* suggests he believed that the blame for his erratic form lay outside of himself, that he was doing more right than wrong, and that all he required was fresh perspective and a new coach and putter to increase his chances of securing a win. Each change was his choice and luck played no part in the solution at all. So despite the media reporting a change in his luck, his savvy decisions meant the superstition called luck had been rendered obsolete.

Psychology is essential to being competitive, which is why it's important to apply scepticism to any belief which is founded solely on the basis of luck. It's intellectually dishonest to attribute the outcome of a deliberate sporting action to luck since luck doesn't prevent the use of our arms, legs, hands, or feet from completing the physical aspects of any task. Instead, physical movements like running and jumping occur irrespective of imaginary constructs such as luck. So what is luck? It is a mental manifestation of human *will* or human *won't*, but what percentage of human psychology constitutes human will?

According to Dutch Philosopher, Benedict de Spinoza, in order for something to be entirely free, it must be uncompelled in all ways and also the cause of itself. Consider the practical implications of Spinoza's interpretation of free will regarding the beliefs we hold dear in sport. If we can't disregard illusionary constructs such as luck, then we are no longer free because we do not possess an uncompelled state of will. How much time does the average athlete spend contemplating how sport might look without luck? Fortunately, I can save everyone valuable time; sport would look exactly as it does now since nothing would change if there's no luck to change it.

How much time do sports psychologists and coaches spend being fully-engaged with athletes in a bid to raise awareness that luck cannot be proven to exist? This has instant ramifications in terms of being able to manage an athlete's aspirations, expectations, and well-being, whilst also establishing coaching rapport. Why aren't sports educators more proactive on the topic of superstitious beliefs since the existence or non-existence of luck is of tremendous consequence given luck is potentially the greatest psychological fallacy in sport?

"Psychobabble attempts to redefine the entire English language just to make a correct statement incorrect. Psychology is the study of why someone would try to do this."

- Criss Jami, *Killosophy* Author

Many athletes rely heavily on luck. Others simply don't care for lucky sentiments as we're about to find out. First though, can we backtrack just a little to visualise the surrealness of the idea of the 20-stone jockey analogy from earlier. Oh, and while we're at it, spare a thought for the poor horse.

"Luck has nothing to do with it because I spent many, many countless hours on the court working for my one moment in time, not knowing when it would come."

- Serena Williams, Tennis Champion

Serena was expressing a wonderful example of an elite athlete's reluctance to concede any credit to luck, despite her former academy owner Rick Macci reportedly conceding during an interview with *Trans World Sport* that *"Richard [her father] was very fortunate. It's lucky to get one in a family but he has two and both girls have that ability."* Rick of course was referring to American tennis sensations, Serena and Venus Williams, and having coached both of them from the beginning, his opinion is at least worthy of note.

Let's begin with Serena's dismissive comments regarding the influence of luck. Where do they sit in accordance with her dad's assertion that both daughters *"possess that kind of speed [so] it's hard to beat them"*? Or when speaking of Venus he later announced, *"there are four main elements required to be a champion: to be rough, tough, strong, and mentally sound,"* and Venus possessed all four, not to mention an equally phenomenal sister to practice with; and if that's not lucky then it's difficult to define what luck is. I will define it, however, as a universal colloquialism for probability and chance.

What were the odds that their father would start them playing tennis with a professional career in mind before they were even five years old? What was the probability that he'd display the necessary mental fortitude to relocate them as kids, along with his family, away from one of Los Angeles' poorest suburbs to Florida so they could enrol at one of America's top tennis academies? He took an incredible risk, and if faced with a similar choice, would we be willing to relocate our families? Initially it appears within these short extracts that luck had everything to do with Serena's rise to prominence, as did her fortunate genetics since if she'd been short and slight of frame it may not have been possible to make the impact she did in the women's professional game.

What if Venus and Serena possessed only three of the four main elements described earlier by their father as necessary to be a champion? What can we conclude from the sisters' good fortune at being bankrolled to attend a top tennis academy to nurture their talents and pursue their dreams? Pretty lucky eh! In truth there were certainly elements of good fortune but so far there's no evidence of the superstition called luck.

Let's consider a more sobering example as experienced by less fortunate kids from the same Los Angeles suburb. Many were equally talented in their own capacity, but due to varying circumstances they were left behind to fend for themselves. Consider the privilege enjoyed by Serena of having an equally talented and driven sister to share her journey. Without access to each other's emotional strength, who can say for certain which one, if any, would go on to enjoy the legendary status they achieved?

"Venus told me the other day that champions don't get nervous in tight situations. That really helped me a lot. I decided I shouldn't get nervous and just do the best I can." This quote by Serena led me to question whether athletes are too often engrossed in curbing their anxiety to just go out and compete and do the best they can. The human psychology need not rely on superstition to counteract anxiety or pull us out of a hole when we're in over our heads and things start to implode, yet athletes continue to embrace superstition to alleviate nerves and combat bad luck. Perhaps that's why Serena's contention that champions shouldn't get nervous in tight situations did not appear to discount using superstition to achieve her goal.

An article by Ryan Murphy in *Men's Fitness* magazine reported some of Serena's superstitious quirks, such as needing her shower sandals at courtside during every match and bouncing the tennis ball five times before every first serve, yet only twice before every second serve. Ryan claimed that she wore the same pair of socks throughout each tournament and blamed major losses on failing to adhere to stringent superstitious rituals and routines. Similarly, an article in *Elle UK* by Imogen van Zaane told how Swiss men's tennis supremo Roger Federer swears by the number eight. She then points to eight consistent towel rubs, eight bottles of water, and eight tennis rackets accompanying him at courtside as demonstrable proof of his superstitious traits.

Superstitions add complexity when simplicity would otherwise suffice. Who can measure the role superstition played on Serena's performances in July 2015 when she became the fourth tennis player in WTA history to spend 250 weeks as world number one? She also entered 2016 having been ranked at number one for 150 consecutive weeks. This was the 3rd longest streak in women's tennis history, and in September 2016 she surpassed Roger Federer's grand slam record to reach an incredible 308 grand slam wins. Earlier she disputed the impact of luck on her magnificent career, but obsessively complied with superstitious rituals and routines which have no bearing in reality other than to make her feel comfortable while she competes.

Superstitions are rooted in alter-ego and offer athletes the courage to adopt various guises and personas. Spontaneity, in contrast, transfers responsibility back onto how the athlete performed. So how prepared is the superstitious athlete to take the necessary steps to regain their zest for spontaneity, impulsiveness, and instinctive awareness given that superstitions tend to thrive best on ambiguity, anxiety, and fear? Serena took the advice from her sister who advocated competing with no presuppositional airs and graces or psychological strings attached. Consequently, her anxiety began to dissipate of its own accord.

Serena's anatomy would not function less efficiently, nor is there evidence to suggest that her performances would dip if she opted to ditch her much publicised superstitions once and for all. Her superstitious beliefs are products of her brain, but if luck does exist, it would be hard to dispute that both sisters are major beneficiaries; yet in terms of their extraordinary abilities, the evidence points to fortunate genetics solely due to probability and chance.

Here is a short extract from my conversation with former Northern Ireland international goalkeeper, Maik Taylor, concerning the much overstated but lesser understood topic of luck. I asked what part luck played in his highly successful, widely travelled, and diverse career. At first he was thoughtful and contemplative before offering the following response:

"Sometimes if you work your absolute hardest, luck tends to go in your favour that little bit more, but I honestly believe that's down to hard work. You're a little bit sharper, you're a little bit quicker. Also, you can jump a little bit higher and then you might make a save, but that's because of all the hard work and preparation that's gone in before. So it might seem a little bit lucky but I think it's down to all the hard work."

I thanked Maik for his insight but decided to enquire a little bit further in search of a more in-depth understanding of luck. I asked, *"You're Maik Taylor, former Northern Ireland International goalkeeper, but what if your height was just 5 foot 7? What part did luck play with regard to your genetics?"* Maik smiled as he pondered the implications but then thoughtfully replied:

"Well obviously genetics are a big factor as it doesn't matter how hard I trained, I would never be Olympic 100-metre champion because my genetics are such that I haven't got fast twitch fibres. So I could never be that quick and genetics do play a huge part in that. Obviously I was blessed with being 6 foot 3, so I'd half a chance because the first thing managers ask these days is how tall is he, irrespective of how he's doing."

Maik's candid interpretation of luck provided further insight into how genetics weaponise the ability to perform at sport. From an ancestral perspective, genetics are a product of chance and probability and can be measured scientifically to study how likely they are to limit or increase an athlete's ability to outperform their opponent. Genetics are instrumental to an athlete's success depending on their advantageous or disadvantageous nature, yet the delusion of luck still affects how many athletes are conditioned to think. This occurs because every sporting action is preceded by a thought and every thought sparks a subsequent reaction, such as luck wielding greater influence than an athlete's actual state of will.

The human brain doesn't opt to ignore our legs when our objective is to stand up and walk, nor does it dismiss the role of our hands when our sole function is to eat by reaching food into our mouths. So how then can our brain so brazenly ignore the fact that the major sporting component we refer to as luck is, in effect, a product of probability and chance and carries no explanatory power. Consider as an example the absurdity of the following game appraisal by Manchester United manager José Mourinho, who insisted he didn't want Bristol City's EFL Cup quarter-final victory in December 2017 to become about luck, but then referred to luck 8 times in his post-match address:

"My thoughts are they were lucky but they fought a lot to be lucky. They win the game in the moment where everybody was waiting for our goal, so I have to say they were a bit lucky. I don't want the fact I say they were a bit lucky to be the main thing. The main thing is that they won and fought hard for that. In the first half we hit the post twice. Marcus Rashford hits the inside and it comes out; they were a bit lucky. They were very lucky to have the goal in the last second but I don't want the fact I used the word lucky to be the most important thing. We know how to win and we know how to lose, so we say good luck to them."

It's hard not to detect a whiff of sour grapes in José's reaction. His implication, however, is self-defeating when closer analysis is applied since somewhere in the haze of his 'lucky' smokescreen, by his own admission, are the following telling facts. *"We hit the post twice before they scored. They fought like this was the game of their lives. In the first half we lacked the intensity they had mentally and physically. For some of us it was one more day in the office. For some, they didn't even want to come to the office."* Yet the most telling factor of José's assertions is that none of these are remotely related to luck. Instead they're all indications of his team's poor finishing quality, poor sense of occasion, lack of physical and mental intensity, and on this particular occasion, lack of professionalism and self-pride.

In a similar vein, consider the advantageous string of events that occurred for the benefit of tennis ace Novak Djokovic. Cast your mind if you can to his bid to secure the 2016 US Open in New York and ask what made him the envy of his forlorn opponents? The answer was watching him breeze into the semi-finals without ever having to break sweat as he only had to compete in two out of five potential matchups to achieve his goal. His good fortune, however, was not solely due to scintillating tennis; instead, three out of five of his opponents conceded to injury.

In quite a startling sequence of events after beating Jerzy Janowicz in the first round, Novak was awarded a walkover in the following round after Jiří Veselý pulled out with a forearm injury. In the next round, he was leading Mikhail Youzhny by 4 games to 2 when the Russian retired with a leg injury. He then swept past British competitor Kyle Edmund in straight sets before good fortune smiled on him once again. This time Jo-Wilfried Tsonga's knee proved so troublesome that he was forced to retire. Pretty jammy eh? It could even be argued, based on the history of men's world singles tennis, that with Kyle Edmund ranked 84th in the world at the time, his threat to Novak was almost equivalent to being granted another bye. Even bookies' odds reflected that an upset by Kyle was not on the cards.

Imagine the freshness Novak brought to the final as opposed to his battle-weary foe. So how should we best categorise his obvious fortune? Was it fate, serendipity, fluke, karma, or simply chance? All of us are entitled to our beliefs; we're not entitled to our own facts, however, since the facts remain facts independent of belief. So irrespective of how athletes view luck, it still has no explanatory power other than being a universal colloquialism for probability and chance.

Many athletes pretend to be luck deniers while complying religiously with superstitious rituals and routines about gods. Yet the idea of a supernatural is also superstition, so they can't have it both ways. It's not logical to believe in a supernatural construct such as a god while denying that belief in the supernatural power of lucky pants is equally viable since the evidence for both, in a falsifiable sense, is exactly the same. Why is it rational to dismiss sports superstitions out of hand just because they lack the same blinkered stamp of approval that athletes often seem happy to bestow on a god? To draw any distinction is not only hypocritical but a logical fallacy known as 'special pleading'.

Something ominous is hovering over every contingency of sport, and the name athletes lazily attribute to this phenomenon is 'luck', despite sharing no consensus as to its meaning. Consider the following scenario reported in *The Sun* in March 2016. It highlighted a wonderfully emotive quote by former Derry GAA boss Brian McIver, following their defeat to Mayo by 1-13 points to 2-12. The defeat left Derry's league survival hopes in tatters, but when asked for his opinion the very animated Oak Leaf boss replied, *"Disgusted, I'm disgusted. Not taking anything away from Mayo but they got a jammy goal and every decision going."*

It was an endearing response from a guy who cared passionately about bringing success to his players, staff, and fans. What it didn't provide is any scientific breakdown of the term 'jammy' since, despite his assertion in the heat of the moment that Mayo got 'every decision going', perhaps Mayo's manager shared a different view. Despite his protest to the contrary, Brian's post-match summation did inadvertently take something away from Mayo's performance by declaring that their goal was jammy and then by suggesting that every decision went their way. His phrasing of events downsized Mayo's technical, tactical, and physical prowess, along with their instinct to capitalise on whatever opportunities came their way.

Brian's tunnel vision failed to address Derry's inability on this occasion to take their chances and defend properly. Therefore, the only pertinent questions are: why wasn't his gripe solely directed at the ineffectiveness of his team, and was he justified in implying that a whiff of conspiracy surrounded their luck? Might he have been better served by accepting that most facets of the game had lain within his team's control? An example of which was recognising that the 'jammy' circumstances surrounding the goal were manifestations of probability and chance.

Only when we start asking these types of questions can curiosity evolve to a point where we're free from any need to posit luck as a convenient scapegoat when events fail to go our way. We can all learn a lot from Venus Williams, who told her sister Serena to do the best she can with the talent she already inherently possesses. We can also learn from the sentiments expressed by former Derry GAA boss Brian McIver, which were not to attribute the causes of success or failure to uncorroborated figments of imagination such as luck since it has no explanatory power and, as such, renders concepts like 'jammy' obsolete.

"Do not take life too seriously. You will never make it out alive."

- Elbert Hubbard, Writer

Superstitions and Faith

"Treat the other man's faith gently. It's all he has to believe with. His mind was created for his own thoughts, not yours or mine."

- Henry Haskins, Writer

'Outside of a dog, a book is man's best friend. Inside of a dog, it's too dark to read.' This is a humorous quote by the wonderful actor and comedian Groucho Marx, whose penchant for comedic timing is peerless. Less comedic perhaps is the following analogy, *'Inside a belief, man's best friend is sincerity, but sincerity is no guarantee against being dead wrong'*. So it's time to inquire as to whether displaying faith in a superstition called god causes a downturn in logic and rationality, thereby sparking an upturn in ignorance and faith?

It seems only fitting that faith takes centre stage when attempting to justify seemingly unfalsifiable topics such as the superstitious belief in a god, since faith is ultimately the reason superstitions exist at all. Faith is also the cause of much idle conjecture due to its reliance on ambiguity, self-delusion, wishful thinking, and lack of self-critique. This was brought to my attention by former Scotland football manager Craig Brown when I asked him to divulge his personal experiences of how superstitious faith permeates sport.

Craig recounted a story of great wit and humour regarding manager Harry Redknapp while Harry was manager of Portsmouth FC. Craig began by acknowledging a player who he greatly admired named Darren Moore and referred to him throughout as a super guy. He said, *"Darren was a big powerful guy. A centre back who at the time was a player at Portsmouth FC, but Darren was also a devout Christian, a born-again Christian. So, one day Harry went into the dressing room before their match with Manchester United and said to his assistant Joe Jordan, 'I think we're one or two players short here'."*

Joe replied, *"Mooro [Darren] has got some of the lads in the boot room and they're having a wee prayer."*

Harry responded with a grin, *"Well, I've just seen the Manchester United team arriving and I think I'll go in and join them."* At the end of the match Portsmouth lost 3-0, whereby Harry said to Mooro, *"You and your prayers, what a lot of nonsense Mooro! It didn't do us a lot of good, we lost 3-0."* But quick as a flash Mooro replied, *"Excuse me gaffer. If I hadn't held that wee prayer it would've been*

6-0."

It was a humorous tale, wonderfully told by an extremely light-hearted Craig Brown regarding a wee bit of prayer and superstition being shared informally before a match. Yet, behind all the banter and good-natured humour, it's worth questioning whether Darren truly believed that his gathering could influence the result of the match by using prayer as his weapon of choice, or was he aiming to convert his teammates to believe in his brand of god?

Many superstitious competitors seek to harness the supernatural for their own selfish ends. Yet the idea of a god-type figurehead interacting with the observable world using visions, dreams, signs, omens, and prayer requires irrefutable evidence of an external agent. Otherwise this type of thinking, although popular, gets us nowhere.

Despite being ambiguous, superstitious faith still manages to wield influence over what athletes do, say, believe, fear, desire, and think. Superstitious claims are not humble claims, but extraordinary claims with no extraordinary evidence to back them up. As such, every athlete who willingly endorses superstition arrogantly asserts that illusion and hearsay are on a par with demonstrable facts.

"How come there's only one Monopolies Commission?"

- Nigel Rees, Author

Any truth about God is purely subjective. All God claims possess similar degrees of sincerity but harbour separate variants of truth. Yet none have a monopoly on superstitious truth; instead, whatever meaning we bestow on superstitions is solely down to us. Furthermore, the idea of separating theistic from generic superstitions, in terms of establishing a proof of concept, is not only ludicrous but bizarre.

Activating a superstitious belief is akin to a gambling addiction, and anyone who incorporates superstition into sport, whether it's having a punt on a horse or beckoning to gods through the superstition called prayer, is a gambling addict and betting junkie, right down to the very last woman or man. Only a gambler places faith in a sports superstition and entrusts the outcome to the will of the gods.

We can counter the urge to feed such addictions by assuming collective responsibility for extending human intellect beyond intellectually dishonest forms of conceit. It begins by awakening to the idea that the universe is big and brazen enough to simultaneously nurture multiple variants of truth, one of which is acknowledging that all superstitions are based on unknowable assertions of faith.

Theism acts as superstition's poster boy, while generic superstition is primarily a moniker for luck, and it appears that no one in all recorded history has categorically deciphered luck. The betting odds for the existence of gods is the same odds as superstition being an actual thing. Both concepts are currently unfalsifiable to the extent that when asked to produce scientific proof for either, athletes resort to examples of sentimentality, while creationism apologists tap dance around not having proof by attempting to poke holes in science and by making shit up.

Superstitions sucker us into believing that they can coexist in harmonious tandem with real events. Yet offering prayers to invisible gods is as much of a gamble as believing that wearing lucky pants can give us an advantage over our foes. When has any god demonstrably intervened and altered a competitive sporting result? And if not, then what practical use is there for an athlete to engage in prayer? Is the role of superstition in sport becoming increasingly obsolete?

What is your personal superstitious win-to-loss ratio, where you proved beyond doubt that superstition helped you to win or caused you to fail? When are you to be awarded a Nobel Prize for demonstrating the prospect of a god to be true, having first undergone the rigorous process of scientific peer review? When did you unleash the earth-shattering breakthrough demonstrating superstition as being a 'thing' which extends far beyond a mere hopeful hypothesis? Let's explore superstition in more detail through insights from former Scotland manager Craig Brown, who is a high-profile Christian working diligently in elite sport.

"I remember listening as a young student in Glasgow to a famous lecturer who gave a televised lecture every Sunday night to an audience. He was a wonderful speaker and I'll never forget a speech he gave one Sunday night about superstition. He said there is no place in the Christian religion for superstition. Now I'm a Christian, though I'm not a devout Christian but I do believe in Christ; and when I heard that lecture, a wonderful lecture, I knew from then on that walking beneath a ladder and lucky numbers like 13 are a lot of nonsense.

There can be no justifications for that in religious terms, and since I heard that lecture I've not paid the slightest heed to superstitions and things like that. I have walked below a ladder since and not worried about it, and I will do what I want on the thirteenth when a lot of people think the thirteenth is unlucky, and you know, things like that. So yes, there are many superstitious players, but I've got to say I'm not one of them."

Of particular interest throughout Craig's response was the stark contrast and imbalance between his ability, willingness, and apparent eagerness to detach from the idea of generic superstitions, compared with his inability, lack of desire, or outright unwillingness to detach from his faith in the superstition called God, despite both types of superstition being one-and-the-same.

Craig seemed happy to align with a god, but less so to align with generic superstitions. This behaviour was common among theists I interviewed, as highlighted by another high-profile Christian in elite sport. I asked former World WBC Bantamweight Boxing Champion, Wayne 'Pocket Rocket' McCullough if, looking back over his career, he considered himself a lucky boxer or a tad unlucky, and whether luck played a role in his successful and high-octane career. Here was his reaction:

"I don't believe in luck. You know, I've got great faith in God, and I just believe if you've got talent, you've got to work hard for your talent. I'm not superstitious either. I know a lot of guys [who are] and a lot of what you're talking about. A lot of guys wear the same socks or the same underwear or something like that, but I wasn't superstitious.

I might have done some things the same way the day of a fight. You know, eat at the right times or sleep at the right times; but perhaps that was more of a routine than a superstition, and as I say, a lot of people have them, but I didn't have any which was a good thing. The only thing I did was pray to God to get me through the fight safely, and to go in there and do my best."

It was all very admirable, yet I wanted to know if it was plausible for his god to appreciate the true essence of professional boxing which is primarily about blood, sweat and tears and athletes knocking seven bells out of each other, often for profit. Did his god favour trash talking between boxers to maximise publicity leading up to a fight, and favour their pursuit of ego and their need to experience self-gratification by way of applause?

"See I've got good faith in God as I say. I'm a good Christian guy and I don't do something like that. I pray before the fight that nobody gets hurt. I never want anybody to get hurt. I never wanted to hurt anybody but I wanted to knock the guy out as quickly as I could. Once, my Pastor in Las Vegas came to my church and

159

prayed that I would knock the guy out, and I did. I knocked him out in two rounds. Afterwards I'd want to thank God that we got through the fight and nobody's hurt, and give thanks to God for that. I wouldn't say the other stuff."

I experienced a feeling of déjà vu due to the glaring similarities that existed between the overall perspectives shared by Wayne and Craig. I refer in particular to the imbalance surrounding Wayne's willingness to detach from subscribing to generic superstitions, falling well short of matching his apparent unwillingness to detach from his faith in the superstition called God. Yet all superstitious beliefs share a commonality; they rely on a concept called 'supernatural' which has no explanatory powers.

We have read a great deal about generic superstitions relating to sport, so in the interest of parity, I cajoled Josh Wagner, a Canadian International football goalkeeper, to share his personal views on superstitious practices as a prominent Christian in professional sport. At the time of our interview in Edinburgh, Josh was a goalkeeper at Falkirk FC.

"My only real superstition is that I always try to pray before games. I believe in the spiritual power of God. I believe that God is very much in this world and I very much believe that he helps me in times of trouble and enables me when I'm playing. I feel it gives me a peace about my game to know it's sort of in God's hands, my personal game and the result of the game. Christianity is very much about eternal life and the fact that we're only in this world for a short time, and that gives me an overall peace about my life and career."

I asked Josh if he scheduled a specific time-frame into his match preparations to pray?

"Yeah, when we get to the changing rooms to drop off our bags and inspect the pitch, that's my time to walk to my goal and have a quick word of prayer with God."

I asked how his teammates reacted to that?

"Some guys don't really understand it. They've never really had faith before in anything, so that can be quite challenging to them. At my old team, I began to take a small prayer meeting before each match with a couple of players. So it's just different ways that people have been brought up and how they react to things of the supernatural I guess."

I then asked how he coped with disappointments?

160

"I think my faith also has a lot to do with that and the fact that I believe we're here for a short time, and during that time our objective is to bring people to know the love of Christ. That sort of gives you a nice eternal perspective rather than a here and now perspective."

Josh's tranquil response left me questioning whether it's practical to dismiss the idea of superstitious beliefs out-of-hand, or was he merely embracing what, for him, was the safest option available because God is the superstition he grew to know best? Superstition is quick to embroil sports psychology in a quagmire of ifs, buts, and maybes. But one thing which was clear from all three interviewees is how willing they were to suspend disbelief in things which seemingly violate natural laws, so long as the 'thing' is an external supernatural agent called God.

"I mean you could claim that anything's real if the only basis for believing in it is that nobody's proved it doesn't exist."

- J. K. Rowling, Author

It's interesting to contrast Craig's, Wayne's, and Josh's Christian perspectives regarding their eagerness to detach from generic superstitions, with their unwillingness to detach from a superstition called God. Most apparent of all is the degree of preference which all three afforded their chosen brand of god, despite all three clearly gambling on an illusion which they cannot physically hear, smell, taste, touch, or see.

Hold on to your hat, since it's time to reveal that the preferred superstitions of many athletes and coaches are being mistakenly classed as guiding principles, but principles are illusionary and do not exist. Instead, guiding principles are 'selfish preferences'; and the reason we deploy the word 'principle' is to feel more at ease when asserting authority by imposing our preferences upon the preferences of someone else.

How's that for a revelation? This is a substantially dramatic twist which squarely places the 'principled' superstition called God on a par with more typical superstitious quirks and bizarre sets of beliefs. There is no such thing as a principle, it simply doesn't exist! Principles are designed to mask and conceal a selfish proliferation of preferential demands. Look inside every principle and therein lurks a preference, and the more principled the claim, the more self-serving it generally is.

To deploy superstition as an active response to fear and anxiety suggests athletes have adopted the pathology of a compulsive gambler, whereby they may as well just visit the roulette table, play a hand of poker, buy a lottery ticket, or roll a set of dice. The odds are the same, irrespective of whether they accept superstitions as gambling vices or refuse to acknowledge that praying to gods is exactly the same as taking a punt. Superstitions are longshots. Not even high-rollers or speculators would dare gamble the bulk of their finances based on the intervention of a god. Nor would they accept faith as guaranteed collateral when sealing a deal.

Try securing a mortgage loan by offering a down-payment of faith as your only collateral and see how far the transaction gets. Ignorance can be bliss, but with this in mind, it's time for the topic of superstition to start getting messy. Few acolytes of religion care to accept that routinely adhering to the superstition called God is comparable to a serious gambling habit. Hence, for some inexplicable reason, the term 'addict' is rarely attributed to an acolyte of God.

Athletes are equally reluctant to believe that wearing their shorts inside out, hopping onto a pitch left foot first, being the last player out of the changing room, or needing to drive to games via certain routes means they too should be tarred with a similar pathology to the gambling addict. Yet, the betting odds against either set of beliefs measurably influencing a sporting outcome or result suggests every athlete who activates a superstition is a gambling addict to their very core.

If superstitious belief has one major drawback, it's that athletes rarely revisit their ongoing relationship to see if they'd be any worse off by dismissing it once-and-for-all. Instead, the general consensus among many interviewees who I canvassed to acquire superstitious insight was to remain true to form and keep on believing just as before. Even though they strived diligently to adhere to their rituals by dotting all the *I's* and crossing the *T's*, they still experienced regular disappointment, not only in terms of bad results, but also due to feeling that the gods had refused to answer their prayers.

One of sport's most impactful Eureka moments is realising that within the sporting fraternity, the superstition called God is considered a principled matter, while generic superstitions are viewed as a matter of preference, as if they carry less validity, less credibility, and are less well-respected than superstitions about gods. Generic superstitions are portrayed as quirky and silly, as if these are behaviours which athletes can just as easily take or leave.

Why are quirky and silly so rarely attached to athletes who actively converse with invisible gods, even though those gods consistently go A.W.O.L when the athlete loses and the shit hits the fan? It seems that the only thing separating principled superstitions about 'gods' from generic superstitions which are quirky and silly, is society's cultural acceptance of theism as a credible art. Otherwise, both sets of superstitions are essentially the same.

Preferences tend to lean in the direction of inclinations, while principles are fixed and unyielding and trick us into believing that our personal preferences have much greater value than those espoused by our peers. In other words, the principles we endorse, adopt, and favour while competing at sport are just shinier versions of our preferred beliefs; but look beneath the surface and it soon becomes clear that a principle is merely a preference in disguise.

> *"Every one of us is, in the cosmic perspective, precious. If a human disagrees with you, let him live. In a hundred billion galaxies you will not find another."*
>
> - Carl Sagan, Astronomer

All of us are wonderfully unique, as are our beliefs and non-beliefs. It's with these thoughts in mind that I grasp my opportunity while working at the iconic Murrayfield stadium in Scotland to ask football pundit and former Chelsea, Everton, and Scottish International, Pat Nevin, if he displayed any symptoms of superstition throughout his long and distinguished career?

"I'm such a dull person to tell you that I had absolutely none. Some things I preferred. I preferred wearing number thirteen as my favourite number in the international squad, specifically to show people I'm not superstitious. I don't think that qualifies as a superstition, but just to show people that you actually made your own fate.

However, I was surrounded by plenty of people who did. I tended to try and blank them from my mind because I knew there were all sorts of guys sitting next to me who'd do his left boot first, then his right boot next, and never put his shorts on until the last second before he went out. There were millions of them.

I mean a lot of them would wear the same shirt every time and that sort of stuff, but anytime it was mentioned to me, I would just look at them and laugh. I'm afraid I'm the least superstitious person in the world. In fact, if anyone said something because of a superstitious reason, I would deliberately do it the opposite way."

Since so many athletes place faith in superstitious quirks, personal artefacts, charms, eccentricities, omens, and prayer to instil self-confidence and to combat anxiety and nerves; and since Pat claimed to have no apparent superstitions, I asked how he managed to combat nerves on big occasions?

"Alan who does the cricket commentary on Sky Sports and I went out and played golf the other day and he asked me that specific question. I said I didn't know because I've never been nervous in my life. I don't know what nerves are. My wife

thinks I'm a complete and utter weirdo but I've never worried about anything. I think the day I did my driving test, or I remember asking a girl out when I was 16, but apart from that I can't remember ever feeling nervous or worried. I always thought it was a good thing because I was always comfortable, calm, and confident.

I've heard so many people saying that nerves are also a good thing because you get your blood flowing, you get excited, you're lively and you're ready and alive for everything, but I don't know, I suppose I always just felt more comfortable being in kind of a slow state where I was completely in control of everything.

I think it was probably somewhere in my mind when I grew up that I just did not actually want that. I didn't want to be nervous. I didn't want to be lacking in control. I always give people this example: if you watch some footballers running out onto a football field all stiff and all tight, and then watch [former Dutch international] Ruud Gullit walking out onto a football field. Cool, relaxed, controlled. That's the way I wanted to be."

So to recap, Craig Brown and Wayne McCullough were swift in their eagerness to align with their preferred superstition called God, but demonstrated a rapid and immediate departure from aligning with generic superstitions. Whereas Canadian goalkeeper Josh Wagner's superstition saw God in everything (including sport), even though a god is not necessarily a thing. All three were quite charming and a little disarming with their grace and humility, but while their insights were captivating, the consistency of their reasoning was skewed in favour of the superstition called God and not even-handed in the spirit of sport which is meant to advocate fair play.

Superstitious beliefs are never clear cut. The mercurial Pat Nevin, for his part, had no faith in superstitions at all, despite being fully conscious of the superstitious culture pervading all aspects of competitive sport. He wasn't beholding to their allure and so they had no control over him. Despite being surrounded by superstitious teammates, he deliberately avoided their psychobabble and was determined to make sure it stayed that way.

Pat displayed no appetite for superstition, barring one barely visible Freudian slip where he admitted going out of his way to do the complete opposite of whatever superstition was being re-enacted by his peers. Yet by actively attempting to prove that he carried no superstitious hang-ups of which to speak, perhaps he displayed a few mild symptoms after all? Otherwise, why go out of his way to respond to behaviours which he deemed as irrelevant and obsolete? Hmm! Let's hope it's not catching.

Consider the following enlightening story of 'let go-ness', about a guru who once sat in meditation on a riverbank as a disciple bent down beside him and gently placed two precious pearls at his feet as a token of reverence. The guru opened one eye, lifted one of the pearls and held it so carelessly that it slipped from his grasp and rolled down the bank into the river. The disciple was horrified and plunged into the river to retrieve the pearl.

He continued to dive into the river time and again but had no luck finding the pearl. Finally, soaked and exhausted, he roused the guru from his meditation and gasped, "you saw where it fell, show me the exact spot so I can get it back for you." In response, the guru lifted the second pearl, threw it into the river and said, "right there!"

"Faith is not desire, faith is will. Desires are things that need to be satisfied, whereas will is a force. Will changes the space around us."

- Paulo Coelho, Author

The story of the guru may seem profound, yet what a joy it is to let go of any needless compulsion for superstitious desires which blocks spontaneity and curiosity from freely entering our mind. Here is a wonderful quote, "Ignorance isn't just what you don't know, it's also what you won't know." This refers to the stuff we refuse to know, irrespective of overwhelming evidence to the contrary such as superstitions not being real, thereby having no impact on how we perform.

It takes a great deal of courage to outrank desire, and more will than our current willingness (willpower) may allow to see superstitions for what they really are, which is mere physical manifestations of faith. But how fluctuating are superstitious beliefs?

"Faith is not something to grasp. It is a state to grow into."

- Gandhi

Consider the dilemma faced by former Olympic and World triple-jump Champion, Jonathan Edwards CBE, as he reflected publicly on his faith as a Christian in the wake of an amazing sporting career. He said, *"It's sort of ironic now I've lost my faith, that my faith gave me the perspective to somehow disassociate myself from the outcome to a degree."*

It was a startling revelation, as hidden in his words was perhaps the key to unravelling superstitious faith. Jonathan was speaking with *The Times* columnist Matthew Syed when he implied that his faith wasn't profound but was a welcome diversion. A diversion which, in his case, meant immersing his mind in Christian

165

principles rather than having to focus his attention on the pressures which accompany being champion of the world.

What did Jonathan mean by *"disassociate myself from the outcome"*? It meant using faith as a smokescreen to reroute his focus and media attention away from the chaos surrounding his sport. Superstitions rely on the human intellect to become inventive, imaginative, and creative; and what is more inventive than imagining God? It required ingenuity on Jonathan's behalf to imagine a god into existence to create a diversion from everyday pressures which were not imaginary but real.

Here is a practical test to determine whether anyone has proven the existence of God. Surely it is logical to assume that after having undergone scientific peer review, the person who brought forth irrefutable proof of a god would've been the face on every 24-hour news channel worldwide, the voice on every radio programme, and the most trending celebrity ever to exist.

Such a story would've automatically eclipsed the small matter of seeing the first man land on the moon. It would've been the most anticipated announcement of all time and one of those moments when we all remembered exactly where we were when the story first broke. Their's would've been the face on every billboard and printed on the side of every bus. It would have been the lead topic of conversation on every street corner, in every workplace, at every sports event, and in every bar, irrespective of language, culture, religion, politics, social status, or race.

This pioneering 'bringer of knowledge' would've been the automatic recipient of a Nobel Prize since the extent of their proof would've been so great that even atheists and sceptics would've abandoned their disbelief and converted to theism. Their findings would've been published in every reputable scientific journal worldwide. Oh, and given their new-found celebrity status, surely the paparazzi would've paid them exorbitant amounts of cash to reveal God's secret whereabouts to the waiting world. So why hasn't this person with access to God been exposed before now? Why keep God under wraps?

Once we come to know something, we no longer have any need for faith. It requires tremendous arrogance to believe that a god wants our team to win at sport or our performance to prevail at the behest of an equally deserving opponent who also believes in the exact same god. This places God in a compromising quandary, wondering what to do next. What is God meant to do when two of his disciples stand face-to-face and toe-to-toe, psyched up and ready to compete?

Consequently, God must deny one opponent in favour of the other. Either way, one opponent is always left questioning why God didn't side with them. Wow, tough call. It's time we began asking these types of questions because, minus extraordinary evidence to back up extraordinary claims, we can pretty much claim anything to be real then tell ourselves that it's true and act accordingly. This brings us full circle, back to that wonderful quote by author and wordsmith J. K. Rowling who expressed, *"I mean you could claim that anything is real if the only basis for believing in it is that nobody's yet proved that it doesn't exist."*

After losing his Christian faith, former world triple-jump champion Jonathan Edwards pondered on whether to forfeit the religious affinity which had so seamlessly enabled him to cope with the increasing demands of elite sport. He competed throughout his successful career using Christian faith as his alter ego, but once he stepped away from competing he began to question whether his alter ego had become obsolete.

This led me to question whether winning perspectives are best gained through the careful deployment of mental diversions? (Jonathan's was his Christian faith). If God really does interact with this physical world, then what was to be gained from intervening in Jonathan's physical altercations with a pit of sand? Doesn't God have better things to do; and isn't this the same God who exerts dominion over all of the sands on earth, including Jonathan's Olympic pit?

It was time to exact a more in-depth exploration of the misleading languages and emotional platitudes in which athletes engage to justify their superstitious beliefs. The temptation exists to substitute logic and reason for personal sentiment and raw emotion when touched by the sincerity of their beliefs. Many reckon emotion is reason enough to assert superstition as being a thing; 'I felt it deep in my heart' is a common assertion. Yet the heart is an organ designed to pump blood throughout the body to supply oxygen and nutrients and remove carbon dioxide, and that's all the heart is evidenced to be.

Nowhere is the heart evidenced to be an oracle of profound understanding. Let's follow the logic; if we need a heart transplant and our donor carries specific beliefs deep in their heart (superstitious or otherwise), does that mean that following a heart transplant operation we're suddenly infused with their beliefs? The answer, of course, is no since the heart is an organ and not an intelligent thinking agent with profound philosophical thoughts.

Feelings resonate in the brain (and not in the heart), which means we have the faculties to unlearn every superstitious thought we have actively 'thunk'. One of sport's most debilitating faith delusions is mistaking superstition for something tangible, as if something worth grasping, worth emulating, and worth seeking to control. Every athlete must face this pertinent question: are they in control of their superstitions or are superstitions in control of them?

How much thought do athletes lend to their state of sanity, knowing in advance that their superstitions will continue to fail them, have no proof of concept, and are merely constructs of their brains? Yet bizarrely, they still focus on the *hits* but not the *misses*, and the following words by Jesuit Priest, Anthony De Mello, form a wonderful pretext as to why:

"Do not attempt to possess things, for things cannot really be possessed. Only make sure you are not possessed by them and you will be the sovereign of creation."

The Non-Science of Faith

"The duality of one is the unity of two."

- Joey Lawsin, Author

The author Robert Brault teases us with two wonderful quotes; the first being, *"Those who avoid the tough choices of life live a life they never chose."* His second entices the growth of personal genius and states, *"Never mind searching for the person you are. Search for the person you aspire to be."* Perhaps as a caveat it's time to consider what percentage of athletes can visualise fulfilling their sports aspirations without first needing to activate a superstitious belief?

'Post hoc ergo propter hoc' (Latin) is a logical fallacy meaning 'after this, therefore because of this', and suggests that since event 'Y' followed event 'X', event 'Y' must have been caused by event 'X'. This is often shortened to 'post hoc fallacy' and should lead many superstitious athletes to question what percentage of success is due to their talent and personal genius as opposed to superstition's influential role? In other words, if an athlete removes superstition from their sporting endeavours, aren't they equally capable of achieving the exact same outcomes as before?

Quotes are easily deployed as marvellous tools to enhance the development of potential life skills such as unlearning beliefs. Ultimately, however, we are the embodiment of whatever information we accept and believe. We are authors of our own identification in a process which begins and ends between our own ears, and so now is as good a time as any to review our beliefs.

"Looking back you realise that a very special person passed briefly through your life and that person was you. It is not too late to become that person again."

- Robert Brault, Author

Throughout all documented history, few epic stories rely solely on the strength and the merit of one lone protagonist. Instead, all the best stories require a villainous spectre or a credible 'other' looming somewhere nearby. Heroes cannot seemingly exist without villains, nor can bad exist without good or sense without nonsense, as we'd have no tangible benchmark to adhere to and no credible 'other' to compare our heroics and abject failures against.

One of sport's many unwritten rules is, *'duality captivates while conflict precipitates'*. In other words, first an opponent or nemesis must antagonise our senses before the hero inside us begins to emerge and attempts to prevail. Almost every great story has a significant other. For instance, who voluntarily chooses to live in fear of a superstition called God without the threat of a significant opposite looming large, i.e. an overbearing spectre, devil, demon, or ominous shadow, or without promise of reward for unquestioning subservience to ideologies of faith?

The concept of theism leads to a dichotomy whereby, if our God's empty threats don't get us first, then His empty promises most definitely will. This is why it's important to keep pushing the boundaries of science to learn and discover new testable and falsifiable stuff. Peer-reviewed scientific discoveries can transition our thoughts beyond superstitious innuendo, ominous shadow, and the ignorance of faith. Peer-reviewed science methodology is currently the most reliable means of debunking the rise of superstitious hearsay and pseudoscience through a process of reasoning, falsifiable evidence, and a willingness to be proved wrong by adapting to new information as it unfolds.

Science offers society repeatable models where the evidence stands alone on its own merit, irrespective of anyone's belief. If superstitions are real, then what proof is there for their existence beyond faith, since faith tells us nothing at all? There is a common misguided societal perception that theism and science share equal notoriety and plaudits, and play off each other to maintain enough kudos to continue to thrive. Yet science is flexible and demonstrates its ability to adapt to new information, which is testament to the ego-strength of science. Theism on the other hand is founded on faith, but its claims of personal revelation are unreliable pathways to establishing truth.

"In this age of specialisation, men who thoroughly know one field are often incompetent to discuss another."

- Richard Feynman, Physicist

Science is descriptive, not prescriptive. Science draws information from what is observable before submitting a hypothesis for peer review. Only then, following repeated testing and unsuccessful attempts at falsifying the hypothesis, is it classified as a science theory and submitted to the public as the best current explanation for what can be observed, but remains open for further peer review. Aiming to eliminate cancer is one example, as is testing hypotheses to ascertain whether the idea of a parallel universe or a multiverse carries any weight.

170

Conversely, theism, unlike science, masquerades as the bastion of absolute truth despite the total amount of peer-reviewed scientific evidence for the existence of gods currently standing at nil.

Scientific theories may fluctuate, but they also embrace the right to be wrong as new information is constantly emerging. Theism, in contrast, remains stuck in the grip of a superstitious hypothesis by failing to provide falsifiable evidence for a supernatural, extraterrestrial god which would leave even the most sceptical of atheists dumbfounded and with no options left open but to believe.

Superstitions are rife among religions, as are arguments among those who advocate for the existence of an afterlife as though it were real. Their trick is to interweave logical fallacy, mystery, and fantasy with science's lack of absolutes to support claims of creationism and pseudoscience. Creationist apologetics use flawed cosmological arguments to poke holes in science, yet even if all science was debunked tomorrow, it still would not confirm the existence of a god. Consequently, preachers revert to the use of scare tactics to heighten anxiety and create alarm among religious punters who place all their chips on an afterlife because they don't want to believe that when they die they are simply redispersed into dust.

Proselytisers of gods who sell superstitious ideas such as an 'afterlife' to gullible flocks are acutely aware that many wish to believe they are going somewhere pleasant once they finally shuffle off this mortal coil, despite knowing fine well that no proof exists to justify such an arrogant claim. The duality of one is the unity of two in terms of athletes who cannot reconcile their superstitious beliefs with falsifiable science rationale or suspend their belief in extraordinary superstitious assertions until extraordinary evidence is available to substantiate and warrant such beliefs.

Religions often position themselves as the humble 'Jekyll' in relation to the spectre of science's 'Hyde' and strategically portray themselves as the heroes when compared to science's villainous cads. Yet belief in a god is superstition and the burden of proof rests on any athlete who believes that a god intervenes in their sport.

"I believe that a scientist looking at non-scientific problems is just as dumb as the next guy."

- Richard Feynman, Physicist

Consider the following tale of a seminal experience by scientist and geneticist Francis Collins, whose ability to apply reason took a turn for the worse while hiking in the Cascade Mountains of Washington. The following quote from Collins appeared in an article on *Salon.com*:

"I was hiking in the Cascade Mountains on a beautiful fall afternoon. I turned the corner and saw in front of me this frozen waterfall a couple of hundred feet high. Actually a waterfall that had three parts to it [which is] also the symbolic three-in-one. At that moment I felt my resistance leave me. I fell on my knees and accepted the truth that God is God, that Christ is his son, and that I am giving my life to that belief."

Few of us can deny that at times nature is awe-inspiring; but where is Collin's evidence that equates a frozen waterfall with a superstitious trinity of unfalsifiable gods? What if he had witnessed a frozen waterfall with countless streams, would he have dropped to his knees and converted to Hinduism? Or if the waterfall had dried up and no water was flowing, would he remain an atheist the rest of his life? Why didn't he test to see if the waterfall freezing was a common occurrence at that time of year? Perhaps the most bizarre aspect of his sudden conversion was dedicating his life to a superstition called God based purely on an unfounded assumption that a common natural occurrence was instead caused by supernatural design.

Such an incredible display of unfounded faith brings us back full circle to an earlier quote by Richard Feynman when he said that a *"scientist looking at non-scientific problems is just as dumb as the next guy"*. Superstitions are symptoms of mental tricknology caused by athletes suspending intellectual integrity in favour of comforting delusions rooted in faith. Facts, however, exist independently of faith or indeed of any subsequent belief, and with this thought in mind I was keen to elicit the personal beliefs of a very tired Craig Clarke of Carrick Rugby Club in Northern Ireland.

I strategically hijacked Craig for an impromptu interview at the finishing line of his first ever triathlon race to ensure I was privy to a captive audience given he was too knackered to run any further. My aim was to explore the pseudoscience secreted behind his superstitious rituals, compulsions, and beliefs. Having undergone such a gruelling and arduous experience, I knew his thoughts would still be wrapped up in whatever inner monologues (self talk) his brain had constructed to complete all three disciplines of the race.

Craig's opening salvo was directed at ensuring I understood that it took every ounce of his resolve and mental resilience just to push his body over the line. Hence I began my benevolent line of questioning knowing in advance that he was fatigued. Here is our conversation as it transpired:

What are your superstitions (if any) leading into sport or any rituals you trigger while preparing to compete?

"Yeah over the years I've had a lot, even down to my lucky shorts, etc. My main thing is I have a playlist on my iPod and I just go away and find a corner to plug in the earphones to try and drift into my happy place, just to get myself in the right frame of mind. But then again I have many, even down to the order in which I do my warm ups."

What would happen if someone were to rearrange your pre-set sports preparation?

"I would find it very, very difficult. It would be very hard for me psychologically to get myself into the right mindset because I set myself times. Right from my very first warm up, I have them all timed right down to the first whistle and if someone messed with that order, I just don't think I'd be in the right frame of mind before I start."

On a scale of 1–100%, can you place a value on your loss of focus when you sense your routine has been interrupted?

"Probably seventy or eighty percent since my routines would be very high up my order of billing, and anyway, in rugby I play at number 10 and I'm very methodical even down to the order in which I do my kicking, so it would be a big issue for me definitely."

When you enter a game feeling frustrated because your focus has been disrupted by say 70% or 80%, to what degree is your performance affected? Can you give me an estimate?

"Probably around 25%, as I would find for the first 20 or 25 minutes of that game that my head would be all over the place, just until I can realign the order of my thoughts back into my own way of thinking. But right at the start from the kick-off it would be a big ask for me, especially during away days when I'm being rushed. That's where I always find for the first 10 or 15 minutes, if that happened, I just wouldn't be on top of my game."

Do superstitious rituals matter?

"For me yes because I've trained like that since I was eight or nine years of age and I've got my mind into the order in which I need to do things so that I feel comfortable. I even have my own routines to come back from my many injuries and my own things that I personally need to do just to get my body and head feeling right before a game. These are things which a lot of other people don't do, but me personally, I have to go through all of this for my head to be in the right state of mind to gain confidence before I start any match."

None of this stuff affects you physically. I mean, at the end of the day, you'll still kick the ball and still aim to complete your passes, tackle, run and compete. So why commit so much time and effort to superstitious rituals and routines? Why not just stop? I know, let's just agree to stop them all right now! What do you say?

"No, I'd get the shakes. I mean personally I just couldn't do it because I've been knocked down so much with injuries that I'm always trying to work my way back up to 100%. So there's never really been a time when I've been at 100% and I'm always trying to get there. I need my head to feel that my body isn't going to break and so I need to go through all this to believe that I can actually do it."

Are you in control of your superstitions or are superstitions controlling you?

"I would like to think I'm in control but after hearing what I've just said, I don't think so."

What if I was to suggest that your superstitions are just rhythmic responses to anxiety and fear with intrinsic meaning which resonate from your past?

"Yeah I believe that because I need to go through all my superstitions just to get my game to flow and to get my performance to flow in a way that I know I'm capable of; and I just feel in my head that if I don't have the right processes of control that I'm always going to fail."

Let's just take a moment to consider a brief montage of Craig's response:

"I'm very methodical. If someone messed with that order, I don't think I'd be in the right frame of mind and I'd be frustrated to a level of 70% or 80% of focus. This may affect up to 25% of my overall performance. My head would be all over the place and I wouldn't be on top of my game. I've trained this way since I was eight

or nine years of age and I need to do that to gain confidence, otherwise I'd get the shakes. I need my head to feel that my body isn't going to break. I'd like to think that I'm in control but after hearing what I've just said, I don't think so. I need my superstitions to get my game to flow and if I don't have the right processes, I feel I'm always going to fail."

This snapshot of Craig's overall response is a damning indictment of the mental discrepancies which he had now discovered for the very first time in his sporting career. Prior to my questioning, he had never been asked to appraise the impact of superstitions on competitive sport. Fortunately, my intrusive line of inquiry managed to create a contemplative environment where he got to converse with the inner workings of his own mind (self-talk). What he discovered, however, was that few things are more exhilarating and exasperating in equal measure than dependency on superstitious beliefs.

Every sports superstition has its own pseudoscience which creates self-fulfilling cycles designed to regulate and ease athletes' innermost fears of how they may perform. Superstitious pseudoscience helps athletes to generate warm fuzzy feelings which temporarily make them feel good. Similar to an addiction to recreational drugs, athletes also become addicted to the sporting high of repeating the rhythms of their bizarre behaviours time and again.

Rhythms are prevalent in every aspect of sport. Elite athletes continue to embrace the assuredness of rhythms to help narrow the odds of things going wrong or increase the probability of things going right. It's all very linear and undeviating. Hence, I felt it was time to ask whether promoting mental resilience as a practical discipline is being underutilised as a coaching tool or being taken for granted amid sporting elite? So I asked County Tyrone's precocious talent and Senior GAA goalkeeper, Niall Morgan, to discuss the psychology behind his current kicking routines. I began by attempting to identify his strategies for dealing with persistent pressure while at its most sustained.

How do you cope with the pressure of sporting anxieties prior to and during a Championship game?

"It's kind of hard to explain and it's probably just down to different routines. I try to leave most of my routines until I'm out on the pitch and if I can catch the first ball that comes in then I'm okay. But if I drop the first ball then the anxiety starts to build until I do get my hands on the first ball that I really need to get."

How do you react to the crowd getting on your back?

"In my first year of County Football it was a struggle. I used to think when you're in the crowd watching that the players couldn't hear a word that was being said; but when it's you out on that pitch you begin to realise how big a factor the crowd is on any game, especially a home-based crowd. Once [when] Tyrone played Donegal in the Championship there were 18,000 in attendance, but there must have been 16,000 Donegal fans all getting on my back and that was difficult, but I've learned to blank them out and to focus on my own game."

Given such factors can induce a high degree of angst, what is the exact purpose of your routines?

"I use routines a lot. The good thing and bad thing about goalkeeping is that you don't really make anything happen. It's more the case that if a forward is coming in to shoot at you, it doesn't matter what you do since ultimately he's going to have the deciding factor on what happens, whereas with free kick taking, I have to decide and I'm the one in full control of what's happening. So I have to make sure that I have my own routines in exactly the same way that every free kick taker has their own routines, and I feel that if my routine is off then I need to go right back to placing the ball and starting again."

Do routines provide you with meaningful rhythms?

"Absolutely, and that's what it comes down to, whether you're in the rhythm or not. Just like musicians, as it's the same with a song I suppose. If you have the beat of the song you feel more comfortable. You very rarely see musicians walking about without music in the background because that's their rhythm and that's what keeps them in time, and free kick taking is kind of the same. So if you're in rhythm and in time, there's more chance of executing a successful kick."

How do you gauge your rhythm?

"I see the mental side of my game as part of my hard work since I can't go into a game unprepared mentally, and I see visualisation as part of my practice since there's no point practicing my free kicks and handling or just practicing the physical side of my game when a lot of the aspects are down to the mental. If I'm going out on the pitch not believing that I can do something [then] it's simply not going to happen and so hard work has to come both mentally and physically."

You talked of visualisation, but what exactly does that entail?

"For me, as a free kick taker, I see it as massive that I visualise every free kick going over the bar before I kick it. True, I don't score them all and they don't all follow the perfect line that I set out for the ball to take, but if I don't see the ball going over the bar first in my head then it's not going to happen and it's probably going to be an unsuccessful kick.

I also visualise each free kick from different angles. With Tyrone, for instance, I'm not likely to be hitting anything close, it's always going to be around the 45 metre mark. So I can picture the whole way along the 45 metre line and I can see myself hitting free kicks from every angle, including which way I'm going to kick it [or] which way the wind's blowing. I have to be prepared mentally for everything that's going to happen. There's no point just preparing for a sunny day and for saving every single shot or for every free kick to sail over the bar. I have to be prepared for wind and rain and for many different things to happen."

For the purpose of clarification, I have defined superstitious routines as a fixed set of actions which, if an athlete is pressed for time, can be condensed without affecting their confidence, focus, or ability to perform at their best. Niall's routines, however, had to be precise or he couldn't envisage a successful outcome. So by this definition, he wasn't referring to routines but to rituals. He appeared to imply that his rituals were synchronised around the rhythm of obsessive timing to ensure that his 'odds' of a successful kick were greatly enhanced. Yet very few, if any, high level place-kickers from any sport are fully aware of their kicking potential in highly pressurised situations when acting spontaneously, without feeling compelled to adhere to pre-set rituals and obsessive routines.

Niall couldn't tell me how it felt to be absent of superstitious rituals and routines because somewhere in the midst of coaching practice, spontaneity upped and left the building and turned out the lights. This is not a demeaning assault on professionalism regarding athletes' common penchant for repetitive practice. Instead I'm just pointing out that the term 'practice makes perfect' is necessarily flawed since many players are prone to perfecting defective practices by becoming increasingly proficient at the things they are currently doing wrong.

Niall retains his rituals because he is hooked on repetition, but what if he were to ditch his rituals for more favourable alternatives when his form starts to dip? He produced no statistics to prove that his ratio of kicking success using rituals was any more effective than that of probability and chance. Nor had he explored the possibility that his kicking ratio could be further improved by dispersing with his rituals as a matter of routine. In other words, how can he determine whether he'd be better off without his compulsive rituals until he gives it a go?

Both Niall and Craig had inadvertently conceded to an air of 'defeatism' by acknowledging that without their rituals, things were more likely to go wrong. Niall explained that if at first he does not see the ball going over the bar in his mind then it's simply not going to happen, thereby resulting in an unsuccessful kick. Yet claims such as these are deeply prophetic and suggest supernatural intervention, as how else can he account for predicting failure before the ball has ever left his boot?

Niall's rituals suggest that every kick is *dependent* on the pictures he formulates in his brain before every conversion attempt, but remains *independent* of spontaneity, talent, execution, and bottle. Consider the consequential nature of rugby player Craig Clark openly admitting, *"I've trained like that since I was eight or nine years of age. I have to go through all of this for my head to be in the right state of mind to gain confidence. I'd get the shakes [if I didn't]. I mean personally, I just couldn't do it. I just feel if I don't have the right processes of control, I feel in my head that I'm always going to fail."*

When did *"I'd get the shakes"* become an accepted behaviour in sport? Craig has been locked into superstition since he was eight or nine years of age, which is when his routines and rituals began. Even when his rituals fail to produce a favourable outcome, he still persists and cannot or will not give them up. Niall and Craig both referred to active visualisations; yet not even the most elite placekicker in any sport can boast a 100% career success conversion rate, irrespective of whatever pictures they project in their mind.

Another prominent form of visualisation is the 'Law of Attraction', but it is mere pseudoscience given it has not been demonstrated to exist beyond the rate of probability and chance. How many times has an athlete actively wished for some aspect of sport to go well but it didn't? Or how many times has a rugby player or American football placekicker visualised striking the ball between the posts, only to see the ball drifting wide or ricochet off a post? How often do boxers visualise landing the perfect uppercut on their opponent's chin only to get knocked out due to dropping their guard, or how often does a sprinter intentionally visualise the perfect start out of the blocks, only to be disqualified for a false start?

If the Law of Attraction is not a superstition we should be able to test its reliability by successfully repeating any chosen scenario at will. Prayer is also a variant of Law of Attraction, but why do athletes who regularly pray to gods to secure a win, fail to ascribe an opposite damning indictment to those same faceless gods who sit idly by as they are soundly beaten? Is it simply the case that athletes are more comfortable subscribing to the fallacy that it's better to stick with the devil they know?

Where is the evidence that an absence of spontaneity in competitive sport always proves more productive than outcomes achieved through repetitive practice? On whose authority should impulsiveness be discouraged in competitive sport to such an extent that we begin losing sight of what it means to be 'us'? When did repetition first become the predominant methodology for coaching, and what became of the athlete with a talent for place kicking who simply steps up to the ball, makes an instant assessment, takes aim, and just kicks the bloody thing?

Granted, it all sounds so unprofessional. Yet how often do athletes measure their success ratio for ritualistic kicking conversions in highly-pressurised situations compared to the conversion ratio of placekickers with no preconceived rituals of which to speak? How can players tell if they are more productive using superstitious rituals unless they replicate similar scenarios using no superstitious rituals at all?

Neuroscientist, author, and renowned atheist Sam Harris suggests there is no evidence that personality was made by a god, but instead it's a product of the brain where all attempts at behavioural modification begin and end. It appears Sam's hypothesis is not specific to personality alone, as placekickers Niall Morgan and Craig Clark were both immersed in kicking rituals to such an extent that removing their rituals seems as unlikely as either of them removing their own skin.

Both players succumbed to believing that reward is inevitable, failure unavoidable, and fate inescapable based on the implementation or non-implementation of pre-set rituals and superstitious routines. Both acknowledged a benefit to establishing rhythms and both stuck to their rhythms just as assuredly as night follows day, even when their form dipped and, metaphorically speaking, they couldn't hit a barn door with a bloody banjo.

Consider the impact of establishing rhythms as seen through the eyes of Japanese footballer Shinji Kagawa, who admitted that nerves got the better of him during Japan's loss to Côte d'Ivoire in the opening game of the 2014 World Cup Finals in Brazil. *"I couldn't get into a good rhythm and I was beaten psychologically,"* he said. It was a surprisingly honest, refreshing, and welcome appraisal from a media savvy professional given that modern footballers are often mollycoddled and ushered away from the public gaze or encouraged to maintain their own counsel.

Shinji shared a key sentiment which proved instrumental in how he performed. He said, *"I couldn't get into a good rhythm"*. Yet unbeknown to Shinji, this practical insight inadvertently uncovered the source of superstition's metaphorical DNA. The secret is out! It turns out that the reason superstitions feature so prominently throughout sport is due to athletes' need to experience rhythms.

It was often suggested during the wonderful era of Brazilian footballer Pele, that the beat of the samba drums being orchestrated from within the crowd, and unbeknown to Brazil's opponents, was dictating the tempo and pace of the game. As the beat intensified, the team upped their tempo and picked up the pace of the game, but as the rhythm of the beat began to slow down, so too in accordance did the pace of the game. The implication was that whoever was orchestrating the crowd could, in effect, inconspicuously dictate the rhythm and tempo of the game.

The subliminal rhythm of the Samba drums mirrors the subliminal rhythm which athletes equate with sports superstitions, except they are swapping the beat of the drums for a series of rituals, odd mannerisms, and bizarre quirks. All superstitions have a unique pace and tempo which athletes feel empowers them with special abilities to influence events before they unfold or helps them to control the emotions they experience prior to or during an event.

The psychology of rhythms is multifaceted and can cause athletes to focus only on winning or losing at certain venues or against certain opponents, or on needing to travel a specific route to a venue as part of an orchestrated ritual or routine. During sports preparations, many athletes feel compelled to adopt fixed psychological norms (rhythms) which create the impression of already knowing their roles and what needs to be done and in exactly which order, and precisely when to do it so that the universal energies will side in their favour and in order for luck to gravitate their way.

"These things are illogical and are not based on any great fact. The way I drove to home games, always the same route and if I didn't go that way I was distracted. I had to prime myself to explain that this was in fact illogical."

- Brian Kerr, Former Republic of Ireland Football Manager

Brian's quote reinforces the hypothesis that elite sports performers are just as odd as the next guy and every bit as susceptible to overpowering rhythms, superstitious angst, and subsequent fear. The impact of rhythms is not inconsequential since habits are rhythmic and impact how athletes perform. Neither Craig or Niall seemed to nurture alternative strategies (plan B or C) to counter negative overtones which arose when they underperformed. Instead, both placed all their eggs in one basket full of 'better the devil you know'.

Niall appeared to break the cycle, however, during an interesting turn of events when he accepted a fun challenge laid down by *Joe.ie*, who featured an article on an impressive exhibition of 'free taking' by Paul Keane of Ballerin GAA. During the challenge, Paul nailed an impressive eight-out-of-nine attempts at kicking the ball between the posts from the 45 metre line. He also successfully converted a 55 metre effort, all in just under 100 seconds. Only a matter of hours had elapsed before goalkeeper Niall took up the challenge and effortlessly swept Paul's efforts aside in a much faster time (approx. 82 seconds) and unlike Paul, Niall didn't miss a single kick.

I draw attention to Niall's impromptu exploits to question the legitimacy of any athlete's dependency on kicking rituals which link visualisation with the Law of Attraction to legitimise the idea that without rituals and routines they may underperform. Athletes who rely on following rituals often mention the hits but rarely the misses, yet the main point of interest during the challenge was that Niall didn't have time to rigidly adhere to his usual rituals since a time constraint of 82 seconds wouldn't allow it. Instead he was forced to exercise spontaneity, muscle memory, and also to fly by the seat of his pants as a result of having to react quicker and think faster than he normally would during a game.

Niall managed 100% accuracy despite having little-to-no time to think. I asked if he and Craig were prepared to discard their rituals but neither seemed overly willing to alter or renounce any part. Instead, both appeared guarded because they believed their routines were integral to winning matches. The result of Niall's kicking challenge raised questions such as, can he still perform with equal competence using only spontaneity as he does using pre-set rituals and routines? The result of the *Joe.ie* challenge suggests he can.

Let's change tact for a moment to ask when athletes first begin to fall foul of sport's most glaring oversight: the absence of fun. Granted, in terms of competitive mindsets, the concept of fun is a relative term and does not refer to an endless procession of joviality, silliness, giddiness, or joy, all of which are unbefitting of the practical demands faced by sport's elite. Fun refers to more reasoned observations such as the overriding factors which first made an athlete fall in love with their sport.

How often do athletes revisit their current interpretation of success and when did fun stop being a factor? When did competing become such a serious proposition for rugby player Craig Clark that failing to activate his rituals 'messed with his head' and gave him 'the shakes'? Superstitions create and counteract anxiety and fear in equal measure, so perhaps athletes should activate the following quote, *'Take your challenge seriously but yourself lightly',* since they can still approach an event with a will to win without adding unnecessary baggage such as rituals and superstitious beliefs.

Superstitions convey an image of emotional dead-seriousness. Don't take my word for it, consider how rarely athletes spontaneously crack a smile amid superstitious rituals or OCDs. Why do so many athletes' sporting mentalities appear top heavy with thoughts of dead-seriousness as opposed to light-heartedness? I discovered the answer at a London seminar where motivational speaker and staunch advocate of happiness, Robert Holden, candidly referred to three rather debilitating behavioural traits.

Robert sought to elaborate on the methods which each trait employs to suck the buoyancy and vitality out of those of us with a lust for living life. So what were these incapacitating traits? He referred to *Oughtism*, *Humouroids*, and *Musterbation*, and it's not easy to forget names like those. *Oughtism* signifies the intrinsic belief that before we can be happy, first we feel that we *ought* to comply with the expectations and demands of our peers. *Oughtism* is a symptom of personal neglect, whereby we display an over willingness to please others or concede to the will of our peers before earning the right to feel happy and content with ourselves.

Humouroids signify a humour bypass, where too often in sport we allow wonderful opportunities to experience light-heartedness pass us by. How consistent are athletes at incorporating a sense of exhilaration, elation, delight, joy, and fun into every contingency of competitive sport, while still managing to meaningfully compete? How much time do they build into sports preparation to exorcise the threat of dead-seriousness by ensuring instead that they take themselves lightly and perhaps even smile?

How many athletes can pinpoint with absolute clarity when sport became such a burden that they no longer felt able to compete without the dead-seriousness of overbearing rituals or superstitious routines? From where did they acquire their superstitious baggage and how much time does an average competitor spend in a conscious state of light-heartedness, either prior to or during competitive sport? Are they too preoccupied by sporting omens or by thoughts of divine interventions to think rationally, or too hung-up complying with *oughtism* and *humouroids* to lighten up?

Why is it accepted as plausible in sporting circles to covet divine intervention from invisible gods but less than okay to be seen to covet supernatural intervention brought about by generic superstitions such as moonwalking onto a pitch, always being last out of the changing room, wearing lucky pants, or kissing lucky charms? Why is belief in a god so commonly lauded as a matter of principle, while belief in generic superstitions is socially downgraded to a matter of preference and considered ridiculous to the point of absurd?

The discrepancy that exists between both types of superstition is a timely reminder of the following quote from George Orwell's novel *Animal Farm,* which states, *"All animals are equal, but some animals are more equal than others."* This is the default position adopted by theism, where belief in a god from a societal standpoint is considered authentic, while generic superstitions are viewed as behavioural quirks or akin to a joke, despite the falsifiable evidence for either being nil. If sports superstitions or prayers to a god really do work, then superstitious athletes should experience success beyond simply the rate of probability and chance; indeed, they should never lose at all.

Rugby player Craig Clarke admitted that up to 25% of his overall performance could be affected if he was knocked out of his stride or out of the rhythm of his superstitious rituals and routines. Yet where did he pluck that number from? Since he knows in advance that form is temporary, why not simply adopt temporary expectations and dispense with superstitions once and for all?

The third type of debilitating behaviour referred to by motivational speaker Robert Holden is *Musterbation*. This refers to the needless and endless friction we self-inflict by telling ourselves that before we can be happy we must first comply with a plethora of arduous rituals and routines, or feel obliged to facilitate the whims of our peers before catering for our own well-being. *Musterbation* gives rise to the idea that we should gratify others before daring to gratify our own ends and needs.

Many athletes feel conflicted by a sense that they must always succumb to superstition's allure. Hence, *Superstitionism* has grown to become the largest religion on the face of the earth. Larger than Christianity, Islam, Buddhism,

Hinduism, Judaism, and Scientology combined. Each of these belief systems falls under the umbrella of superstition, thereby *Superstitionism* is the figurehead under which theism and deism are comprised. It would be more realistic if census forms were updated with immediate effect so that the column marked 'Religious Denomination' was replaced by 'Superstitious Denomination', since theism is the world's largest superstitious belief system of all.

> *"It's not enough to make bold statements of fact just because they cannot be disproved."*

> - Derren Brown, Illusionist

Many athletes are keen to adopt a sport scientific approach to affecting the outcomes of competitive sport. Others believe sporting outcomes are driven by fate or by pseudoscience such as the Law of Attraction, or by the supernatural will of interfering gods sticking their oars into matters pertaining to sport. Luck is also a form of superstition since everything we believe about luck is effectively a guess. Superstitions are propagated by correlations of randomness, patterns, and rhythms, but neither Craig or Niall appeared over-anxious to look beyond the intransigence of the patterns and rhythms of their rituals and routines. Instead, both lent a disproportionate sense of value to the idea that rituals are integral to triumphing at sport.

Not once did either player mention spontaneity, or trusting their instinct, or being impulsive, or testing the reliability of their intuition during the cut-and-thrust of competitive games. Craig implied that he felt less likely to experience injury as a result of being better mentally prepared. None of his examples were scientific, yet he believed that his superstitious rituals aided his numerous recuperations back towards fitness; while in the same breath he admitted to being knocked down by injury so many times that he never really functions at 100%.

Craig hadn't measured the extent to which his superstitious rituals had aided his endeavours to stay fit and play well over sustained periods of time, and in retrospect, his superstitions did not appear to be much of a recuperation tool at all. Meanwhile, Tyrone star Niall Morgan's reliance on rituals, routines, and visualisations has catapulted his talents to the pinnacle of county football in Gaelic sport, or so he appeared to believe. Yet belief means 'unknowing' which is, by definition, the primary reason it's called belief.

Would Niall be less effective if he kicked his frees on impulse alone? Would he become a liability to his team if he elected to kick using only his instinct as a guide, particularly if he embraced spontaneity as his overriding methodology by only kicking according to how he felt at any given time? How easy is it for athletes to become agents for change or to transition their mindsets beyond a fixed set of beliefs? It may help to consider a post-match analysis which occurred in 2017, when football pundit Roy Keane lambasted Celtic FC for failing to learn lessons in European football after losing 3-0 to FC Bayern Munich. Despite Roy highlighting Celtic's technical and tactical errors, a more in-depth analysis suggests psychology played a major role in halting Celtic's European progress.

The prospect of psychology playing its part appeared evident in a news report two years prior to Roy's scathing appraisal, in which former Celtic FC Manager Ronny Deila spoke on the subject of facing an uphill struggle to establish Celtic FC as a constant fixture and competitive force in the UEFA Champions League. His response left many fans scratching their heads in wonder at whether he was starting to lose the plot. The whole saga was best illustrated by a newspaper headline questioning whether Ronny *'Had been out on the sauce?'*

The headline wasn't meant as a slur on Ronny's conduct or a reference to alcohol. It referred to the culture shock experienced by many Celtic players when he declared that ketchup was to be banned from their canteen menu. The story was leaked to the media where it was viewed by many sceptics as a smokescreen to create a distraction from Celtic's poor run of results. In reality, Ronny's futuristic vision for his squad in terms of diet and match preparation was so detailed that it even monitored what his players were opting to spread or pour onto their food. He stated:

"To be professional is to be a 24-hour athlete and I really think Scottish players are open to new things; but are we talking Scotland or are we talking Europe? To win in Scotland we can still do the same things as before, but to succeed in Europe we have to adapt to Europe. If you tell me that a player can be three or four kilos too heavy and play against Ronaldo, then good luck; I get irritated discussing it.

If you want to get to the Champions League, you fucking have to look at the Champions League. Look at the European level and you have to understand the fitness is unbelievable. If you see Gareth Bale, that's Champions League level. The fitness in the Champions League is unbelievable and if we want that we have to look outside the country, not inside. That's because the levels are not inside the country but outside."

Ronny had identified how his players needed to extend beyond their comfort zones and display enough courage to start looking inwards before targeting European success. He was aware that a much bigger picture lay beyond the confines of Scotland, but he also implied that some Celtic players appeared stuck in a cosy, Scottish kind of optimism by not demonstrating the propensity to see beyond the parochial nature of Scottish football towards a much bigger picture of competing in Europe, except this time on European terms.

Ronny sought to disrupt the comfortable mentality of certain players to meet with European football's more exacting demands. He also sought to increase their sense of self-discipline regarding their diet and overall approach to become more industrious, professional, and efficient. This approach applies equally to athletes who are stuck in the comfort zone of superstitious beliefs, as they too are tasked with demonstrating the ability to see beyond the parochial nature of their rituals and routines.

"I have six locks on my door all in a row. When I go out I lock every other one. I figure no matter how long somebody stands there picking the locks, they are always locking three."

- Elayne Boosler, Comedian

The mentality of superstitious athletes is intrinsically locked in such a way that attempting to unpick their beliefs as a means to an end only complicates matters further and brings about an end to their means. What makes an otherwise rational athlete point to the sky in acknowledgement of an imaginary god when they win a race or score a point, a try, or a goal? Theism is the unjustified proposition that superstitions are real, but with no falsifiable evidence to prove such an extraordinary ideology. Superstitions about gods require a leap of faith, yet this shouldn't cause shock or consternation since qualifying as a religion isn't difficult as was evident in a much-publicised tongue-in-cheek event which occurred in England and Wales.

The Office for National Statistics stated that 390,127 citizens declared their religion as 'Jedi' on the 2001 Census forms. This represented 0.7% of recorded religious affiliation, surpassing Sikhism, Judaism, and Buddhism to name but a few. Yet irrespective of the novelty factor, this carried significance as Jedi was elevated to the fourth largest reported religion in those particular regions at that time. While conventional religions are traditionally revered, the Jedi religion was ridiculed and mocked by those with little or no sense of humour as being merely a stunt. Oddly however, unlike Jedi acolytes, theism is not considered a stunt.

This was a quite extraordinary discrepancy given theism is immersed in mitigating bias, the most eloquent of which are hearsay and bluff. The whole premise of theism is founded on faith and relies on hope and wishful thinking. Sadly, hope has its roots firmly lodged in optimism, coincidence, probability, and chance, all of which are factors which no theocratic religion can reasonably dispute although many still do. The keywords of the superstition called theism are 'faith' and 'belief', yet the concept of God, in a supernatural context, carries no explanatory power.

Superstition's greatest trick of all is to first conclude answers and only then seek to add a supporting premise once belief has been well and truly formed. We live in a space between appearance and reality where the best magic is not designed to trick us but to entice us to believe. Theism never wavers, inasmuch as our only choice is to believe... or else. All belief in a god has an accompanying 'or else' to encourage ideological compliance, just as generic superstitions compel us to 'touch wood' or 'cross our fingers' while remaining optimistic that things will work out for the best.

> *"It's no accident that the symbol of a bishop is a crook and the sign of an Archbishop is a double cross."*
>
> - Gregory Dix, Monk

Not only do superstitions possess us, but more-often-than-not they maintain a stranglehold on us till we die. Give that a moment to sink in. Superstitious beliefs only cease to exist when we cease to exist since there's no longer a brain to carry them around. Worse still is the notion of taking our beliefs with us to the grave without knowing for certain that they carried validity, but imagine instead if our superstitious beliefs were to die before us. We'd be free to experience the exhilaration of fresh perspective.

Losing track of a superstitious belief should be roundly applauded since if we continue to do what we've always done then we'll always get what we've always got. Superstitious beliefs can spread like a virus and each one offers a glimpse into the overriding psychology of what makes us tick; but be careful that superstitious *ideas* do not spread into superstitious *ideals* since the ointment to cure such an affliction often proves rather awkward to apply.

> *"We all wear masks, but the time comes when we cannot remove them without removing some of our own skin."*
>
> - Andre Berthiaume, Author

Consider the following newspaper article by Graham Nickless which referred to AFC Bournemouth's Russian Chairman Maxim Demin's refusal to attend matches because he thought he was cursed. Even after one of the most successful weeks in the club's 115-year history when they romped to an 8-0 victory over league opponents Birmingham City FC, he still refused to attend. Maxim's curse only surfaced following Bournemouth's ground-breaking achievement of securing a League Cup quarter final slot for the first time in their history when Cherries boss Eddie Howe revealed:

"He thinks he's a jinx. I had to text him at a certain time before the game. I have to do certain things to follow his superstitions. I try to convince him to come but he rarely watches because he thinks he is bad luck. He has invested all this money into the club and isn't even here to enjoy it."

Maxim's paranoia provides a startling insight into the power superstitious values exert upon the mentality of sports protagonists with regards to their rituals and subsequent routines. Eddie used every piece of rationale he could muster but still could not persuade Maxim to overcome his fear. Albert Einstein once stated that it's easier to split an atom than a prejudice and the same, I contend, applies to superstitious beliefs.

The human brain is continually processing reason in a 24/7 operation which never stops for a vacation or takes a break. The memory is accustomed to sifting nonstop through unique human variables to interpret which patterns, rhythms, or trends hold explicit meaning integral to us. The human memory is infatuated by details, but what exactly do the details reveal? What hidden intricacies are already secreted inside our brain?

Consider the astonishing story of shop floor worker Jason Padgett who in 2002 was involved in a bar brawl where he received a blow to the head and was knocked unconscious. Following his release from hospital the next morning, he began seeing the most incredible things such as water flowing from his bathroom tap in perfect perpendicular lines. *"At first I was startled and worried for myself but it was so beautiful that I just stood in my slippers and stared,"* he explained to the *New York Post*. It later transpired that his blow to the head had triggered a condition called 'Acquired Sudden Savants Syndrome' (terminology for stuff which scientists only partially understand).

It was a condition similar to that portrayed in the 1988 film *Rain Man*, and as a result, Jason, who now mixes in highly exalted company, was estimated to be one of only 32 reported Acquired Sudden Savants worldwide. It was such an incredible transformation that it led to an article in the *Daily Telegraph* questioning whether there is a savant inside us all. Jason's visualisations showed no signs of abating, inasmuch as he became obsessed by every shape in his home, from the rectangles on windows to the curvatures on every spoon and from the patterns of leaves on the trees to the patterns of cream swirling round in his coffee.

Next, Jason began to notice elaborate geometric shapes within everyday common objects. He even began, with no prior knowledge of complex mathematics or science, to create amazing drawings of geometric fractals. Isn't the human brain amazing, given that he inadvertently began illustrating the incredible geometric patterns which form the building blocks of everything currently known in the universe. This includes a startling visualisation of 'Hawking Radiation', which is the substance emitted from within a micro black hole.

Unsurprisingly, Jason is currently recognised as a leading math thinker of world renown. Experts even suggest his condition is further proof that all of us have potential for astonishing feats of mental prowess, if only we were aware how to further untap the right-hemisphere of our brain. It seems like an incredible travesty to characterise an extraordinary phenomenon such as Sudden Savants as being merely a syndrome or condition. Yet, until science yields further information, it's as good an explanation as we've got. Although Jason's transformation was staggering, it only further typifies how little is collectively understood of the untapped potential of the human brain.

Jason's neurological transformation was not the result of anything supernatural but a symptom of the incredible human genius already in-situ inside his brain. One leading hypothesis was that this was a result of his left brain being affected by the blow to his head and 'going dark', while the circuits which kept his right brain (hemisphere) in check disappeared into the shadows. This effectively meant that the area of his brain associated with creativity had the freedom to operate completely unchecked. Hence the latent potential, which lay secreted and dormant in his brain for so long, could finally emerge from its slumber and amaze us all.

It has often been said that with our thoughts we create our reality, so why not seek to augment every conscious act with curiosity since Jason's story provides increasing grounds for optimism that each of us is a living, breathing dichotomy whose psychology has only been partially explored. There is nothing necessarily supernatural about the 'going dark' hypothesis because brain states are natural, if not somewhat bizarre; yet we cannot escape from the thoughts which go on in our minds unless or until we replace each thought with an alternative thought.

Consider the athlete who maintains that he is suffering from depression. He says he is depressed but he isn't necessarily since depression is primarily a brain state for the redistribution of human will. He is experiencing something akin to deflation and so he is deeply disheartened. Yet, as is often the case with human emotion, his feelings fluctuate, ebb and flow and seem so increasingly vivid that in his mind they begin to sprout legs.

What caused him to enter a downward spiral? Did he trip and fall at the final hurdle or fail to make the final cut? Was he robbed of his 15 minutes of fame or did he let down his teammates by failing to fulfil their expectations and demands? Did injury cut short his career or his temperament fail him once too often or his gambling spiral out of control? Was he simply unable to cut the mustard or let down once too often by his faith in sports superstitions, prayer, or gods?

We must make up our own minds as to the cause and as to whether any of the aforementioned scenarios also apply to us. Who can fathom the sense of disillusionment he may have experienced due to having no avenues through which to empty out his debilitating emotion, trepidation, and fear? So what was dragging his mind towards thoughts of deflation? The answer is his subjective interpretation of truth.

Let's explore this hypothesis in more detail and refer to the athlete in question as James, whose pact with depression was a natural phenomenon induced by whatever personal value he placed on the sincerity of his beliefs. The problem with sincerity is that it's no guarantee against being wrong. So let's begin with a question. Who among us can remain depressed for 100% of the time? Is such a feat even plausible? Who among us has the wherewithal to maintain anger, disappointment, rejection, dejection, or deflation for 24 hours a day, 365 days a year on a continuous loop? Who on earth has the willpower to sustain such energy, let alone the strength, inclination, focus, time, or will?

What happens when we're asleep? Are we still depressed while we are sleeping or dreaming or experiencing orgasm? What becomes of our thoughts of depression at times such as those? Or are we being lied to by self-serving experts and gurus who have successfully managed to build an industry on peddling expertise, but whose real expertise lies in peddling jargon and a cocktail of pills? Are we too easily enamoured by gurus who accommodate 'symptoms' but make no effort to eliminate 'causes'? Why was James so intent on keeping his mental state of deflation intact, especially once it became clear that his downbeat emotions were not serving him well?

A simple story of let-go-ness

One windy day, James felt at quite low ebb while sitting on a doorstep with his head buried deep in his hands. He was feeling despondent and somewhat deflated when all of a sudden an empty crisp bag caught his eye as it blew down the small corridor of streets where he sat. The bag began to swirl around in circles with wild abandon and with no apparent means of escape until, as if from nowhere, a playful puppy emerged and eagerly began chasing the bag but could not seem to catch its elusive foil.

So spontaneous was this light-hearted moment in time and so completely organic, that for a few fleeting moments something incredible occurred. Not in any supernatural sense, but more in terms of a transformative experience. It seemed, without rhyme or reason or prior indication, James momentarily lost track of all previous patterns of thought which had led him to feelings of deflation, dejection, and depression, and instead he broke into a smile. So preoccupied were his thoughts with the current innocence, joyfulness, and playfulness of the spirited puppy, that James actually forgot he was feeling depressed.

With his thought patterns now briefly disrupted, James unconsciously discarded his debilitating emotions and replaced them with light-hearted emotions. Hence, in that one brief window of opportunity he became detached from his state of deflation, misery, and despair. He also detached, albeit momentarily, from his previous premise of subscribing to a life devoid of fun, as on this occasion he became detached almost to the point of elation and inner-contentedness, all because he'd forgotten he was feeling depressed.

How does it feel to recognise that, for one brief and beautiful moment in time, James allowed spontaneity, calm, contentedness, and even light-heartedness to outrank incapacitating beliefs, thereby freeing his mind from its acidic state, and as an immediate consequence he began to smile? In that one fleeting moment he lost track of feeling depressed and his mind was enthralled by light-hearted emotions which were much more conducive to his emotional health.

Unbeknown to James, his guard had slipped and, as if in defiance of his unconscious efforts to remain deflated for 100% of the time, he instead demonstrated a propensity to be happy and spontaneity lay at the heart of the cause. There is nothing profound about human emotion. Centuries ago Gautama Buddha stated that, *"The world is full of suffering. The origin of suffering, the root of suffering is desire. Eliminating suffering consists of eliminating desire."* By desire this interpretation implies eliminating the things which we believe our happiness depends on.

Suffering in sport often occurs due to our egotistical weight of expectation manifesting as sporting 'wants' and 'desires', yet the only reason superstitions exist in the first place is because athletes hope for something advantageous to occur or to experience relief while they are suffering. Yet this brings them full circle back into the bosom of *oughtism, humouroids,* and *musterbation* by prioritising faith in external concepts before coaxing and nurturing the best from themselves.

Very rarely do athletes make any decision without first mentally calculating what others might think or what they may say or whether they approve, and the cause of their indecision is the search for applause. Athletes often care more about what others think than what they actually think about themselves. Furthermore, any failure to meet with their own expectations can induce thoughts of deflation, insecurity, and dejection, and compel them to flirt with thoughts of depression which depreciate their interpretation of 'self'.

"Life and Jah are one and the same. Jah is the gift of existence. I am in some way eternal, I will never be duplicated. The singularity of every man and woman is Jah's gift. What we struggle to make of it is our sole gift to Jah."

- Bob Marley, Iconic Songwriter

What links an emotion to a superstitious belief? Is the duality of one the unity of two? Why did Niall Morgan and Craig Clark persist with their respective rituals when they lost, or got injured, or fell out of form? Why stay locked into patterns (similar to James) in which their propensity to be happy is so easily altered by probability and chance? What halted the progress of some Celtic players in the eyes of former manager Ronnie Delia, from transitioning beyond their parochial mindsets where they did only enough to be successful within the confines of Scottish football? What stopped them from adapting to the challenges of European football?

Why do athletes allow *Won't-power* to outrank their *Willpower*? Is the most glaring oversight in sports psychology the failure to acknowledge that emotions fluctuate, oscillate, and waver? No athlete is transfixed by emotional constructs or mental states such as superstitious belief or depression for 100% of the time. It is time to adopt the mentality of a changeling since the only reason karma (yet another superstition) always finds us is because we're always standing rooted in the exact same place. To illustrate this point further, consider the story of a woman who contemplated moving to a new house:

"What's the problem today? You loved that house yesterday, what could have changed in such a short space of time?" asked the estate agent.

"This would be my thirteenth time moving house," the woman said apprehensively.

"Good grief, what was wrong with the other twelve. Was it your neighbours?" gasped the estate agent.

"No, I've been very lucky as my neighbours could not have been nicer," she replied.

"Was it the location?"

"Nope, all twelve locations were wonderful in their own right."

"Then what was the problem?" he enquired once again, a little perplexed.

"Well, my neighbours were all really nice and the locations were all I could've hoped for but the problem was that, no matter where I went, 'I' kept turning up."

Therein lies the answer as to why superstitious sequences, patterns, and trends keep us locked within circular beliefs. The woman could not get away from the thoughts in her head. She was constrained by a debilitating fear and by mental presuppositions which still haunted her memories, thereby making it difficult to transition beyond her accumulated past. Even though it's a tale, it's still a sobering observation which begs the question, how many of us are currently stuck with accumulated mental baggage which belongs in the past?

When was the last time any of us sought to disrupt our current superstitious ideologies with renewed understanding that every act can be an act of self-improvement and that the key to unlocking life is recognising that life isn't locked? The key to unlocking our personal genius and discovering whatever latent potential is currently secreted inside our brain is best described by revisiting Elayne Boosler's quote, *"I have six locks on my door all in a row. When I go out I lock every other one. I figure no matter how long somebody stands there, they are always locking three."*

In the field of psychology there is a self-identity status called 'Identity Foreclosure'. It refers to the stage of discovery where individuals arrive at an identity but haven't explored other options or ideas as to how that identity was formed. They must then undergo an identity crisis (called Identity Moratorium) to disrupt any premature sense of mental foreclosure and to arrive at a genuine sense of self. Athletes often foreclose on superstitious ideologies and become locked into superstitious identities without any means to demonstrate whether their superstitions are even real.

Either Elayne's quote is the purest form of cynicism or it is genius at its absolute best since superstitions are grounded in circular logic which locks us into self-replicating illusions on a continuous loop. Athletes gravitate towards superstitious reasoning as an alternative means to excel at sport and also as an aid to interpret the world; well perhaps not the whole world, just *their* world. This explains why every time superstitions show up on our radar, '*we* keep turning up'. So how can we disrupt the process of prematurely foreclosing on superstitious identities? It may help to consider Einstein's realisation that *"We cannot solve our problems with the same thinking we used when we created them."*

Counterstition

"There are 24 hours in a day and 24 beers in a case: Coincidence?"

'Counterstition' is the sense of paranoia experienced by athletes when superstitions and conspiratorial beliefs converge, especially when events fail to go their way. On other occasions it's the sense of elation athletes experience when the planets appear to align in their favour. Some athletes, however, see conspiracy in pretty much everything and so retreat to Counterstition in a bid to explain events, often even before the event has occurred, while others see beyond sport's trivialities by learning to value each precious moment during which they are fortunate enough to compete.

All of us can learn to appreciate the unique set of talents and characteristics which life has bestowed on us without feeling indebted to unfathomable illusions such as fate, karma, providence, fluke, or luck. Yet the truth rests uneasily somewhere in between. In other words, some of us can remain completely unfazed by the mediocrity of the day, while others feel aggrieved and completely bamboozled by just about everything sport throws their way.

"Referees are afraid to give decisions for Chelsea. Why? In other matches we see the same thing and it doesn't happen. Clear penalties are not given and it's one and one, and one, and one. The penalty is a giant penalty and he is afraid to give. Like everybody is afraid to give, so no penalty."

- José Mourinho, Football Manager

We are the embodiment of whichever information we accept and believe, as was evident by the following post-match assessment from former Chelsea F.C Manager, José Mourinho, which was widely reported on social media as being akin to a seven-and-a-half-minute rant. He may have believed that his subjective appraisal of what transpired during Chelsea's 3-1 home loss to Southampton FC was accurate, but he still saw fit to create a smokescreen of conspiracy theories, paranoia, clairvoyance, and superstitious rationale.

"It's amazing where the paranoid mind can take you."

- Bill Ayers, Educator

Counterstition is always at its most prevalent when conspiracy theories, random assertions, and general assumptions haphazardly converge, as was seemingly evident in the following montage of extracts from José's post-match response:

195

"I repeat that if [the] FA wants to punish me they can punish me. They don't punish other managers but they punish me. Even in the Champions League which is a game which is not three officials but with five, you are not given a penalty. I can also know what you are thinking, what you are saying in the studio, what people imagine."

José appeared stricken by a touch of paranoia, or perhaps he had shrewdly concocted a superstitious agenda as a means to an end. So brace yourself, since we are about to witness two types of truth being played out simultaneously. One dealt with the facts while the other was a construct of José's imaginative mind, but apparently it all felt very real to him.

The first type of truth is the 'actual truth' which alludes to the *clarity* of José's perceptions, while its nemesis is the 'awful truth' which alludes to the *accuracy* of his response. The actual truth is constructed from falsifiable evidence, while the awful truth implies that, irrespective of any facts, José preferred to believe whatever he liked. So let's analyse some extracts from his response to identify if any aspects of confirmation-bias were hidden within his 'awful truth'.

"Diego Costa is suspended [and] the first negative thing that happens, my team collapses. The team mentally and psychologically is unbelievably down. It looks like good players are bad players. We didn't show our quality [and] one mistake and lack of concentration [led to] one goal. Their second goal is an individual mistake. Their third goal is another individual mistake. They are in such a low moment that they collapse.

I think the players should assume their responsibility and there are other people in the club who should also assume their responsibility and stick together. When you go down to so many individual mistakes and fear to play, I think it's clear that we are being punished by too many individual mistakes and as I was saying, sadness brings sadness. Bad results, they attract bad results. The team needs to play with a free brain and a free spirit and unfortunately for them this is not happening."

It's worth mentioning how, amongst football pundits on *Sky Sports* and on *BBC Match of the Day,* the controversial penalty to which José referred remained highly contentious despite being reviewed several times in slow motion. José also failed to mention that Southampton FC had equal cause to be angry, given on two separate occasions (and the pundits agreed) they were denied two equally valid penalty claims of their own. Yet rather oddly or perhaps conveniently, José seemed to suffer a memory lapse, as neither claim got a mention in his blinkered post-match surmise.

Further post-match analysis provided irrefutable proof that the cause of José's footballing woes lay a little closer to home than at the doorstep of linesmen and referees. It was a classic case of 'Counterstitious' tactics being played out right in front of our eyes. The view of many observers was that José's insinuation of some form of vendetta by referees (although he never openly used those words) was evidence of paranoia and conspiratorial thinking.

The moment José cast doubt that there may be more to each penalty decision than meets the eye, he inadvertently veered towards 'Counterstition' by encouraging paranoia to grow its own set of legs and form conspiratorial truths. So much so, that his assertion (or self-delusion) appeared reminiscent of this humorous quote: *'Do not interrupt me when I'm talking to myself',* since his post-match analysis suggested that the only person seeing a conspiracy was him.

"Your living is determined not so much by what life brings to you as by the attitude you bring to life; not so much by what happens to you as by the way your mind looks at what happens."

- Khalil Gibran, Poet

If one lesson is apparent from the study of human psychology it's that once the brain is exposed to being bamboozled for an extended period of time, it very quickly dismisses and rejects all previous evidence of any bamboozlement having ever taken place. This happens because human beliefs are formed by emotion, yet emotions fluctuate and are notoriously chaotic, unruly, and unstable at best. This is why a belief tinged by emotion is neither impartial nor the most reliable pathway to truth.

"Once you give a charlatan power over you, you almost never get it back."

- Carl Sagan, Author - *The Demon-Haunted World*

Consider September 2013 at Croke Park in Dublin, where in front of a packed arena and a thoroughly exhausted crowd, the Dublin GAA County players were down on their knees and out on their feet as they had just battled their way through a bruising war of attrition. It was a massive struggle of epic proportions, but also a tight and enthralling encounter against a resurgent County Mayo team. Dublin eventually managed to overcome Mayo to win their second All-Ireland Senior Gaelic Football Championship (Sam Maguire Cup) in the space of three years.

Dublin's win by the slenderest of margins effectively meant that a season's worth of planning, commitment, enterprise, and personal endeavour all converged into one slender point as being the difference between winning-or-losing, but in the end the best team won on the day. Or perhaps not! As despite their winning endeavours, both the management and players from the Dublin team appeared to suggest during post-match interviews that mysterious forces beyond their imagining had a hand in the final result. A question therefore arose as to the mysterious nature of why Dublin won so narrowly on the day? Was Counterstition the culprit? Let's look and see.

To gain insight into the world of Counterstition, consider a post-match interview by Dublin player Bernard Brogan who scored twice on the day and declared, *"I'm empty, very tired but I'm delighted. I'm wrecked."* His reaction was perfectly understandable given he had left every ounce of endeavour out on the pitch. Yet less obvious to many observers, perhaps, was the unconscious innuendo that lay within his otherwise routine post-match assessment:

"Today I just got a bit of luck, if you're in the right positions you might get some scores. I just wanted to get something on it for the first one but they can go anywhere. Thank God on the day it went in. My second goal in the 54th minute was a case of being at the right place at the right time."

Contrast Bernard's comments to those of victorious Dublin boss Jim Gavin during his post-match interpretation of events where he reportedly claimed that his team were playing against Mayo *and* the referee. Gavin pointed out that the Cavan whistler had awarded 32 frees to Mayo but only 12 to Dublin and then said *"that's just beyond me. I can't understand that, I really can't. It's not only today, opposition players are getting more frees than we are."*

In the space of two short but emotionally charged All-Ireland championship winning interviews, the public were confronted by claims of luck, conspiracy, risk, resilience, and hope; as well as chance, probability, divine intervention, bewilderment, disbelief, victimhood, coincidence, and outright relief all playing their part in proceedings. Phew! Yet quite incredibly, this was two members from the same winning team. Imagine if they had lost?

It's extremely unlikely that luck, conspiracy, or divine intervention would have been high up the agenda in preceding team talks (if mentioned at all) or identified by the manager as being integral to the result. And yet after the match, within two emotive appraisals, both luck and conspiracy stand accused of raising their heads above the parapet to interfere in a GAA event. Now that is extraordinary.

Counterstition does not mean causation, but is purely anecdotal and combines paranoia with the realisation that despite exhaustive efforts on everyone's part to cover all bases, every sports performance is vulnerable to the mischievous nature of mixing conspiracy with superstitious concepts such as fate, fluke, destiny, providence, and luck. This is particularly true of how Bernard chose to interpret the final outcome of the game.

"Today I just got a bit of luck. Thank God on the day it went in," said Bernard Brogan. Yet all we can deduce from his post-game appraisal, in a falsifiable sense, is that either he intentionally undermined the extent of his own immense talent or he failed to give himself enough credit for the innate instincts and talents which helped him to win the All-Ireland title; or maybe he really did get lucky. There is no way of knowing for certain since we have no means to determine what luck actually is. Perhaps one further possibility, given the civic sense of occasion and the emotion and passion from the Dublin fans reverberating around the stadium, was that Bernard's God had opted to wear the blue of Dublin that glorious day.

Tricknology:

"Most of our problems are related to the mind, so we have to work to reduce our destructive emotions."

- Dalai Lama

I asked former Northern Ireland international footballer Sammy Clingan to describe his superstitious rituals prior to competing. His response was poignant, extremely touching, and a little disarming. In fact, the very nature of his heartfelt answer made my question seem intrusive, but how else was I to learn of the many secrets behind the meticulous preparation which goes on in the mind of sport's elite, or of the behaviours which fuel their imaginations to rise above hurdles too exacting for lesser mortals to surmount? So in the end, I had to ask.

"Before a game I always bless myself and say a prayer to someone in my family who has died recently and stuff. Just so they are looking over me in the game and I think that gets me through the game."

Sammy's response threw a metaphorical spanner into my inquisitive works. His insinuation of divine intervention having an impact on how he performed, plus his optimistic belief that the concept of prayer could influence sport, left me with more questions than originally anticipated regarding the value which athletes willingly attribute to bizarre superstitious compulsions, audacious absurdities, placebos, habits and quirks. Do superstitions possess arbitrary powers which add measurable value to how an athlete performs, and can they free-up their thoughts from experiencing duress?

Are superstitious beliefs practical? If so, what are the origins of such beliefs? How often does the outcome of a superstitious practice exceed expectations or stand up to the scrutiny of peer review? Does superstitious belief conceal something sinister in terms of undermining our confidence to think and act according to things we can actively verify, as opposed to things which we merely believe to be true as a result of faith?

"I bless myself before each half, but I don't know if it's a superstitious thing or a religious thing. I just don't know."

- Shay Given, Republic of Ireland Goalkeeper

What makes athletes adopt bizarre superstitious practices? I asked former WBC World Bantamweight Boxing Champion Wayne McCullough whether he had actively encountered superstitions in practice during his highly successful career. Here is an extract from his response:

"Some of the guys in the amateur boxing team had to wear the same socks. They never washed the socks either, they just wore the same socks over and over and never washed them and I'd always say, 'but what would happen if you got beat? Would you burn the socks or something, or throw them out?' But they just kept on wearing them. It was just like a superstition where even though they lost they still wore the socks. I think it's a psychological thing where they needed to wear them. It's like 'I need these socks'. It's like people having a rabbit's foot or something. They need it."

Philosopher Sir Francis Bacon famously stated that *"the root of all superstition is that men observe when a thing hits but not when it misses."* This supports Wayne's astute observation that superstitions and boxing just don't add up. Yet, thanks to his observations we can gain further insight into how superstitions emerge from the realm of obscurity to influence how certain boxers interpret the world. Why were those amateur boxers so psychologically ill-equipped to resist or repel the magnetic pull of recurring beliefs? Is it because superstitious compulsions, if left unchecked, can offset an athlete's mental equilibrium by engulfing their mind in fallacious beliefs?

Becoming hooked on a belief can be careless but isn't unusual, but asserting a belief as a fact without verifiable evidence is gullibility. So, I issue a challenge as a practical test of mental integrity, intellectual honesty, and also as a means of distinguishing nonsense from sense. How long it is plausible to maintain a superstitious belief? Moreover, in full-contact sports such as boxing, might superstitious delusions prove hazardous to an athlete's health? Consider the following declaration:

"It's time to test that chin. I'm gonna test that chin. I've hurt every single opponent I've been in the ring with. This is God's plan. I lost my first fight at the start of my professional career; since then it's been God guiding me to this Saturday. I'm spiritually, mentally, and physically strong. I'm a strong man right now, I'm coming for him."

Those were the fighting words of former IBF Intercontinental Boxing Champion Eric Molina, as reported on *Sky Sports News* prior to challenging Heavyweight Champion Deontay Wilder in a bid to win his coveted WBC crown. Yet Eric's comments were merely a further example in an increasingly long line of sport's elite who see fit to attribute their sporting achievements to the will of a superstition called God. But was Eric's gesture morally and ethically practical? In other words, if gods do exist, is it fit and proper for any god to act as a willing advocate of combative sports?

Is it 'godly' to condone the ferocity of two warring combatants knocking seven bells out of each other to entertain a baying crowd? Would a god of true divinity wish to endorse egotistical concepts such as eyeballing and trash-talking as being necessary evils in a lucrative sport where opponents go in search of the 'legal high' of hogging the limelight, while plummeting to whichever depths are deemed necessary to ensure that the spotlight remains firmly fixed on them?

Boxing is entrenched in aesthetics, image projection, bravado, brutality, ego, and greed; plus the odd bitten ear. So is God a narcissist who cannot be happy until the spoils of every bloody and unscrupulous success is dedicated to him, if god is a 'him'? Are sycophantic tendencies the characteristics of a god? Wouldn't that be egotistical on God's behalf? Or is he hedging his bets and covering all bases by inadvertently placing a crafty wager on every opponent on the sly?

What makes athletes consciously seek intervention from supernatural entities or worshipful deities which hail from origins unknown? Why give rise to the escalation of intrinsic self-talk (inner monologues) which emanate from the voices they hear in their minds? What leads them to believe the 'trustworthiness' of their own self-talk, given self-talk is corrupted by external influences? How trustworthy is self-talk in the cut-and-thrust of competitive sport, and when athletes are fully engaged in self-talk, to whom or with what are they conversing and who or what have they determined is answering back?

How do any of us measure the quality of a conversation when talking to ourselves? Self-talk gives the appearance of conversing in third-person, as if someone or something outside of *us* is looking back at *us* and interacting with *us*. Yet, who gave this third-person permission to grab centre stage and dictate how we should think and act? When was the last time we attached a use-by-date to a superstitious belief to measure whether our expectations are being met or if its usefulness has long since expired?

It's not enough to be sold on the premise of belief since any fool can believe and most already do. Yet, where is the proof that superstitions work? I mean tangible proof that is both demonstrable and falsifiable beyond simply believing that they do, and beyond buying into subjective wishful thinking and the wishy-washiness of faith and hope? Otherwise our superstitions should be allowed to elapse, expire, and respectfully die. Why, in the 21st-century, are we still crossing our fingers, touching wood, pulling a wishbone and making a wish?

Boxer Wayne McCullough offered wonderful insight into the many quirks that boxers employ to feel comfortable in their own skin. One of which was his teammate failing to place a use-by date on washing his supposedly lucky, sweaty socks. In doing so, the boxer failed to acknowledge that the sweat he secreted when winning became instantly invalid from the very first moment he experienced defeat since that was the point when the spell was broken. After which, hanging onto the idea of accumulated luck was no longer valid. Yet are we really so different? How rational and trustworthy are our beliefs? Consider the following humorous tale:

A politician once visited a mental institution and asked the doctor, *"How do you determine if a patient should be admitted or not? I'm very interested to see how you evaluate their state of mind."*

The doctor replied, *"Well, we fill up a bathtub with water and give each patient a teaspoon, a teacup, and a bucket and ask him or her to empty it out."*

"Oh, I get it!" said the politician. *"A typically sane person would use the bucket since it's much bigger and so naturally faster?"*

"No," replied the doctor. *"Any rational thinking person would simply pull out the plug. So would you like a bed next to the door or by the window?"*

This is a tale tinged with humour but with serious overtones given each of us carries transferable baggage, convertible fears, and an intoxicating form of madness which is primarily exclusive to us. The same madness persists when we turn a blind eye to pledging allegiance to superstitious delusions which we can't hear, smell, taste, touch, or see. Belief is always one step away from knowing, which is primarily why it's called belief, but the moment we know anything for certain is the moment we are able to discard belief.

To empty out a belief isn't easy. Consider a typical Thursday morning in radioland as former *talkSPORT* radio presenter Colin Murray received a call from an avid listener as part of his *Colin Murray and Friends* morning phone-in show. *"Here's Charles in Hull,"* Colin tells his listeners before broadcasting one of the most bizarre stories ever encountered during their time on the hugely popular show. Caller Charles, who was originally from Scotland, then went on to say:

"When I was younger I was a bit of a rebel. I grew up in a Rangers family and me and my dad never used to see eye-to-eye. So just to wind him up on my 13th birthday, with my birthday money I bought a Celtic top. Now I came home with this top and he said, 'You put that on and you're out [of this house] when you're 16'. So I said fair enough and I chose to support Celtic simply because of that threat, and that's how I ended up in Hull.

On my 16th birthday I had to go [leave home] and that's the God's honest truth. I never spoke to my dad in 17 years until I had my little boy. I never ever agreed with that whole thing; it is forced upon you that you must support this team or believe in their beliefs. So, I thought I'd rebel against it but I didn't think it would go as far as it did to be fair."

Wow! If ever a story bordered on insanity this was it. Seventeen years of quality time lost to a father and his son which can never be recaptured. All as the result of his dad's inability to see beyond his biased belief in a religious (sectarian) divide. His behaviour was teetering on insanity, yet his fervent addiction to tribalism bears a striking resemblance to the insane rationale which accompanies athletes' addiction to superstitious beliefs. Many athletes display the same sense of intransigence and belligerence because they believe they have less chance of winning without superstition backing them up.

This incredible story highlights the potential dangers that lie in wait to entrap the psychology of athletes who are lacking the foresight and ego-strength to attach user-dates to their continuing faith. This story of estrangement is a quite sobering lesson for us all as it shows how easily the past, if we allow it, can still envelop the present by enslaving our thoughts in arrested development, thereby ensuring our minds are no longer ours to make up.

Go to any zoo and look at an elephant, crocodile, lizard, rhino, or hippo and experience how easy it is to become rapidly transfixed by an overwhelming sense of antiquity since each majestic animal acts as a current reminder of primeval throwbacks to a bygone age. Being in their presence can feel somewhat surreal, yet no less surreal than being caught in the gaze of superstition's restricting glare since superstitions appear equally timeless. Indeed, if left to their own devices they are every bit as adept as an elephant at creating a sense of having been with us forever, as if they are a part of what makes us *us*.

It's important to challenge the validity of faith-charged emotions which are tinged with nostalgia, along with any mental construct that is powerful enough to accommodate theists, but also many atheists, under a unified banner called superstitious belief. We do not conquer superstitions by facing them down, standing toe-to-toe in a combative stance, or by matching their seeming inflexibility by adding further belligerence of our own. Nor do we combat superstitions by routinely capitulating to their ever-increasing psychological demands. We eliminate superstition with curiosity and scepticism, and where better to start than with a popular curse?

The Commentator's Curse

A clear separation exists between omens and their supernatural counterparts such as lucky charms, rituals, spells, potions, amulets, and even prayer. Omens manifest as warnings which precede events through prophetic signs or intuitive signals. This is where omens differ from other superstitions since omens are not said to cause an event while charms, spells, curses, incantations, potions, prayer, a lucky rabbit's foot, and other superstitions of this ilk are said to exert a supernatural influence which violates the natural order of events.

To be under a spell or curse, or to kiss a lucky charm, or pray before an event is viewed by many athletes as a precursor to summoning supernatural assistance from somewhere beyond their physical realm. Omens and premonitions are not said to exert such powers, but instead merely indicate that there are external powers or mysterious forces at play of which they need to be mindfully aware. But hang onto your hat because premonitions and omens are just skimming the surface, and perhaps the most prophetic anomaly of all is a name we may recognise; say hello to the 'Commentator's Curse'.

The curse refers to a strange and recurring phenomenon where sports commentators and pundits espouse high praise for an athlete's majestic sporting performance, only to be forced to retract their previous words as no sooner does praise fall from their lips than the eye-catching performer trips and falls flat on their face. Commentator's Curse is such a random coincidence of comedic timing that we are often left flabbergasted as to the odds of things going so wrong with such immediate effect.

What are the odds of a player who is currently playing the game of their life making an error so basic and out of character from their quality of performance up to that precise point, that it causes a commentator to splutter and choke on the rotten timing of his or her words? Yet this occurs so regularly that pundits have given it a name. Hence the Commentator's Curse with its penchant for comedic timing was born as a humorous anecdote within live sporting commentary, and here are a few examples of where it appears to be doing its worst:

"Rooney is a shadow of himself." This was uttered by commentator Morten Bruun just seconds before former Manchester United player Wayne Rooney scored a spectacular bicycle kick against derby rivals Manchester City.

"And Lennon is going all the way." This was uttered by an excitable and expectant commentator as footballer Aaron Lennon raced through on goal in a one-on-one situation before tripping and falling flat on his face.

"I'm looking at Alastair Cook. I know it's early [and] they will say Commentator's Curse but I'm watching his movements and his movements are so much better now than they were last year." These were the words of cricket commentator Michael Vaughan moments before his co-commentator Ed Smith declared 'caught', as Alastair Cook's day came to an abrupt end.

"It's been the perfect response from England. This has been the perfect response, no problem, keep dominating. The only thing they (Iceland) have got up front is the

big boy Sigthorsson." These were the thoroughly damning words of former England manager Steve McClaren just as the 'big boy' Kolbeinn Sigthorsson smashed a low shot past hapless England goalkeeper Joe Hart. *"Oh my word!"* was all that McClaren could say in response as his heart sank and his chin dropped to his knees.

Some consider the Commentator's Curse to be laughable. Others ponder its effects with a little more care given the immaculate timing of such inexplicable bad luck. This is evident among commentators and pundits who view Commentator's Curse as an offshoot of probability or chance, in contrast to those who view the curse as paranormal, as if bad luck or bad karma is biding its time and waiting patiently somewhere in the ether for the correct moment to pounce.

Many commentators have been made to sound foolish by messing up right on cue while broadcasting live on air. But why try to explain chance, probability, and coincidence as being a curse? Are they verbally portraying themselves as sharp shooters or simply shooting themselves in the foot? Perhaps the curse is part of a wider conspiracy which is working in tandem with supernatural sources to achieve maximum embarrassment in the world of punditry.

If the curse is a figment of imagination, then why do pundits refer to it by name? The Commentator's Curse or Commentator's Nightmare is how it's affectionately known. Yet, if it isn't coincidence, then surely we must assume that it's being driven by something ethereal and extra-terrestrial or at least by something external to us; yet what type of intelligence could orchestrate such an anomaly?

The primary purpose of superstitions is to affect our luck, just as the primary purpose of the Commentator's Curse is to give rise to the assumption that the words we utter can supernaturally evoke a sporting mishap in the natural realm. It creates the impression that an intelligent agent is conspiring to embarrass commentators and pundits in front of their peers. Yet, if it is a curse, then what is the source of its power?

As part of an ongoing process to appease human ego, athletes seek to create ingenious methods of moving the unknown into the realm of what is known. One example is naming superstitions since names help to personalise and sanitise how the brain interprets experiences it cannot decipher. In other words, adding names to our fears does not change the content, but it does alter the context of how we perceive and interpret fear. The author and renowned atheist Christopher Hitchens stated, *"That which can be asserted without evidence can be dismissed without evidence."* Just as Albert Einstein surmised, *"If the facts don't fit the theory, change the facts."*

Collectively, the human ego has grown increasingly adept at softening the impact of whatever blows come our way, and the easiest route to achieve such a goal is to assign names to our fears. This ingenious means of mental 'tricknology' lends a friendlier face to things we find troubling, thereby softening the impact of whatever threat is most prevalent in our mind.

Consider the devastation which took place in Southern Haiti on October 2016 as villages were submerged under several feet of water. According to an account by *Reuters,* more than 800 people lay dead in the aftermath; while the *BBC* reported the most powerful Caribbean hurricane in a decade, whereby an estimated 30,000 homes were destroyed. So what was the response to this culprit of mass murder and wanton destruction? Quite incredibly it appeared that the preferred coping mechanism for subduing trauma and dealing with human calamity was to downsize its awesomeness by granting it an inoffensive and non-threatening name, which in this case was Matthew.

Just by adding a sense of familiarity to fear, we can minimise or negate any potential for worsening psychological impact, similar to the subtle wartime illusion called 'friendly fire' which in retrospect isn't friendly at all to the unsuspecting recipients of stray bullets, missiles, or bombs. Hurricanes are similarly endowed with friendly names, not authoritative or aggressive sounding names such as Warlock, Havoc, Mayhem, or Chaos, but names with a non-threatening veneer which trivialises the trauma.

Few names convey less of a threat and appear less passive than Matthew, Harvey, Paula, Gilbert, or Max. 'Girl or guy next door' style monikers such as Katrina and Mitch (also hurricanes) are commonplace for impending atrocities but play a pivotal role in shielding public anxiety behind warm fuzzy feelings of neighbourly names. Yet girl-next-door Katrina reportedly caused 108 billion dollars (US) of carnage, while regular guy Mitch claimed an estimated 10,000 lives.

So why is this methodology relevant to sport? It's because adding monikers to occurrences which we may not fully comprehend is already commonplace in sport. Names such as Commentator's Curse and other superstitions are now mainstream sporting terminologies. So much so, that if we were to witness an athlete behaving irregularly or erratically during their lead-up to compete, few of us would even bat-an-eyelid, see fit to remark, or feel any sense of concern for their state of mental health. It is almost as if, by attributing such irrational forms of behaviour to being superstitious or a bit OCD, we have formulated an adequate explanation which makes their behaviour seem okay.

In order for the Commentator's Curse to not only exist but be effective, there must first be a supernatural causation (agent) hard at work whose job is to prime luck, coincidence, fluke, and chance to trip up pundits at their earliest convenience the moment a prediction falls from their lips. Hence, paranoia is rife among sports punditry and is evident through sayings such as *"I'm reluctant to say they're playing well just in case I jinx them,"* or *"I think she'll go on and win it now; mind you that's probably the kiss of death."*

Consider the comedy value in the following quote from a sports commentator who sheepishly admitted live on air, *"The timing of her trip was so immaculate that I swear it felt personal and was aimed at me."* His admission came after mistiming praise for an elite hurdler whose foot struck a hurdle and caused her to fall at the very moment the praise left his lips. Yet how arrogant must he be to assume that something 'supernatural' cared about what sentence came out of his mouth? Whatever next?

Fortunately, we don't have to look any further for an answer than Murphy's Law. This is the hypothesis that anything which can go wrong will go wrong (eventually), whereas its counterpart Sod's Law requires that it always goes wrong with the worst possible outcome and at the most inopportune moment imaginable. Welcome to the conspiratorial world of Sod's Law. Or perhaps 'Odd's Law' seems more apt to describe a scenario whereby the thing that we least desire to happen, invariably does.

Is Sod's Law an extension of Commentator's Curse or a subset of the superstition called 'Law of Attraction'? Why does an athlete who says, *"I hope I don't trip over a hurdle,"* really mean, *"I don't want to trip, but I bet that I do"*? The Law of Attraction gives rise to sayings such as, *'if you think that you can't then you're right'*. This sentiment is further embellished by American self-help author Oliver Napoleon Hill who professed, *"whatever your mind can conceive and believe it can achieve."* The Law of Attraction suggests that 'thoughts really do become things', and few athletes have not at some point or other succumbed to belief in this law.

These are pseudoscientific laws of undeterminable origin, and yet have evolved to become a permanent fixture in popular sporting culture where perhaps they're best known for merging worst case scenarios with improbable odds. Who hasn't heard someone say, *"It's just typical, the one thing I didn't want to happen just happened."* Or what about sayings more directly related to sport such as, *'It's Sod's Law! We talked about keeping things compact before the game but ended up conceding in the first minute of play. What were the odds of that?'*

Is this type of language ringing any bells? Perhaps we should be deafened by the infernal chiming of warning bells trying to tell us that by adding names to random sporting occurrences such as Murphy's Law and the Commentator's Curse, we are lulling ourselves into believing that coincidence happens by design. This is why it's important to apply scepticism to popular superstitious laws and to measure their consistency over an extended period of time since, unless we can replicate these laws in practical situations for up to 100% of the time, then there are no laws and we are the sods, and not just any sods but silly sods for allowing ourselves to mistake random coincidence for intelligent design, when all we are doing is making shit up.

So why do sports commentators and pundits only draw special attention to laws and curses when an athlete's behaviour fails to concur with their predictive speech? Why do they rarely mention the countless number of times when the action unfolding before their eyes panned out exactly as predicted and nothing went wrong? It is intellectually dishonest to assert pseudoscientific laws as anything more than hypothesis without first testing to see if they're rooted in fact. So let's take a closer look at one such example (Sod's Law) in action:

"The funny thing is Gennady (boxer Gennady Golovkin) was sparring with this body protector on. He was getting ready for a fight and he didn't want any injuries [so] they offered me one (a protector). I've never used one [and] so I thought it'd get in the way so I said, 'No it'll be alright, I won't need it'. Sod's Law, I ended up cracking a rib."

- George Groves, Boxer

"I had a European title fight all lined up to fight Sebastian Sylvester. I would have [taken] that as I was quite capable of knocking him out. [So] that was in the pipeline but then I had the car accident and all that fell through, and the fighter who ended up fighting Sylvester knocked him out in the fifth round. It's Sod's Law really."

- Scott Dann, Boxer

In competitive sport the superstitions just keep on rolling-off the conveyor belt, and next into the spotlight is the 'Second Season Syndrome'.

> *"Harry Kane will have questions marks against him. Second season syndrome*
> *strikes often in young players and I see a season of disappointment."*

- Stan Collymore, Football Pundit

At some point in an athlete's career or a team's evolution, they step up a level in competition and quickly come to the realisation that the honeymoon period lasts for roughly a season or for a series of events. Perhaps their good form will continue for an unspecified period until eventually, as expectations heighten, they will be forced to confront the superstition called Second Season Syndrome head on.

'Are you worried by the prospect of Second Season Syndrome?' is one example of superstitious paranoia and alludes to the loss of a surprise factor for the upcoming second campaign. The more this question gets asked, the more it becomes many players' and teams' new sporting reality, yet closer scrutiny of this syndrome reveals that inquisitive journalists are effectively saying, *'You're in trouble now that you've lost the element of surprise because your opponents will have sussed you out'.*

Many managers, coaches, and athletes embrace Second Season Syndrome as an opportunity to sneak their excuses in early, just in case their second season fails to unfold according to plan. They are aware that it's always much easier to pass the buck onto an unsuspecting third party than to bear the brunt of their own ineptitude or carry any burden of underlying guilt. Second Season Syndrome, however, is yet another superstitious construct, and as such, cannot speak in its own defence which is why it's the perfect socially acceptable scapegoat on which to distribute a disproportionate share of any blame.

'It's not my fault it was Second Season Syndrome,' managers sometimes imply, as if all their planning has been ostensibly hijacked by something obscure before the second season has even gotten underway. Incredibly, the madness doesn't end there as examples of strange sporting anomalies are commonplace. One of which came to light during a crucial football World Cup Qualifier at Wembley between England and Poland.

With both teams aiming to qualify for Rio 2014, an intriguing conversation developed as television presenter Adrian Chiles happened to comment on the prospects of young English starlet Andros Townsend's expected role in the team. This was only his second senior cap and Adrian questioned whether the young English player could live up to the hype despite the hostile atmosphere generated by the fervent Polish fans.

Andros had amassed tremendous media interest as a result of his impressive debut just a few days earlier, and in response Adrian posed the following question to his fellow pundits, *"Andros Townsend, is there such a thing as Second Cap Syndrome?"* Of course the truth is, *'No Adrian there isn't!'* Nor did such a concept exist in the public consciousness until you invented it right there live on air. Yet, as a result, 'Second Cap Syndrome' began cropping up in sports conversations as a matter of routine and is now an accepted part of sports terminology and referenced by pundits far and wide. Thanks to Adrian's thirst for curiosity, a new superstition was born.

To adhere to a superstitious practice only proves that each of us is as prone to intoxicating madness as the next guy; but exactly how far does our madness extend? It was interesting to gain insight from former elite athlete and uniquely talented Gaelic football star, Seán Cavanagh, who at the time was captain of a hugely successful County Tyrone football squad. Seán is a three-time All-Ireland Championship winner, five-time Ulster title holder, and five-time All-Star winning footballer. He also captained Ireland during the wonderfully entertaining International Rules Series versus Australia.

To top it all off, Seán was a deserving winner of BBC Northern Ireland Sports Personality of the Year in 2008 when he finished ahead of legendary jockey Tony McCoy and golfer Rory McIlroy, which is quite a feat given Rory has since scaled the dizzy heights to become number one in the world. Now that's impressive! So I asked him what role superstitions had played (if any) during his game preparation, and this was his response:

"A big part yes they do. Even to the extent that I remember at the All-Ireland semi-final which we played in 2003, and it's common I think in sport, that I had a pair of sports underwear that I'd worn during every Championship game up to the final. I remember I was in Dublin on the morning when we were due to play Kerry at Croke Park, and I realised I hadn't got them. So I had to phone my mother and she had to travel out from the Citywest Hotel early. I mean really early that morning to make sure I got the lucky underwear, and I think there were a couple of occasions like that.

You know, confidence is a big thing in any sport and players go through the same routines, and whenever you go through that same routine and it works, you gain confidence from it. Once you gain confidence from something, you're going to get the best out of your ability. I know within our [former] team there were guys that went through the exact same routines and had the same superstitions. Philip Jordan used to tap the door frames. Stephen O'Neill would read books. Eoin Mulligan would lie and sleep and you know that there are guys who go through the same things with superstitions before every game. So certainly those methods have worked for guys I know and it doesn't work for some other people, but certainly it plays a part."

I asked Seán what would happen if he didn't get his lucky underwear on time.

"I know it's crazy to think about it, but automatically your preparation is kicked out, and if that preparation is kicked out, your head and your confidence perhaps gets kicked out of gear a bit. I mean, if I hadn't got my lucky underwear I'd be thinking, 'God these new underwear, are they going to give me the same freedom, and are they going to give me the same luck, or are they the reason why I'm going to kick a wide? Was it because of the lucky underwear? It's these sorts of things that are hard to define whether you are or aren't a high-level sports person, but it's these wee issues which are obviously never talked about that sometimes make the difference, and it does give you that wee bit of an extra lift or extra confidence. So I think superstition does make a real difference."

Finally I asked Seán to give me a percentage, in terms of an actual figure, to which the failure to acquire his lucky underwear on time may affect his attention and focus both before and during his game preparation.

"If I were to put a number on it, I would imagine superstition probably plays as much as 10 - 20% of my preparations [during the] lead-up to a game; because I get into my own wee routine and I get set in my ways and so certainly it would annoy me. For instance, I've seen me getting up out of bed at perhaps two o'clock or three in the morning before a major sporting event, simply because I'd been lying in bed thinking about something that I needed to do or should've been doing. I couldn't leave it till the morning because I'd always done it the night before. So yes, you do get into those routines and yes it does make a difference."

This was an incredibly revealing insight into Seán's pre-competitive psychology and an invaluable journey into the unspoken relationships between that which is deemed rational and reasonable or deemed irrational, ludicrous, and borderline

212

insane. Seán's actions were typical of many sports competitors. Yet, how did it ever get that far and what hijacked the 'power' within his empowerment to ensure he lacked the necessary willpower to repel his superstitious beliefs?

The reason superstitions exist is because athletes believe they can affect their luck and can help tip the balance of fortune in their favour by coaxing it away from their hapless peers. Superstitious philosophy is merely a fail-safe which athletes employ in their ongoing quest to secure success, yet they only subscribe to superstitions because they think there is something in it for them. Once they begin to believe a thing for bad reasons however (since there is no current mechanism to measure the supernatural), then what is there to prevent believing in things for bad reasons from becoming an ongoing characteristic trait?

A Kind of Hush

Consider the following analogy. Years ago, dentists used a product called novocaine to numb our mouths and dull our senses as they set about us with drills and various sharp instruments. Novocaine has since been superseded by numerous other products but still remains a popular generic term for anaesthetic to this very day. Novocaine, however, creates a similar impact to that experienced by anyone who carries a superstitious belief.

Consider the scene from the dentist's chair as we lie keenly observing the dentist smile and listen attentively as she talks reassuringly. Yet we are so numb from novocaine that we are unaware that the blood is trickling down our jaw. We are being bamboozled by chemicals and hoodwinked by a reassuring smile into believing that we are okay, when in reality we are damaged and bleeding.

> "Numbing the pain for a while will make it worse when you finally feel it."
> - J.K. Rowling, Author

Superstitious beliefs create the same effects as being under the influence of novocaine by appearing as plausible and innocuous solutions to anxiety and fear. Superstitions leave us numb to exercising spontaneity by dumbing down our capacity to think independently beyond things which are rooted in sentiments of faith. Superstitious beliefs fool us into believing that they are effective and serving us well, except similar to the effects of novocaine, we are numb from subservience and too mentally sedated to care whether our beliefs are actually true.

Questions often abound as to whether athletes can function with impunity and aplomb while under the influence of superstitions. To explore this topic further, consider the build-up to the Turkish Open in 2014 as reported by *Sky Sports News*. The report was a celebration of golfing legend Colin Montgomery's ground-breaking appearance at his 600th European Tour event, whereby he spoke of his pride at reaching such an incredible landmark. Yet he also displayed an inner resistance to facing up to the pattern of inconsistencies which had blighted an otherwise stellar and distinguished career by failing to win at major events.

Of particular interest was his stated belief that 'bad luck' was the cause of his failings, despite statistical evidence suggesting that his problems lay much closer to home. The topic of not winning at major tournaments appeared irksome to Colin, mainly because the media never seemed to let him forget. Here are some of his thoughts as part of that insightful yet often bemusing interview discussing the reason why not winning major tournaments was the only blemish on an otherwise perfect career:

"It's been some journey and I have enjoyed every minute of it. I'm very, very fortunate to reach 600. That means I've played 30 tournaments for 20 years which means, by definition, I've got to be healthy to do that. I'm very fortunate to say it was always [just] that piece of fortune that goes a winner's way and I never had that in Majors. I just never had it in Majors. I can say for the next 20 Major winners, they're all going to have a little bit of fortune.

Whether it's the second round at the 7th hole or the 72nd hole, whatever hole it is, they all add up and there's that bit of fortune that turns things. Whether it's for you or whether it's unfortunately against your opponent, there's a bit of fortune and you need it. You need that and I don't think I got that in Majors. I got that in European Tour events fine. I've been very, very fortunate in my career, just possibly not in the Majors."

Irrespective of whether Colin's response was a measured reaction or emotional retort, it is interesting to note that he used the term 'fortunate' seven times, or eight times if we include his use of 'unfortunate'. This merely served to catapult the mystery called luck straight to the heart of his losing equation and raise further questions such as whether fortune really does favour the brave. In other words, was fortune really the problem, or did he fail to display enough bravery throughout 20 years of competing at golf's major events?

Was it simply a question of failing to maintain his 'bottle' when the pressure was on? Throughout Colin's interview he displayed a subtle form of intellectual dishonesty by blaming misfortune. Why wasn't he questioning his mental resilience, decision making errors, or whether he made too many technical mistakes? Was he really the victim of poor fortune or was he using misfortune as an excuse to disguise his recurring inadequacies while under public scrutiny and mental duress? Did Colin find it easier to interpret the absence of good fortune as meaning that he was the victim of bad luck throughout his major career?

Why imply that poor fortune caused his golfing strife? Was he actively avoiding the responsibility of not owning up to potential flaws in his overall game or with his psychology? Or if the superstition called karma is true, hadn't Colin's karma presented him with numerous opportunities to win at major events through empowering him with 20 competitive years of longevity and health? Was the purpose of his karma all along to allow him to rectify earlier golfing wrongdoings until finally he won a major event? Isn't that partly what karma is about?

What made Colin assert that his talents were curtailed by poor fortune, i.e. bad luck? Did he use luck as a scapegoat to deflect from his stubborn resistance to accept any blame? Was his overuse of the word 'fortune' aimed at undermining the winning achievements of his more successful peers, each of whom held their nerve and their game together (unlike him) when the pressure was on and it mattered most? Perhaps he really believes that his previous ill-fortune was the consequence of fate, karma, coincidence, fluke, or luck, but did his assertion reflect the facts?

Another question which remained unanswered was whether Colin was trying to engineer the facts or if he actually believed the things he was saying. Did his assertion of fortune imply superstition and did he make his assertion knowing in advance that claims about fortune are hard to disprove? The type of fortune of which he spoke is undeniably a superstition, but what compelled him to believe that fortune was a consistent factor in every major tournament demise? Or what compels us, for that matter, to believe that touching wood or crossing our fingers is compulsory to achieving success? Or if it isn't compulsory, then why do it at all?

Consider July 2014 during the Commonwealth Games in Glasgow as 18-year-old freestyle swimmer Siobhan-Marie O'Connor was asked during an interview how she planned to prioritise the upcoming events throughout the competitive week. Her reply was typical of many sports competitors with superstitious beliefs, but also odd and compelling and a little disconcerting given her youthful age. *"Every race is important to me, touch wood, fingers crossed"* she replied, thus confirming the subliminal capitulation of yet another young and impressionable mind to the contamination of superstitious hearsay. Yet what was the origin of her superstitious surmise?

Does the idea of touching wood to trigger good-fortune hail from a fictional ideology which we'll call 'Treeism'? Did Treeism form a pattern of mental 'tricknology' which duped Siobhan-Marie into believing she could summon good fortune just by touching wood? If Treeism is real, does it work in cahoots with 'Cross-your-fingersism' which sounds like a belief system for willing contortionists? Yet Cross-your-fingersism is a process where hope springs eternal at the behest of a single act of the hand. Imagine if it was true, that we could guarantee success by simply adjusting two of our fingers so they overlap. It would be an extraordinary phenomenon.

Touching wood and crossing fingers is a superstitious farce with no proof of concept, as was Siobhan-Marie's wishful Commonwealth surmise. The process of unlearning superstition is best summed up by the following quip, *"You've got to cut through the bullshit to get to the cool shit."* This may also have served during turbulent times as a useful mantra for my next interviewee, Northern Ireland footballing legend Keith Gillespie. Keith is one of the original 'Fergie Fledglings', which was an amazing crop of young British footballing talents who climbed through the ranks at Manchester United FC to scale the dizzy heights of footballing stardom and set the footballing stage alight.

I can personally testify that, as an international player, Keith lit up many rainy evenings for tortured souls such as myself who once sat defiantly but slightly dispirited in the terraces at Belfast's Windsor Park. I therefore felt humbled at the prospect of participating in an honest and frank conversation to gain unique and exclusive sporting insight regarding the impact of superstitious beliefs on his preparations to compete.

Keith is the successful author of a wonderfully honest and powerful biography called *How Not to Be a Football Millionaire,* in which he speaks candidly of having to cope with an all-consuming gambling addiction earlier in his career. In the book he describes the resulting toll which his gambling addiction exacted on both him and his family. So it's safe to say that he knows how it feels to experience both the exhilarating highs and incredible lows which a career in the spotlight can impose on sporting elite. To begin the conversation, I first sought to explore the extent to which he was prone to superstitious behaviours and this was his response:

"Yeah, I always wear long sleeves. I've actually got quite a few. If I've done something the previous week and we've won, for instance if I had beans on toast

and we won, I'll make sure I have it the following week and if I've worn a certain type of trainer, I'll wear the same trainers again. So I am pretty superstitious when it comes down to it.

It's just something that gets in your head and I actually make sure that no matter what, I will follow it until we lose, but something I will always do is wear long sleeves. I don't know why, it's just something that I've picked up along the way and I just feel more comfortable in my mind when I know I'm wearing long sleeves."

While listening intently to softly-spoken Keith, I found it difficult not to be stricken by his humility. Since despite his much-publicised gambling addiction, this guy managed to forge a successful career both inside and outside of football and turn his life around. So in retrospect, he can look back at his transition with great pride. Oh, and did I mention he's a Northern Ireland footballing legend who once crowd surfed with *BBC Radio 5 live - Fighting Talk* presenter Colin Murray (another Northern Ireland legend) at Euro 2016? Perhaps I'd better move on.

Every interviewee whom I spoke with to compile this information appeared to optimistically believe that they constantly retained ownership and complete control over their own mind, including how they currently think or have previously 'thunk'. But what makes them so sure they are correct? How can they rationally claim to be in control of their behaviour if their behaviour is irrational by default and is therefore seemingly controlling them? What if they are wrong and instead it transpires that they have mistaken ownership for followership?

Superstitions thrive when external sources and imaginary forces are allowed to exert more control over us than we are able to exert on ourselves. Perhaps we think that's impossible as surely we'd notice? Well, let's put it to the test. So, to lighten the mood, consider the following challenge. Simply read the following facts and decide whether to agree or disagree:

1. You can't tickle yourself.
2. You can't count your hair.
3. You can't breathe through your nose with your tongue out.
4. You just tried No. 3.
6. Once you tried No. 3 you realised that it's possible, only now you look like a dog in heat.
7. You're smiling now because you feel foolish.
8. You skipped No. 5.
9. You just checked to see if there is a No. 5.

I accept this is all a bit gimmicky, but it's merely intended as a piece of fun. Yet for those of us tricked into following suit by its humorous content, we've just learned that the mind is rarely its own master. Indeed, it took very little effort to hijack your focus and redirect your thoughts. This bears similarity to the unconscious deception causing Keith's brain to sum up his personal experience of superstitions by admitting, *"I don't know why, it's just something I've picked up along the way."*

Keith was inadvertently referring to a process called redundancy, whereby his mind was too preoccupied with subjective beliefs to apply scepticism. As a result, he was unable or perhaps unwilling to consider that his superstitions had never been evidenced to work. We are all susceptible to mental redundancy, but as an example, try to visualise jumping into your car and driving to work, only to ponder on your arrival how you ever managed to get there at all since you cannot remember passing *that* building site or *those* roadworks. Nor can you recall crossing *that* junction or stopping at *that* set of lights, yet quite incredibly you still arrived safely at your destination.

That was a typical example of mental redundancy, where because your mind was preoccupied or you were still half asleep, you missed seeing the journey taking place in between. A similar process appeared to edge Keith from a position of rational awareness to the irrationality of debilitating compulsions and superstitious beliefs. What fuelled his unshakable desire to only wear long sleeves and why did he stick rigidly to believing that a specific set of trainers had supernatural powers? Keith was being played by ambiguity, and so is every athlete who activates a superstitious belief.

How do we rid ourselves of experiencing any need to adhere to superstitions in sport, since demonstrating a willingness to eradicate superstitious behaviour is highly commendable, but transferring willingness into doingness isn't so easy? Superstitious beliefs exist in a void between appearance and reality where athletes allow *won't power* to outrank their *willpower* until *won't* emerges as their overriding belief. Both *willpower* and *won't power* are equally potent, but which one has most impact depends solely on the athlete's state of will.

Won't power forms an integral part of the human psyche, but it's only the emotions and value which athletes attach to superstitious beliefs that determine whether those superstitions *will* or *won't* become surplus to how they perform. Every superstitious belief is tinged with emotion, yet no better means exists to purge superstitions than to acknowledge that no one can experience the same emotion for 100% of the time. Emotions are temporary, but from within such a state of mental flux, perhaps we can generate enough psychological leeway to revise our daily odds.

How many of us can remember the last time we accurately appraised the odds of our superstitious beliefs? What evidence convinced us that those beliefs were serving us well and what is stopping us from reappraising our superstitions as of right now? Isn't it time we began to care whether our superstitions actually work? They're not difficult to measure since a fact remains a fact independent of faith or belief. Faith cannot be trusted, nor is it a reliable pathway to discovering truth.

Former international footballer Keith Gillespie and GAA stalwart Seán Cavanagh were both gracious enough to reveal that something felt amiss from their sports preparations when they failed to comply with their superstitious rituals and routines. Both appeared to believe that ignoring their superstitions meant they were vulnerable to being punished retrospectively by destiny's wrath by way of experiencing misfortune, catastrophe, calamity, and other forms of bad luck.

Although numerous athletes endorse superstitious thinking, many still believe they are not being overwhelmed by its allure. However, this hypothesis was quickly dismantled on hearing Seán Cavanagh admit to getting out of bed at 2 or 3 a.m on the morning of major events when he should have been resting. So dress it up or make light of it if we dare, but Seán and Keith's fascinating insights beg for an answer to the following question: do we have control of our superstitions or do superstitions have control of us?

"The quality of everything we do: our physical actions, our verbal actions, and even our mental actions, depends on our motivation."

- Dalai Lama

Superstitions are motivated by probable cause, and that cause is fearing the probability of things going wrong just by failing to activate a fixed set of behaviours. Consider former Liverpool FC 'Captain Fantastic' Steven Gerrard's so-called mild OCD as revealed by his wife, *"He's got this thing about washing his hands. He washes them, I'm not joking, fifteen times a day."* If this is true, then from where did he acquire such a fetish for cleanliness? What is the origin of his behaviour, and if pressed for an answer could he even recall when or why his compulsion first began?

Competitive athletes are prone to eccentric behaviour. Yet where is the evidence for a fool's belief that the Commentator's Curse is a viable explanation for the convergence of two random but totally separate events? Where is the proof that the next time an athlete or a team enters a second season at a higher level and experiences a less than auspicious start, that it's down to a 'Syndrome' and not due to tactics, resources, or personnel? Steven's hand washing fetish may appear odd in the eyes of casual observers, yet is it any more odd than the prospect of Seán disrupting his sleep before a major final by climbing out of his bed at 2 or 3 a.m just to tuck a piece of kit into his bag?

Did Seán's superstition portray him as being thoroughly professional and meticulous or just bloody odd? It may take some deep-seated unravelling to untangle Steven's obsession with hand cleanliness or to unpick the unedifying truth behind Keith Gillespie's obsession with long sleeves. Furthermore, Keith has probably heard it said a 1000 times that he was mad to gamble to the extent that he did and risk losing everything, given he had so much to lose. Yet none of us can escape from the thoughts which go on in our minds unless or until we replace each thought with an alternative thought and the willpower to match.

Here is a thought which we all can peruse. Superstitions are akin to the behaviour of hypochondriacs who display the audacity to modify, adapt, and even invent separate variants of truths as their functioning norm. The hypochondriac thinks nothing at all of twisting partial truths into convenient truths, and similar to many athletes who attempt to justify their superstitious truths, asserts a reality which flies in the face of conflicting evidence and displays the audacity to advocate for things which cannot be measured or independently observed.

The sports hypochondriac primes their environment for failure. Every sports competitor has played alongside or competed against the sports hypochondriac. I refer to the athlete who reinvents injuries even where they don't exist, or amplifies the extent of their discomfort to experience sympathy, or at the very least empathy, often in order to replicate a comforting sense of self-absorbed ritual and routine. Some athletes use hypochondria to serve as a practical tool to prepare for failure, so that if they fail to succeed, their excuse is already lodged in the psychology of their peers and no one can say they weren't warned in advance.

A hidden undercurrent lurks beneath sport hypochondria. It is the unheralded question as to how sports hypochondriacs are meant to react once they actually win, as this is similar to questioning how superstitious athletes are meant to react when they lose. When the sports hypochondriac wins, they feel entitled to receive extra plaudits given how miraculously their body held together just long enough to see the job through. However, the danger with sports hypochondria is sustaining a sense of heroism which encourages the feigning of even greater injuries next time around.

There is an obvious crossover between hypochondria and superstition, inasmuch as both raise the question as to who is culpable for the way athletes manage or mismanage compulsive beliefs. The sports hypochondriac spins a convenient reality which ensures they are never personally to blame; it is practically genius as this way their feigned ailments and injuries are always at fault. We can contrast this behaviour with converts to theism who spin alternate realities to those preached by hypochondriacs of sport, except the God hypochondriac does not take front-and-centre stage, yet is always at fault due to the superstition called sin.

Sports superstitions are afforded a similar courtesy when athletes underperform, as for some unexplained reason their superstitions are never to blame. We could synchronise our watches in perfect alignment with the neurotic predictability of the sport hypochondriac's need to redirect and apportion blame, but why do athletes feel drawn to such rhythms, sequences, and patterns? Is it because randomness feels innately uncomfortable and so they invent narratives to add familiarity to things which they cannot fully explain?

Sport mirrors our lives in microcosm. Consider for instance our eating habits (patterns) at Easter time as we attempt to devour a creme egg. Try to observe the precision of each meticulous ritual since each of us is a gastronomical artiste at work with our own unique method of consuming the egg. Or the quirky British obsession for debating what goes into the teacup first, is it the tea or the milk? Or for how long should we boil the perfect egg? It appears that irrespective of whether an athlete's obsession is for wearing long sleeves or for getting out of bed needlessly at 3 a.m. to tuck a piece of sports kit into a bag; the human psychology is eccentric to the point of being borderline insane.

One Hell of a Messi

Consider the following dichotomy as reported during a pre-2014 World Cup warm-up match between Argentina and Slovenia, whereby four-time World Player of the Year Lionel Messi gave Argentina a vomiting scare. Messi had only just arrived onto the pitch for the second half of the match when he was immediately sick. This wasn't the first time, however, as the FC Barcelona superstar had repeated this behaviour at least six times prior, thus mystifying experts as to the cause. Yet in retrospect, the expectations surrounding Messi to maintain his extraordinary standards every time he stepped on a pitch were immense.

Such were the expectations surrounding Messi that his manager Alejandro Sabella insisted, *"In these moments there is anxiety. It is difficult to remain calm."* Perhaps being sick *was* Messi's method of remaining calm, but if so, does the prospect of throwing up six times (that we know of) prior to performing on big occasions constitute a superstitious ritual? If not, then surely it must come pretty damn close. So what was the cause of Lionel's anxieties or of the debilitating emotions which his mind and body seemed so determined to empty out, or we are missing the point altogether?

Was Messi's ritualistic vomiting a physical reaction to how it actually feels to be Lionel Messi, whereby he is permanently stuck in an exalted position of unparalleled pressure, far beyond that which most athletes can realistically comprehend? Was vomiting his means of achieving mental purification, thus purging his stressors from within while simultaneously increasing his odds of performing to his very best? Is there any mileage in the fact that having expelled his pre-match anxieties by throwing up, within four minutes of stepping onto the pitch, yep you guessed it, Messi scored?

Superstitious behaviours appear rhythmic by design, and it appears that the regularity of vomiting before games was Messi's method of staying calm. Perhaps the learning from his sickly dilemma is best summed up by the following pearl of wisdom from the 14th Dalai Lama of Tibet. *"There is no surer way to amend your goals than to alter the pace of expectation,"* since expectations define our state of psychology and consequently our state of health.

The human brain is continuously striving to make sense of, get the gist of, and figure things out, but what happens when superstitions are no longer enough or when sincerity is no longer reciprocated by way of results, especially during critical and defining moments when we need results most? What happens when faith no longer cuts the mustard and *Counterstition* infiltrates our subconscious thoughts by leading us to believe that supernatural forces are sabotaging our chances to excel? *Counterstition* is the label I attach to the process experienced by athletes who, in the face of overwhelming adversity, can't help but believe that they are dealing with supernatural odds.

The following tabloid newspaper snippet concerning Northern Ireland's and Ireland's leading gymnast Luke Carson may help to shed light on why *Counterstition* is the cause of much anxiety and stress. In the article Luke confessed, *"Doctors have told me this latest injury could spell the end of my career as an artistic gymnast. I'm totally devastated. I feel like my world has stopped. Everything I dreamt of achieving as a seven-year-old gymnast has gone."* Luke (23) had been training for the 2013 World Championships when he landed badly and shattered a tibia bone during a vault warm-up routine.

This was Luke's second major setback since just twelve months earlier he was ruled out of the 2012 Olympic Games in London. His unfortunate story highlights the convergence between random misfortune, coincidence, probability, and the unpredictability of chance. To add insult to injury, it transpires that this was his second piece of misfortune in a ridiculously short space of time, as prior to his second tibia injury, he had just been informed by his governing body that his sports funding was to be cut. He was reportedly told that he *"did not meet the agreed minimal performance standard required to be eligible for funding."* In response he implored, *"I was unable to meet the minimal performance targets as I was still recovering from my 'first' tibia fracture."*

Luke was back training with Team GB when his second major injury occurred, yet his double-edged dilemma raised many questions. How well was he prepared psychologically to cope with his dreams being offset by one of the worst injuries that any gymnast could ever wish to comprehend? Was his career-threatening injury further exacerbated by a potential weakness in his leg as a result of the injury sustained one year prior, and had sheer bloody mindedness encouraged Luke to ignore the potential for his worst-case scenario to ever arise?

What practical contingencies had Luke put in place to cope with failing to qualify for yet another major championship? He later expressed that, *"the difference between the impossible and the possible lies in a person's determination. I have not reached my potential yet due to bad luck. I'm going to change my luck."* His sentiment was extremely optimistic as he appeared to believe that with enough faith and determination, *nothing* is impossible; while in retrospect, his forced retirement from international athletics proved beyond doubt that some things clearly are.

Over-optimism in sport is both rife and impractical; as is many athletes' common habit of turning a blind eye to fearing the worst. What percentage of focus did Luke commit to developing a robust mental strategy to cope with misfortune, and what were the immediate choices he faced as his childhood dream lay in tatters and his career hung perilously by a thread? Luke was facing the threat of *Counterstition*. This is a largely typical human response whereby after weighing all the odds, he must surely have felt that the gods had conspired against him or that fate and karma had colluded with luck to sabotage his career.

What else could he assume, when for a second time in succession he had witnessed his efforts at rehabilitation and his re-emergence onto the world stage effectively implode, leaving him to adjust to his fluctuating emotions from the inconvenience of a hospital bed. Luke's story is compelling, and the short documentary *The Hard Way to Success* chronicles his incredible fighting spirit. Yet how plausible was it to remain rational and reasonable throughout his obvious trauma without harbouring a grudge and some animosity towards his governing body for axing his funds?

Try putting ourselves in his shoes. Who wouldn't have felt as though fate had deliberately conspired against us? Luke must surely have felt that his governing body were sadly lacking in patience, empathy, and faith, since at times such as these, facts seem irrelevant compared to his sense of worthlessness, betrayal, and pain. What interest had Luke, at this particular time, in hearing that his governing body was handcuffed by protocols, bureaucracy, and red tape? Very few of us who have suffered major injuries or long-term disruptions throughout the course of our own sporting careers wouldn't fully empathise with his dilemma or feel that luck had colluded, connived, and conspired to bring his career to a shuddering halt.

"Sometimes you just need a scratch of luck."

- Sean Dyche, Football Manager

At some point during proceedings, it must have been difficult for Luke not to feel as though the universe had conspired against him in some form of personal attack. His story is one of only a few instances where as author I have sought to inject such a large degree of poetic licence, but only because I feel that most readers will share a large degree of empathy with Luke. I also wanted to highlight the obvious comparison between sports pundits who imply that a random convergence of events is tantamount to a Commentator's Curse. Many pundits seem convinced that just because a coincidence seems so accurate and precise in nature and timing that the only plausible explanation is that luck is trying to trip them up.

Sod's Law is yet another example of where *Counterstition* is viewed as having instigated a personalised attack. So much so that many athletes believe they are the victims of a supernatural hex or jinx, as if they are pawns in one of sport's many supernatural elaborate plans. Two things remain constant to human ego.

First, when events go against us, it's increasingly difficult not to take things personally. The second is the continual failure to recognise that when information-bias rears its ugly head, the threat of confirmation-bias is always one step behind to prop up our assumptions, irrespective of facts or evidence to the contrary.

Counterstition is the sense of paranoia which manifests when random events merge with thoughts of conspiracy, particularly when events fail to go our way. Such a sense can feel personal to the extent that we begin seeing sequences and patterns (confirmation bias) which support our beliefs. Consider the patterns which must have formed in Luke's psychology, such as the coincidence that his 2nd major injury within the space of a year led to his 2nd withdrawal from a 2nd major competition which invariably led to his 2nd major heartache due to a 2nd major assault on his career caused by bad karma and luck.

Welcome to Luke's world of *Counterstition*, or at least to my use of poetic licence as to what it must have been like for him to experience so many coincidences converging all at once. Try telling Luke that luck wasn't his enemy or that fate was his friend; or perhaps his excruciating landing had nothing to do with luck whatsoever. Luke had practised that jump hundreds of times prior to his fall and yet, due to one incorrect landing, his world had imploded; but was it due to bad luck, fate, chance, probability, coincidence, or simply the result of his own carelessness? Luke's fall was captured on camera and so his performance can be evaluated from take off to landing. This means that the surefootedness of his run up, positioning, and landing can be easily assessed to see where things went wrong, and yet nowhere in this process does luck factor at all.

We read earlier of former Warrington Rugby League star Paul Wood's reported OCD where he wrapped and rewrapped his hands with bandages up to ten times before every game. It doesn't require much imagination to visualise his teammates taking-the-piss during dressing room banter. Nor is it difficult to imagine the mutterings and sly comments from teammates who witnessed his bizarre rituals during the lead up to every match. Comments such as, *"keep that bandage on this time and just get out there and bloody play"*, must surely have been commonplace. Yet, irrespective of banter, intended malice, or repeated attempts to wind him up, his response was quite simply *"I can't."*

It appears the line between what constitutes a superstition and an OCD is becoming increasingly blurred. The idea of luck is also ambiguous. Who or what was the catalyst for Team GB athlete Luke Carson announcing his retirement from elite gymnastics in 2015 at only 26? Should the blame fall on Luke for failing to execute the perfect vault or was it partially the fault of his governing body for exerting too much pressure by way of deadlines he couldn't meet?

As testament to his spirit of bouncebackablity, it's worth noting how in April 2018 at the Commonwealth Games in the Gold Coast, Australia, Luke helped shake gymnastics to its core by coaching young Northern Ireland gymnast Rhys McClenaghan to gold in the pommel event ahead of the reigning Olympic champion, England's Max Whitlock. Luke came full circle by exporting his talent with no cause to denounce the superstition called luck.

Why did José Mourinho choose to ignore clear deficiencies that were otherwise evident in his struggling Chelsea football team? As I listened to José subtly berating referees' decisions, I was reminded of a classic quote by comedian Kenneth Williams who quipped, *"Infamy, infamy! They've all got in for me."* Yet behind the smoke and mirrors, José also talked of how his players were lacking in confidence, had failed to take responsibility and instruction, and were not doing as they were told. None of which are even remotely related to conspiracy or luck.

Spare a thought for Dublin GAA boss Jim Gavin who found it tough to cease-and-desist from questioning the referee's decisions even after winning an All-Ireland title. This caused me to wonder who he might have blamed if they'd lost? Would he have blamed his team's deficiencies, his own inadequacies, the referee, or luck? Or what conclusion should be drawn from former Tyrone GAA star Sean Cavanagh's stated inability to feel completely at ease playing football without his lucky underwear? It's also interesting to note how he couldn't stop smiling throughout our conversation at how ridiculous it sounded to openly express his superstitions in words.

Former rugby star Paul Wood habitually craved the next bandage. Yet, his belief was artificial at best as his additional bandages had no practical value. Or consider his thoughts when he then fell victim to an excruciating sports injury which resulted in the loss of his right testicle during a turbulent period when even his marriage fell apart. Consider how conspiratorial such an awful convergence of events must have felt to Paul at that particular time? Or, if we were in his shoes, might we also be inclined to believe that the sporting gods had conspired against us?

How we view luck affects sports preparation and consequently how we perform since we are the embodiment of whichever information we choose to accept and believe. So welcome to the world of *Counterstition*, where one person's idea of rationale clearly impinges on another's interpretation of insanity, while the truth lies somewhere in between. *Counterstition* is real! It exists in the mind of every competitor who feels fate, luck, or karma has not acted in their favour as a result of supernatural design.

"What we don't understand we can make mean anything."

- Chuck Palahniuk, Novelist

A Neuroscientific Nudge

"The only Zen you find on the tops of mountains is the Zen you bring up there."

\- Jules Renard, Author

There is a story of a medical patient who once suffered from a terrible dose of flu, and nothing the doctor prescribed seemed to bring any relief. *"There must be something you can do to cure me,"* snapped the patient, clearly perturbed.

"I have a suggestion," said the doctor. *"Go straight home and take a really hot shower, but before drying yourself off, try standing naked in a draft and the longer you stand for the better."*

"Will that cure me?" asked the patient, a little startled and taken aback.

"No," replied the doctor, *"but it may induce symptoms of pneumonia and that I can cure."*

How often do any of us stop to consider that we're surrounded by gurus who offer us remedies to conditions of which they are the primary cause? Alternatively, it's estimated that, intrinsically as humans, we say between 300 and 1000 words to ourselves every minute (self-talk), so perhaps the gurus causing our conditions are us. So why waste time and effort telling ourselves that the cure for the anxieties we experience in sport is superstition, as this kills any impetus to embrace spontaneity and stifles any attempts to establish a natural cause.

Superstitious beliefs embroil athletes' mentalities in an undercurrent of subservience to self-perpetuating habits which are hard to shake-off. Consider UFC Fight Night 59 (Ultimate Fighting Championship) and the effect of superstitious innuendo being actively played out to a worldwide pay-per-view audience live from Boston. Following the second-round stoppage of fighter Dennis Siver, rising Irish superstar Conor McGregor moved one step closer to realising his lifelong dream of being crowned UFC Featherweight Champion of the World.

To achieve his goal, Conor would have to defeat unbeaten champion, Brazilian José 'Junior' Aldo. Knowing this, and immediately following the post-fight announcement of his victory over the hapless Siver, Conor scoured the Boston arena to seek out Aldo whom he knew to be somewhere in the crowd. Even veteran UFC fight commentator Joe Rogan was using all his media savvy to raise post-fight intensity by beckoning to Aldo to join McGregor in the centre of the cage.

Rogan was aiming to instigate a face-to-face clash of posturing, trash talk, and bravado to whet the appetite of the fans. As a seasoned commentator he would be aware that a stare-down is priceless in terms of promoting the next main event, but also to raise the hairs on the back of the necks of excitable fans. Sadly the spectacle failed to materialise as Aldo respectfully declined. *"Don't be superstitious,"* Rogan shouted at Aldo, yet his seemingly random remark ghosted over the heads of most in the crowd. It did not escape the attention of McGregor, however, who in typical extrovert fashion, seized on the frenzy of the moment to grab some one-upmanship over his potential foe.

Conor wrongly mistook the reigning world champion's refusal to step into the octagon as an overwhelming indictment of fear. Then following a spontaneous outburst of adrenalin-fuelled bravado when spotting Aldo's face in the crowd, he sprang from the cage to confront the champion, face to face. Having scaled the menacing octagon walls, he ran into the crowd in a moment of undeniable theatre which caused even the unflinching champion to smile. Conor hadn't planned, however, for the disarming nature of Aldo's amicable smile which reduced his vitriolic attempt at intimidation and provocation to no more than an act. The fact that Conor appeared as the only aggressor made the whole altercation appear so one-sided that it momentarily left him with egg on his face.

Conor quickly retrieved the situation by once again asserting that José's snub to meet face to face in the octagon was an obvious sign of weakness. Hence the battle lines were drawn with Conor seemingly holding all the aces. Or so it appeared until the timely intervention of UFC President Dana White, who quickly pointed out that Conor's assertion couldn't be further from the truth. *"He [Aldo] wants this fight so bad,"* enthused Dana. *"He wanted to get into the octagon to do the interview but he's superstitious and won't go into the octagon unless it's specifically to fight."*

José's somewhat awkward but surreal scenario was a wicked indictment of the far-reaching impact of superstitious belief. It also confirmed that athletes remain as impaired by superstitions in the 21st century as at any previous time throughout history and that UFC fighters are no exception to the rule. José's superstition radically altered the nature of his behaviour, yet minus the antics of Conor McGregor, it may never have fully come to light. This raises a question as to how many of us are impacted by superstitious beliefs which are all but invisible to our peers?

José couldn't define with any earthly authority the direct line of punishment or retribution which lay in store if he prematurely stepped into the octagon prior to an actual fight. Yet why would any supernatural essence, divine agent, or extra-terrestrial entity give a damn either way at the probable outcome of a terrestrial MMA fight? When did superstition become an external thinking agent with the prowess, intelligence, and acumen necessary to determine which athletes to assist, which to ignore, and which to completely disregard? Why is no one providing definitive answers?

According to UFC President Dana White, José wouldn't break his superstitious code. This makes no sense, however, as how could his superstition have known it was being deceived? Do superstitions possess the conscious faculties necessary to sense if or when they are being duped? How should athletes refer to superstitions? Should they call them a 'they' or an 'it'? Can a figment of someone's imagination ever truly be consciously aware of an athlete's indiscretion behind its back? Does superstitious belief act as confirmation of mild schizophrenia? How is it even possible that if José was to betray his code and step into the octagon with McGregor prior to a fight, that some months later he would suffer from the delayed effect of a renegade superstition with a long memory and which had followed him from Boston still bearing a grudge?

Do superstitions possess the faculty for ego, whereupon they deliberately work against us if we fail to fulfil their terms and conditions? Likewise, do they intentionally work in our favour if we demonstrate subservience through faith that they're real? Wouldn't these types of occurrences indicate that superstitions are 'intelligent', as would their ability to track our thoughts and behaviour across varying demographics and times? Or consider instead the popular pseudoscientific superstition known as 'Law of Attraction'. Where has it been proven that a conscious thought acts as a prerequisite or precursor to the thought manifesting as a physical thing?

Do thoughts have the capacity to become physical things? Or given Aldo's fear that breaking his superstitious code may come back to haunt him, is it time to ask whether superstitions are not only intelligent but can also experience hurt and betrayal just as we do? How else can they come back to bite us unless they also get miffed, harbour feelings of vengefulness and spite, and possess the capacity to implement sanctions which they deem appropriate if we don't follow suit? Oddly, all of these are human traits, yet each raises a question which every athlete or
230

coach should ask: are the things they believe regarding superstition actually true?

Do superstitions possess a conscious faculty for expressing anger or delight or for exacting revenge or retribution? It's important to ask these types of questions as how else can we measure whether our actions cause supernatural displeasure or feed into a supernatural ego thus making it smile? Do superstitions possess willpower or some observable means of punishing Aldo's potential indiscretions? How would his superstition be able to tell if he'd crossed the imaginary line and stepped into the octagon prior to a fight? Perhaps this line of questioning seems somewhat surreal, yet Aldo's pre-fight reluctance to enter the octagon only further exacerbates the extent of delusion which many athletes are prepared to believe.

Athletes often modify their behaviour to accommodate the terms and conditions of bizarre beliefs. José Aldo's example further typifies how easily superstitious or theistic dogma can hold us transfixed in unknowing states. Many athletes claim to be guided by spirituality, but spirituality is also a mental construct with no explanatory power. Athletes frequently adopt spirituality to harness experiences which they do not or cannot fully express or comprehend. Spirituality is not defined by religious practice, just as a sporting performance is not defined by superstitious faith. It is, however, definitively superstition, as is the idea of a supernatural since beyond tales of personal revelation, no falsifiable evidence for either exists.

Without the benefit of observable and falsifiable evidence, how can anyone tell if a superstition actually worked or if the outcome of an event was caused by an intelligent supernatural agent with powers to respond to our selfish demands as we continue to search for a definitive sporting edge? How can harnessing belief in the supernatural help to identify the unknown cause of an event when the term supernatural tells us nothing at all? Faith isn't a virtue, nor is it a reliable pathway to truth, while hope, for its part, is an offshoot of optimism and the success rate for optimism is tantamount to that of probability and chance.

How often do athletes feel truly elated by activating a superstitious belief, and if not, then why bother at all? Is it because superstitions are forces of habit? Or how about you? When was the first time you consciously concealed the extent of your superstitious beliefs from the prying eyes and ears of curious peers, lest they think you had lost the plot? This process of concealment demonstrates an awareness that superstitious beliefs lack credible evidence and the bizarre behaviours which you view as normal may appear to others as somewhat eccentric and downright weird.

UFC fighter José Aldo's reported fear of stepping into an octagon prior to a fight highlights a similar dearth of rationale. Oh, and just for the record, José subsequently lost his world crown to McGregor after being dethroned by his very first punch. This story conveys an extraordinary dichotomy, insomuch as it's difficult to rationalise why José's fear of losing and getting punched in the face appeared minimal when compared to incurring the wrath of a rogue superstition prior to the fight. Go figure!

Can an athlete transition beyond superstition? The answer seems to be yes, and one solution is found in the world of neuroscience which is typically viewed with increasing regularity as an emerging interdisciplinary science and allied to disciplines such as linguistics, physics, and psychology. So I sought a fresh perspective and current insight from the very gracious Amy Brann, who is a thought leader in the fields of neuroscience and human potential and author of thought provoking books such as 'Make Your Brain Work', 'Engaged', and 'Neuroscience for Coaches'.

Amy is passionate about pursuing research opportunities to advance the practical applications which neuroscience can bring to any business. Yet, given the flexibility of the human brain, I began to explore how neuroscientific models could be adapted and replicated to enhance sport. Irrespective of our personal motivation or sports orientation, the one thing of which we can always be certain is that we're always accompanied by our brain, therefore the brain seems a logical place to begin. I asked Amy to explain why athletes experience difficulty breaking free from superstitious compulsions, addictive habits, and subsequent beliefs. I also sought her opinion as to what transitioning beyond our current habits might entail. This was her response:

"Our brains are largely plastic by nature, so are very able to change and so the habits we have we can change to make into habits that really support us, as well as habits that we really want to have. However, this process is hard and the reason it's hard is because our brains are very efficient and effective and they want to groove into all kinds of neural networks.

Perhaps we can imagine it as being a bit like driving around a racecourse. If we drive around a racecourse enough times we entrench our pathways upon the course and the benefit is that the next time we want to drive on that particular racecourse, it's nice and easy for us to get straight back into the grooves. If we want to take a different path, say we want to drive on the outside lane as opposed to the inside lane, that becomes more difficult to do since our wheels are stuck
232

within the grooves. So change is possible from a habits perspective, but we need to do it slowly and we need to apply some dedication if we wish to affect our outcomes.

Say if we are looking to change a habit, the first thing I'd recommend is looking at why we want to change that habit, thereby getting really connected with what the new habit is going to bring to us. Next we'd look to see if there is anything we need to do to minimise the downside of letting go of our old habit, and once those things are all out of the way we would then take a series of very small steps.

So, if for example we were to start going to the gym in the morning before work, then I'd suggest the first step would simply be to set our alarm clocks to go off 30 minutes earlier. Don't get out of bed! Just set the alarm clock for 30 minutes earlier and do that for a few days until we feel that yes, we can do this now - we can awaken at this time every morning. The next step would be to actually get out of bed and to do that for a few days. Then we would start doing something to make it easier to progress things that wee bit further again.

We call it 'nudging' within the neuroscience community and it would perhaps be to leave our gym clothes on the floor right beside our beds so that when we get up first thing in the morning, our gym clothes are right there and it's just really easy to put them on. So just do that and get into our gym clothes for a day or two and then actually hit the gym a couple of days down the line. That would be one way to start changing a habit from a neuroscientific perspective."

Next I asked Amy what stops us from making the necessary adjustments once we are aware that our superstitions aren't working or serving us well:

"I think sometimes we become extremely attached to our habits and equally attached to the things we do, and so sometimes it's just about doing something differently one time, just to see that nothing bad happens, particularly from a superstitious perspective. Say it was knowing that you had to wear your lucky pink socks to win a race. Then perhaps you'd want to experiment by not wearing your lucky pink socks and just see how things go.

Of course the downside or risk is that beliefs are very powerful and they affect our behaviours and if we believe that wearing those pink socks is going to win us the race, there is a danger we may alter our behaviour simply because we are not actually wearing our lucky pink socks. So it may well be that first we have to change our beliefs before we attempt to change our behaviour."

I thanked Amy for sharing her insight and began to ponder on two observations which immediately sprang to mind. First, change always requires an element of risk. Next, it's important to utilise positive self-talk to clarify in our mind that nothing bad is likely to happen just by choosing to do things a different way. It's not dissimilar to agreeing to lose an appendix when it becomes inflamed and causes pain. Eventually we accept that it's time to detach and let it go.

Repelling a habit seems relatively straightforward; all it requires is a measure of self-discipline and will. Yet if change is so simple, what stopped us from transitioning beyond any debilitating beliefs we currently hold? Why is it the case that when athletes deviate from a superstitious ritual and something goes wrong, they are quick to imply a supernatural causation while blatantly ignoring more obvious causes - 'natural' causes? What does this tell us about the fragile nature of how they think? It tells us there's a need for helpful solutions such as Amy's process of neuroscientific 'nudging' to ease them past dependency at a pace which is comfortable for them.

"Transformation can come in the mysterious guise of shape-shifting, or through a simple change of mind"

- C.R. Strahan, Author

Superstitious belief is an optimistic or pessimistic means of fast-tracking prophecy and is potentially transformative depending on whether or not a prediction comes true. Having undergone a process of thinking, believing, and behaving as if a prophecy will come true, then the damage may already have been done since the brain still underwent an initial process of not knowing for certain what might transpire. The following snapshot from an article in *Time* magazine by Eric Barker best sums up the impact of an unknowing brain: *"Sometimes it seems like your brain just sits around creating lousy feelings and worries. You want this, you're frustrated about that, you're annoyed about some other thing. The list never stops and it makes it impossible to be happy."*

Eric's article highlights research conducted by Harvard Social Psychologist, Daniel Gilbert, who concluded that *"a wandering mind is not a happy mind. People spend 46.9% of their waking hours thinking about something other than what they're doing, and this mind wandering typically makes them unhappy since mind wandering is an excellent predictor of people's happiness."* As yet, no one fully knows what percentage of time is taken up by our minds wandering into the realm of omens, superstitions, premonitions, and prophetic beliefs. What we *do* know, however, is that dwelling on prophecy can leave an indelible mark etched on our brain.

Further research conducted by Matthew Killingsworth, PhD, asserts, *"How often our minds leave the present and where they tend to go is a better predictor of our happiness than the activities in which we are engaged. Our wandering minds are generally the cause [and] not the consequence of unhappiness."* This caused me to question if the mind wandering towards a prophetic belief is part of the cause as opposed to the consequence of experiencing disharmony and subsequent 'dis-ease'. The way athletes perform at sport often mirrors their life in microcosm, insomuch as the characteristics they display in their everyday lifestyle will most probably follow them into competitive sport.

Art imitating life is not uncommon. An example of which is pretending that deciphering prophecy is an actual art, as illustrated by the following bizarre rationale which was reportedly proposed by former Prime Minister of Thailand, Thaksin Shinawatra. He believed in astrology to such a degree that when asked to comment on escalating political tensions he told reporters, *"Be patient with the headache inducing situation until July 2, as Mars moving closer to Saturn causes the headache. When Mars leaves, the situation will ease."*

Imagine the impact in Western society if a politician announced that the solution to easing an outpouring of political tension and social unrest was to wait for the convergence of Mars and Saturn. What do we propose as our first reaction? How much confidence would any of us retain in the politician once it came to light that their decision was rooted in superstitious belief. Moreover, it would most likely affect our vote next time around.

One further example of self-induced prophecy was former world champion and Team GB diver, Tom Daley, who became embroiled in OCD (Obsessive Compulsive Disorder) to counter his fear of a dangerous dive which filled him with dread every time it came around. Tom confessed, *"I hated the dive. If you say what has been the scariest moment of your life then I would allegedly say every time I stood up on that board to do that dive. I became this massive OCD freak when it came to the day I was doing those dives. I couldn't walk across three drains without thinking the world was going to end. If I didn't sleep well I thought the dive was going to go wrong or if I didn't eat the right things, etc."*

Tom was referring to his infamous twister dive which had already failed him at the 2012 London Olympics, and once again the same fear had returned to haunt him during the lead up to Rio 2016. As the pressure intensified, his mental state deteriorated to such an extent that not only did his twister dive fail him, but this time his whole repertoire fell apart at the seams. During preparation he admittedly placed a tremendous psychological value on various compulsive behaviours - *"I became this massive OCD freak when it came to the day."*

Tom embraced OCD as a coping strategy when the time came to execute his terrifying dive. His approach shared some commonality with the sentiments of former Sunderland FC Manager, Gus Poyet, who while nearing the end of his tenure at the club stated, *"I don't believe in luck in the long-term."* This suggests that luck can be triggered on an on-and-off basis to alleviate poor form, just as Tom sought to trigger some short-term assistance by embracing OCD-like tendencies on the day of *that* dive. His honesty was commendable regarding his approach, but what evidence exists that OCDs are effective? Unless OCDs are intelligent thinking agents, then by what means can they issue Tom with a temporary day-pass to success before seemingly retracting their good grace at will?

What exactly did Gus mean by dismissing luck in the long-term? How long is long-term and how short is short-term and how can we be sure if we are correct? Many athletes experience mortal dread at the thought of ending up on the wrong side of prophecy, omens, and superstitious beliefs, or feel obligated to comply with the meticulous demands of their adopted OCDs. Others are scathing and dismissive of supernatural charades and apply curiosity and old-fashioned scepticism to debunk faith-based beliefs.

Neither faith nor belief are necessarily admirable virtues, but what is often forgotten is that the overall objective of both is to arrive at a knowing state since knowing trumps every form of faith and belief and is therefore integral to becoming 'aware'. Many athletes performing under duress appear happy to grasp at even the most questionable of solutions to experience relief. Some wear lucky numbers, boots, or pants, or facilitate weird rituals or odd routines before they are able to feel at ease, while others call on supernatural entities such as gods to pull them out of a hole.

Oddly, a discrepancy still exists between superstitions deemed as generic and those solely devoted to gods (theism), yet both are equally prevalent throughout sport. So why does conventional thinking fail to bestow the same collective respect upon generic superstitions as is duly dispatched to those which are rooted in stories of apparitions and gods? Why does scepticism surround the wearing of lucky pants, t-shirts, boots, or other curios, quirks, potions, or charms which supposedly pave the way for athletes to interact in an implied supernatural realm?

Why draw a distinction between the idea that wearing a rabbit's foot around our neck is lucky (although not particularly lucky for the rabbit), and the idea that a meddling god of divinity can instigate a sporting success? The same quality of evidence exists that rabbit feet are lucky as that which exists to prove a meddling god ever stuck its oar into terrestrial sporting affairs. Surely it would be dishonest of any god to disrespect sport's general rule of fair play by displaying bias, yet many athletes believe this occurrence is common. Consider UFC Fight Night 59 at the TD Garden Arena in Boston, where fighter Benson 'Smooth' Henderson was adjudged to have suffered a unanimous defeat to his opponent and good friend outside of the octagon, Donald 'Cowboy' Cerrone.

The judges' decisions at ringside were deemed widely controversial to say the least, and many MMA (mixed martial arts) fans were left scratching their heads in disbelief. Prior to the post fight announcement, Benson was publicly buoyant and upbeat, only to be left stunned by the decision but also by the margin of defeat as all three judges adjudicated that Cerrone won unanimously on all counts. Despite his obvious displeasure at the ruling, Benson, who was also a devout practicing Christian, sought solace by placing huge public emphasis on the enduring nature of his Christian beliefs. So rather that swear and cuss, he delivered the following bold revelation, *"I can do all things through Christ who strengthens me. I just want to say for the record that it is what it is."*

Although Benson felt sincere in his bold assertion, on this occasion he was entirely wrong since Christ was either unwilling or simply unable to wield enough influence to sway the only thing of significance inside the octagon, which was the result. So, why did his personal Christ fail to ensure that the judges would make the correct call and what role, if any, does scepticism play in Benson's divine delusion? Surely he was entitled to be critical of his Christ's no-show at the event and for abandoning his professional fighting interests. Instead, it only served to highlight that he seemingly cannot do all things through Christ.

Throughout Benson's dilemma, what became of the pseudoscientific superstition known as Universal Law of Attraction? Surely it too was negligent, having failed to deliver on its promise of reforming the energy produced from Benson's ultra-positive state of mind and unyielding faith into a physical win. Rarely does such a fierce and combative competitor display such an immediate sense of optimism having experienced the devastation of defeat. So if a thought really can manifest as a thing, then why did the Law of Attraction go missing in action when the universe should have automatically responded to Benson in kind?

Was it simply a matter of conflicting perspective? Perhaps the Law of Attraction really did fulfil its obligation as supposedly laid out by cosmic law and was instead drawn to a superior energy source and force of will as exuded by Benson's stronger-minded opponent 'Cowboy' Cerrone. In other words, perhaps the Law of Attraction was more powerfully drawn towards Cerrone's much stronger sense of will. Perhaps Cerrone's power of attraction so outweighed the impact of Benson's faith delusion that the universe found itself more attracted to him.

Benson provided no answers as to why his personal Christ lacked the necessary guile, capacity, or know-how to sway even one judge. This isn't meant as a flippant observation but to highlight the speed and impetuous haste by which athletes concede emotional sincerity to superstitious constructs, irrespective of whether those constructs are rational, irrational, comical, outrageous, or just plain daft.

"Tell people there's an invisible man in the sky who created the universe, and the vast majority will believe you. Tell them the paint is wet, and they have to touch it to be sure."

- George Carlin, Comedian

Why do relatively intelligent and rational thinking athletes concoct invisible constructs deemed worthy of worship, while stubbornly refusing to drop all affiliation with superstitious bias when a desired expectation does not come to fruition, a prayer fails to materialise, or a superstitious ritual, artefact, or compulsion fails in its anticipated effect? If an athlete is truly intelligent, then why hang on to the coattails of nostalgia or to the fading embers of wishful thinking which have long since petered out? Why not simply let go of the superstitious conventions and customs bequeathed to us by our forefathers as part of *their* legacy from a bygone age?

Try being sceptical of our forefathers' intelligence by not allowing ourselves to be suckered into complying with superstitions that belong in the past. Often it was they who taught us that the answer to self-determination lies outside of ourselves. So perhaps their unintelligence is the reason we exist on the cusp of so many unverifiable superstitious beliefs. At what point do we stop overvaluing the thoughts and opinions of external gurus, thereby undervaluing ourselves, and stop looking to surrogate sources of intelligence to tell us who, what, when, or how to believe, perform, or behave? Instead, try to avail of curiosity, evidence, reasoning, and freedom of will. Learn lessons from previous disappointments and bask in the exhilaration of spontaneity, fresh perspective, and experiential methods of discovering conclusions by ourselves.

When did you last have an original thought? Consider the impact of spending a lifetime devoid of original thought. This is not as far-fetched as you might imagine since athletes who succumb to superstitions cannot cite intelligence as a reasonable pathway to establishing truth. Intelligence is vastly overrated when it bears no resemblance to reality at all. Yet, who hasn't done stupid stuff 'intelligently'? Moreover, some of the most heinous crimes ever perpetrated on humanity occurred at the behest, or as the result, of extremely intelligent people.

There is nothing unique about intelligence since all thoughts are corrupted by emotional, metaphorical, or ideological gurus saddling our thoughts with information-bias, skewed interpretations, prophecy, dogma, and fear to lead us to succumb to highly unintelligent and yet significant demands. Self-determination is generally retrospective since we must first draw on our prior experiences before formulating intelligent beliefs. Hence intelligence is rarely of our own making but is more likely comprised of remnants from the past masquerading as original choices.

"Now what is intelligence? It is when your senses and your consciousness calculate on the spot. Senses will say one thing. Consciousness will say something different. And when you can put it together, two and two, that is intelligence. The mind becomes a monster when it becomes your master. The mind is an angel when it is your servant."

- Yogi Bhajan, Entrepreneur

How angelic are our minds? Are they monsters which control us or angels of obedience and circumspection? Consider this marvellous lyric by a band called The Rainmakers from a song entitled 'Snake Dance': *"And the angels and the devils are playing tug-of-war with my personality."* Likewise, superstitious beliefs play tug-of-war with our senses and all we must determine is whether or not we actually care if our beliefs are true.

Consider the psychology of Formula One racing driver Max Chilton, who at age 23 availed of the services of an Olympic Mind Coach to help manage heightening expectations for the fast approaching 2014 British Grand Prix. *"I have been encouraged to visualise driving laps of the British Grand Prix before I go to sleep,"* said Max in response to previous anxiety which he experienced one year earlier during his first competitive F1 race at Silverstone. He admitted to feeling overawed by the sheer enormity of the event, but also constrained by strict F1 rules designed to restrict testing prior to each race. So he opted instead to practice visualisation and his focus became trained on visualising racing 'actual' laps on the Silverstone track, except this time from the comfort of his bed. Here is his assessment of visualisation:

"I have not used a simulator for Silverstone this year. I just shut my eyes and try to visualise the perfect lap. I start running through a few laps before going to bed and before I get up. It's all very relaxing. I sit there with a stopwatch timing a lap. I'm getting better and better at it and when I do that before qualifying, I am usually within a tenth of a second of the lap time. It is just about getting your mind right and it's also free practice. I could've done 100 laps in my head before the race even starts."

It was a revealing insight into one of Formula One's racing elite, particularly his candid revelation of mentally envisaging and then re-enacting a complete rerun of an actual Silverstone lap, as though it was actually happening in real-time. Max had mastered the art of channelling his focus to within one tenth of a second of an actual lap time out on the track, which by any standard is incredible accuracy. He also attested to visualisation enhancing his ability to stay mentally attuned for the full duration of every race and to feel calmer and noticeably more at ease with the ensuing demands of Formula One.

The skill of visualisation primed Max to feel better coordinated, sharper, quicker, and more composed. From a coaching perspective, the neuroscientific process of 'nudging' his emotions beyond self-debilitating doubt enabled him to discard needless psychological clutter which, in turn, led to a more productive state of mind. It was also further proof that we cannot escape from the thoughts which go on inside our minds unless or until we replace those thoughts with alternative thoughts. Max used visualisation as a practical tool to ensure he would not be overawed by the Silverstone juggernaut for a second time around.

UFC fighter Benson 'Smooth' Henderson opted for the superstition called 'Christ' to act as his aid for achieving sporting greatness, while Max Chilton opted for practical visualisation techniques to tap into his latent genius. He used visualisation and not superstition to exorcise demons from one year prior, and visualisation requires no attempt to violate any known physical universal laws unlike superstition which requires the existence of a supernatural which defies every physical law of which we're currently aware. Hence by natural means only, Max nudged his psychology from a position of weakness to a position of strength.

Consider the Zen proverb which states, *"Try as we may, we cannot see our reflection in boiling water."* Similarly, try as we may, we cannot see the true value of personal genius while ensconced in a state of superstitious disarray. We cannot repel what we cannot see and many athletes struggle to see that emotion and sincerity, but sadly not evidence, are guiding their superstitious beliefs despite sincerity being no guarantee against being dead wrong. All faith-based beliefs are tinged with sincerity, but the more we grant superstition enough leeway to ride roughshod over our will, the less sceptical we become towards ideologies and dogma with no explanatory powers to justify faith.

Even as you read this very sentence you may still outright refuse to believe that you are not in complete control of your thinking or that you lack the appetite, willpower, or stomach to launch a full-scale enquiry into why you find it so difficult to transition beyond superstitious belief. For those of you, however, whose minds remain open to enquiry, sport empowers you with wonderful opportunities to reinvigorate and uncover a brand new you. So I offer a challenge; I challenge you to think an original thought! Go on! It's so easy it's almost patronising. Or is it?

Where exactly did your mind travel to extract your original thought? Did you find yourself drifting towards or away from a hidden cache of involuntary beliefs over which you had little or no control? Did you only feel able to draw on thoughts that were already deeply embedded in your psyche, as if lying dormant and playing possum while awaiting their chance to spring out of the cake (your brain) and shout *"surprise"*. Yet so few of your thoughts are particularly surprising since at best you are merely regurgitating, repositioning, and redepositing stuff that already exists in the inner recess of your mind.

Every thought you experience is tinged by emotions which lead to beliefs that feel sincere. Superstitions are also tinged with sincerity, which is why many athletes are prone to feelings of contentment, anger, and guilt. Superstitions are generated by raw emotion and so athletes are systematically duped by whatever emotions they are experiencing at any given time. Sometimes they pray or point to the sky as a token of acknowledgement to invisible gods who play hide-and-seek. Others seek intercessory blessings from those very same gods by way of human messengers who pretend to know deeply profound stuff that the rest of us don't, but when pressed have no choice but to backtrack to faith which we've already established is not a reliable pathway to truth.

Who among us accepts that superstitions work in tandem with supernatural sources? Are they still fit for purpose in the 21st century or might it be that, despite their feel-good factor, they possess a more sinister nature than we care to admit, closer perhaps to the stuff of nightmares given that any failure to comply increases anxiety and fear? From interviews I conducted to compile this information, most athletes were beset by some kind of fear, so their primary purpose for adopting superstitions was to shield them from fear. The purpose of a shield is to glance and deflect, just as the purpose of superstition is to glance and deflect encroaching anxiety from penetrating an athlete's psychology to detrimental effect.

Since time immemorial, human awareness has come under attack from a barrage of superstitious artillery, ambushing our thoughts from strategic angles at the behest of gurus using sharp tongues, complex jargon, and mind-numbing dogma as their weapons of choice. Gurus thrive in this age of social compliance by encouraging vulnerable mentalities to die on their shields (sometimes metaphorically, sometimes not) and to fall on their swords in reverence to the power of ambiguity. It is time to wake up to the realisation that social compliance, when used incorrectly, sparks social reliance and as a result the collective awareness of many athletes has grown increasingly reliant on external gurus who ensnare them in faith delusions masquerading as facts.

Here's a question. Exactly how long does it take before anyone can claim that they have finally come to know a belief to be true? What is the exact timeframe for such a process, and who among us has installed failsafes such as deadlines and cut-off points for demonstrating that a sporting outcome was solely the result of superstition and that the same superstition is capable of repeating the same outcome time and again? Once we finally know a thing for certain, we no longer need faith. Hence it's unreasonable to hang on to faith forever with no tangible proof that the wait is worthwhile. That's why it's important to apply scepticism to external pied pipers and to equip every claim that's reliant on faith with a practical timeline, whereupon it's discarded along with the trash once it fails to manifest as a fact within a predesignated period of time.

The reason why karma (also superstition) continues to find us is because we're always stood in the exact same place. Some athletes profess karma as the moral arbitrator of sport by way of colloquial sayings such as 'what goes around comes around'. Others think this sentiment refers to luck, yet neither concept is proven to have interacted with terrestrial sport or caused an athlete's comeuppance. So what keeps athletes rooted in superstitious belief or affords gurus who peddle ambiguity a free hand to further indoctrinate unknowing acolytes with ideological beliefs about placing their trust in invisible friends? The answer is a failure to apply scepticism.

To help redress the balance, next time in sport when someone says that X was the cause of a particular outcome but provides no supportive, substantive, or falsifiable evidence to justify their claim, ask them why they assume their proposition to be true. Try to nudge them discreetly towards an assumption since assumptions grant footholds in conversations and affords everyone leeway to revisit and reframe the facts; but try not to hold on to an assumption since neither assumptions nor presumptions are reliable pathways to establishing truth. The only clear benefit of an assumption is that it stops just short of the worst option of all, which is the scourge of accruing an uncorroborated belief.

UFC fighter Benson Henderson's earlier alliance with divinity is a perfect example of uncorroborated belief. He transcended the boundaries of scientific reasoning by suggesting that a divine figure called Christ was actively engaged in his fighting endeavours in the UFC. Thankfully, despite his bold proclamation and through the wonder of live media, we watched the effects of *Superstitionism* unfold as he publicly 'bigged up' his personal Christ. Perhaps such bravado may have led to universal praise if he'd won, but instead it exposed him to harsh critique because he failed; yet he can't have it both ways. What also seemed odd was his reluctance to direct any blame towards Christ for going AWOL. Perhaps he was too preoccupied viewing defeat through Christ-tinted glasses.

Wearing superstition-tinted glasses is not merely a trait exclusive to Benson. Many athletes who agreed to be interviewed to assist in compiling this body of work were also ensnared by supernatural bias, while others outright refused to acknowledge superstitions as practical, beneficial, or real. Curiosity is essential to maintaining a safe distance between scepticism and delusional superstitious bliss. So why does athletes' intelligence fail them so miserably when it comes to emptying out the emotions they attach to the power of everyone else? The power of everyone else is the false sense of kudos they attach to the idea that everyone else seems more powerful than them. This sets the extremely dangerous precedent that they can only achieve at the behest of sources external to themselves.

The power of everyone else fails to acknowledge the incredible powers already incumbent inside each of us. Many athletes imply (as did Benson) that terrestrial outcomes are contingent on the mercy of divine decree. Hence, it's important to sleep with one eye open to stay alive and alert to the regularity with which human memory keeps reminding our minds to offer more credence to external sources and factors than we're prepared to acknowledge already exists as personal genius inside ourselves. Any fool can believe, but *knowing* can free us from stockpiling unnecessary clutter since once we come to know anything, what further need exists for belief?

Superstitions should operate with time restrictions; after all, we place time restrictions on pretty much everything else. Optimism is one thing, but to recklessly display faith with no prospect of knowing is not only ludicrous but dumb. The superstitious brain is being starved of spontaneity. So to counter this imbalance, let me introduce an aspirational construct called 'Drunken Consciousness'. The primary objective of drunken consciousness is to counter the alliance that exists in the minds of many athletes between wilfully accepting superstitious irregularities as normal behaviour, and becoming too comfortable reasserting and re-enacting unoriginal thoughts.

Drunken consciousness is the most accessible means of experiencing spontaneity first-hand. It does not mean being comatose in an alcohol-fuelled stupor, but being in a state of spontaneous awareness as seen through the sobriety of experiencing everything as though it were for the very first time. It sounds contradictory perhaps, the idea of being sober and drunk at the same time. Yet nothing feels more intoxicating than the elation of a eureka moment which is free from the trappings of all prior beliefs.

Try to recall the last time you felt exhilarated; chances are there wasn't a trace of superstition in sight. So how does drunken consciousness actually feel? Consider your first roller coaster experience and your thoughts being scrambled by an exploding kaleidoscope of adrenaline-fuelled life. Try to recall how every supercharged emotion left you feeling as though you may self-combust, as if your brain was a firework primed to explode. You felt captivated by every exaggerated sensation, and as the roller coaster continued to dip, dive, swerve, climb, and tumble, every previous point of personal reference which you held dear evaporated as the shock scattered your senses, leaving you in a daze.

The ride caused you to grimace but also to grin, wince, and laugh hysterically while your face contorted. Perhaps you can still recall the embarrassing squeals and screams of unconcealed delight as the terror filled, panic-stricken elation caused a plethora of contrasting emotions to erupt. You underwent the full range of undignified emotions, each littered with uncharacteristic behaviours such as staggering gingerly from the chaotic scene of the white-knuckle ride in no fit mental state to recall with any clarity which emotions took precedence throughout your adrenaline rush.

What was your predominant emotion? Was it fear, raw excitement, none of these, or a combination of each? You never felt more alive yet feared you may die, yet this is how spontaneity is supposed to feel. Even devout believers found themselves involuntarily blaspheming the superstition called God just to make the ride stop, while simultaneously hankering for it to continue. You felt riveted by terror as your hands gripped the safety bars in a conscious bid to cling on for dear life, while the blood drained from your fingers and rushed straight to your brain making you feel giddy, a little woozy, and so light-headed that you thought you might faint.

Did your eyes shed involuntary tears of laughter? Were your ears pierced by the prevailing screams of shock and delight from euphoric peers? Can you still recollect the eclectic mix of madness and mayhem, the likes of which you had never experienced before or perhaps since? Finally, the roller coaster ground to a shuddering halt, yet even then the abruptness of the halt left you dazed and confused as you were caught in a moment, disorientated and feeling inept. Yet that feeling you had as you stepped away from the ride was of being completely and utterly detached from every mundane distraction in an otherwise unspectacular life. That feeling was spontaneity. The initial shock left you inebriated on drunken consciousness, where just for that wonderfully disconcerting moment while your mind was in turmoil, you never felt more at one or at ease with yourself.

Your first roller coaster ride was a mind-altering memory which is unlikely to dissipate until you die, but when was the last time during sports preparations that your brain underwent a similar sense of disruption, whereby all your previous points of reference got blown away? When were you last shaken out of the comforting brain state of adhering to fixed superstitious beliefs or your thoughts so disrupted that when they finally regained clarity, there wasn't a superstition in sight? The roller coaster ride is a simple analogy of how it feels to experience spontaneity, but also an example to which many of us can relate.

Welcome to the world of drunken consciousness, where the best way to visualise the elation of 'thinking originally' is to recall the extra sensory experience of your first ever roller coaster ride. It's not easy to escape from the thoughts in your mind once they are entrenched, nor is it easy to ignore addictive traits as demonstrated by the spellbinding effect of the roller coaster ride. You couldn't wait to get off, but yearned to climb straight back on, back into the intoxicating madness as though it were a drug and you needed a fix. Stepping off left you starry-eyed in a dreamlike state as your seemingly hallucinogenic experience emptied out every previous point of reference and opened your mind to fresh perspective.

It is said that the human brain is unable to entertain two contrasting thoughts at exactly the same time. This suggests that it's impossible to fixate on a superstitious thought while simultaneously entertaining one that's original. If so, it's important that ambiguity is not allowed to outweigh spontaneity as highlighted by the thrill of the ride, which not only unlocked your senses but momentarily prevented your thoughts from reverting back to type. All it took was a diversion for you to embrace spontaneity with open arms.

The most practical catalyst for achieving original thought is recognising that superstition destroys spontaneity, whereas thinking originally and organically destroys superstition at source. The universe is as mysterious as it is curious, as is every hypothesis regarding what may or may not lie beyond. We are, however, just tourists and current custodians caught in this physical realm at this specific time. Considering such a backdrop of ambiguity, why weigh ourselves down with the mediocrity of actively performing superstitions in sport when we could be experiencing the meteoric effects of no longer dancing to the tune of bizarre and haphazard, delusionary beliefs.

"Yeah, I think we deserved a bit of luck. Of late it's not really gone our way."

- Jermain Defoe, AFC Bournemouth Player

At the time of this quote, Jermain was still a player for Tottenham FC and was referring to a rare piece of good fortune which he apparently believed was long overdue; but when did he become an authority on luck? As I pondered on how to structure this chapter, his throwaway comment kept niggling at the back of my brain, as did many similar random utterances until finally I felt compelled to openly question whether anyone can tell with any authority if they're deserving of luck?

"The luck came our way, so we'll take it. You have to earn it. You have to stay in the game. Lady Luck shone on us today with the goal that we got but I think we earned it."

- Chris Coleman, Football Manager

At the time of the quote, Chris Coleman was not only the National manager of Wales but had also acted as an authority on luck because he made an unsubstantiated claim that luck can be earned and is therefore a thing. As did Northern Ireland international footballer, Kyle Lafferty, when he said at the start of the 2016 European football championship in France that *"every team in the world is due some luck at times"*, yet when did Kyle become an authority on luck? From whom or from what did he acquire permission to stockpile bankable supernatural credits which he could seemingly access at will to make frequent withdrawals in the currency of fluke, fate, karma, and luck? Is every team in the world due a modicum of luck or is it merely a product of wishful thinking?

Does stockpiling luck operate in a similar vein to collecting Air Miles or retail loyalty points or, in Kyle's optimistic scenario, is luck freely redeemable from somewhere in the ether where it's held in cold-storage for a rainy day? How could he tell if his team were deserving of luck, and when did luck sign-up to Jermain's binding list of contractual demands? The greatest question in all of known history is what is the question I haven't yet asked? An example of which for superstitious athletes is questioning the extent to which partial truths impact the impartiality of their stated beliefs? Every superstition has a partial truth, but athletes nit-pick the bits that back their assertions while ignoring the bits with potential to disprove their beliefs.

Consider one athlete bragging to another, *"I've worn this lucky rabbit's foot in my last three races and won all three."* At face value the foot carried no physical validity at all, and yet the idea of winning three races in a row with the foot in tow often seems compelling to non-sceptical minds. Alternatively, consider the dichotomy created between 'absolute truth' and 'partial truth' by the superstition known as Universal Law of Attraction. It isn't hard to *partially* recognise that if we actively pursue positivity in sport, then positivity is increasingly likely to manifest as our truth since we're already predisposed to seeing positivity in every endeavour we attempt. The same applies to actively pursuing negativity, only this time negativity is more likely to manifest as our *partial* truth.

So far the evidence points to the Law of Attraction as being nothing more than an optional name for life's already purely natural process which works roughly at the rate of probability and chance. Motivational speakers at business seminars rarely mention the rate of suicide among business colleagues whose companies collapsed despite imploring the ether to send something positive their way. Or what of family members who wished, hoped, and even prayed with all their might that cancer would disappear from a loved one, but it didn't and eventually they died. Or what of the athlete who actively channelled thoughts of positivity before a race but lost anyway.

The Law of Attraction raises two important questions. First, what is the Universal Law of Attraction? Second, is it a supernatural phenomenon, whereby whatever energy we actively project attracts a similar energy back towards us, or is it yet another superstitious partial truth based solely on confirmation-bias whereby we see only that which we choose to see? Superstitions thrive on ambiguity, and superstitious athletes rarely care if the things they believe are actually true.

Consider the prospect of catching a lump of burning coal in your hand. You would juggle it gingerly in obvious panic and drop it to the ground with immediate haste to avoid being blistered and horribly scarred before finally breathing a sigh of relief. The upshot is simple, you couldn't let go of the coal quick enough, but why does the same tenet rarely apply to the speed by which athletes let go of delusional beliefs? Why, once a superstition has fallen into their lap, do they try to juggle its all-encompassing effect rather than simply drop the compulsion, thereby decreasing any potential of becoming dependent or mentally scarred? Why does it seem easier to let go of a lump of burning coal which they can actually smell, touch, and see, than to drop an imaginary mental construct?

Letting go of a belief isn't easy, while finding practical alternatives to supplement that belief can prove twice as difficult. This was indicated by the following concerns reported in a tabloid article entitled *United call in Zen master to help fix stars' heads*. It told of former Manchester United manager Louis van Gaal's attempt to play mind-games with his talented array of stars by inviting a Zen master to give an address at United's Carrington training HQ. Van Gaal seemingly believed that Thai-boxing Guru, Grandmaster Sken, could improve his players' patchy form and that the principles of calmness, respect, discipline, and Dhamma (the knowledge of Lord Buddha and his wisdom) were just the tonic his players required.

Van Gaal's squad learned meditation skills to help channel their focus. He believed this could lead to fewer injuries, greater concentration, and better overall results. According to the article, Master Sken's main principle states that *"True strength lies in gentleness, and mastery of the world begins with mastery of self."* A source in *The Express* also added, *"It's an unusual decision to focus on the emotional angle of training rather than the physical."* United, however, had faced several confidence sapping blows and Van Gaal appeared willing to grasp at anything with

248

the potential to improve their overall game. The article also reported how Van Gaal believed that having a clear head in football is just as important as being physically fit.

Van Gaal sought an innovative approach to solving a psychological problem, yet two things are apparent from this intervention. First, gurus exist in multiple forms and various guises. Next, the influence of gurus can be easily categorised into one of two of the most prominent effects of light: either the glow that illuminates enlightened awareness or the glare that obscures scepticism and curiosity. We just need to figure out on which side of the coin our external gurus consistently land. So let's begin by defining what it means to be enlightened in competitive sport.

Sport is as much about managing fear as it is about feeling elated, yet many superstitious athletes are losing the impetus to lighten up. Who among us hasn't, at some time or another, sought to rid ourselves of a tiresome and draining emotion in a conscious bid to lighten up, only to find that we could not? The most practical pathway towards enlightenment in sport is to follow a process of transformational change. This is perhaps best described by the following saying, *'Take your quest seriously but yourself lightly'*. Activating a mental state of 'let-go-ness' is key to a light-hearted frame of mind.

As author of these written considerations, I am often accosted for my opinion on whether it's wrong to lambaste superstitious beliefs given so many athletes heavily rely on them to guide them through personal anxiety, trauma, fear, and self-doubt. My response is consistent, relative, and concise. Athletes often confuse sincere beliefs as justification for subsequent actions. Yet superstitious belief is a mental lottery of karma, faith, wishful thinking, coincidence, fluke, and luck.

Consider the impact of the following quote, *"If you always do what you've always done, then you'll always get what you've always got."* Now let's invoke the superstition called karma as a learning prop to explain it in more detail. There is a common saying often linked with karma which states, *"what goes around comes around"*. Yet the only reason karma supposedly finds us is because we're always stood in the same bloody place. So in order to disrupt our karma, we must actively instigate transformative change. Similarly, we cannot transition beyond superstitious belief unless or until we evoke curiosity and spontaneity, otherwise we'll continue to get what we've always got because our brains are still doing what they've always done.

Here is a delightful quote from yet another unknown author who cordially suggests, *"We learn something from everyone who passes through our lives. Some lessons are painful, some are painless; but all are priceless."* Most priceless perhaps is learning an invaluable lesson from the following quote by poet James Russell Lowell, *"The idol is the measure of the worshipper."* In hindsight there is substance to his words since idolising any form of superstition means athletes get the idol they damn well deserve.

"I water you, you water me; we grow together."

- Brandon Nembhard, Writer

Theatre of Reversed Effort

"I got lost in thought. It was unfamiliar territory."

- Unknown

During a Sky Sports News report, former AFC Bournemouth captain Tommy Elphick revealed a string of bizarre pre-match rituals which he saw fit to incorporate into his game. An example of which was headbutting the woodwork! He sheepishly explained:

"I have to headbutt the post [and] tap it a certain amount of times with both boots and say a few little words to myself to get myself ready. It brings me comfort. A sports psychologist noticed what I was doing and said he thought it was a good time [for me] to have a chat with myself. I'm very superstitious and I touch wood before I leave the house in the morning. I also have a certain amount of potatoes and broccoli for dinner."

Tommy wasn't alone with outrageous superstitious disclosures. Consider the boldness of the following declaration by Celtic FC defender, Efe Ambrose, while recounting the role of divine intervention in a 2015 Scottish League Cup triumph over Dundee United FC. Efe praised God as having played a key role in helping to lift his first ever Scottish League Cup trophy. *"I feel great and delighted to win the League Cup. I thank God for the trophy. I give all glory to God and dedicate it to him because he made it possible."*

Efe's incredible (if somewhat delusional) claims didn't end there. The *Daily Record* reported how Efe's transfer to Celtic FC was a result of God's work, following the unravelling of a potential deal with Manchester City FC. He seemed happy to recount how his hopes had been scuppered because his parent club had refused to let him stay any longer in Manchester on trial. *"It was disappointing but things have now worked out well for me. God chooses what he wants and it was to be Celtic. That is why I am here."*

Efe's claims of supernatural intervention didn't end there. He next forecast to *MTN Football* in 2015 that God would help Nigeria beat hosts Congo in an upcoming must-win AFCON tie. He said the Super Eagles (Nigeria) were ready for battle in Pointe-Noire and believed God would favour his team with a win. *"We are fully prepared for the game against Congo. I am calling on God and I believe he will bless us [and] crown our efforts with victory against Congo by his grace."*

There is little disputing Efe's optimism. Sadly it isn't matched by the disappointing role played by his god, whereby just five months later the *Daily Record* reported Efe as having been ejected from the Nigeria squad for the upcoming two games, despite the squad being enlarged to include 27 players. It appeared scant reward for his unflinching faith, but it does raise the question as to why his god didn't choose to intervene on his behalf?

Despite God's supposed grace, Congo beat Nigeria 3-2, and interestingly, Efe then claimed in a report by *SL10.ng* that too many errors cost them the game; but hang on a moment, as here comes Efe's punchline right on cue: *"I won't point accusing fingers at anyone because my philosophy is we win as a team and we lose as a team. We are sorry. We as players have resolved to make sure it doesn't happen again and by the grace of God it won't. So I won't say we're going there [to play South Africa] for a win or a draw, but by the grace of God we won't be disappointed at the end."*

Oh dear God, please make it stop! Oops, Freudian slip. Let's take a quick breather and dust ourselves down to consider Efe's stated philosophy following defeat. He said they win as a team and lose as a team. Earlier, however, his stated philosophy was fixated on winning by the grace of God. He even disclosed that he would call upon God to crown his team's efforts with a victory. Given the unsatisfactory nature of the result, and despite refusing to point an accusing finger of blame in the direction of specific players, he did admit to the team holding talks among themselves. So a blame game did appear to take place behind closed doors.

Oddly, however, at no point did Efe suggest that part of the blame lay with God. This is not only irrational but downright weird since if God's not to blame for experiencing defeat, then how can God be praised when he wins? Why involve God at all? Efe's failure to rebuke God to any degree for Nigeria's shock defeat means he loses credibility when praising the same god because Celtic contested a cup and won.

According to his philosophy, Efe *should* point an accusing finger at God since they lost as a team and God was part of that team. So the finger of blame should be pointed at God, but not from a position of seclusion behind closed doors, instead he should be equally willing to take God to task in full public view; he can't have it both ways. Efe was sincere in his belief that God interacts through the medium of sport. Sincerity, however, is no guarantee against being dead wrong.

Where was Tommy Elphick's proof of a supernatural convergence after headbutting the goalposts, routinely touching wood, or eating a precise amount of vegetables before every match? Where is the proof that his eccentric behaviours are in any way advantageous to how he performs? What are the odds of Tommy being able to mentally transition beyond his superstitious beliefs, or are superstitions transferrable? Did he leave them behind at Bournemouth when he transferred to Everton FC, or did Everton get a bargain by acquiring two for the price of one, whereby Tommy and his superstitions were part-and-parcel of the same package deal?

If sport is a drug as is often suggested, does the self-professed theist Efe Ambrose qualify as an addict of hallucinogenic faith? Was he experiencing mood-altering highs of self-delusion as a result of opting for superstition as his drug of choice? Why did he seek supernatural solutions to earthly predicaments and, despite his gushing sentiments, what on earth does a god have to gain by orchestrating the outcome of a Scottish Cup match? Was his god unaware that Barcelona or Real Madrid may have been in action that very day? Hey, just saying!

Given the extent of global pestilence, people displacement, war, famine, our rapidly expanding universe, and the increasing threat of solar flares escaping from the Sun, one might reasonably assume that Efe's God had more important things to occupy its mind. So where is his evidence that a god was the reason Celtic won the 2015 Scottish league cup? Why did he display no recollection of alternative facts such as Celtic's resources being vastly superior to Dundee United's, or Celtic entering the match with superior league form and having more winning experience throughout the squad? Even the bookies declared Celtic as overwhelming favourites to win before a ball was ever kicked.

Considering the overwhelming statistics in Celtic's favour, all they did was fulfil their vastly superior potential since anything less would have been considered a shock. Despite Efe's sentimentality clouding his judgement, if a divine occurrence were to take place, no doubt supernatural order would soon be restored by the 'blue half' of Glasgow (a polarising term) by fans of Rangers FC, who could never accept that a god would display the affront and audacity of wearing the green and white hoops of Celtic FC.

Superstitionism *is* a religion, with sometimes exhilarating but often debilitating effects. As such, questions arise as to why sports superstitions such as wearing lucky socks or headbutting the goalposts are derided by mockery and scorn or still viewed as a topic for ridicule or as a whimsical myriad of hocus-pocus? Why do athletes who view generic superstitious practice as an exact science still attract ridicule, while others who maintain a theistic approach (the belief that a god is guiding their sport) attract little or no ridicule at all, despite the God hypothesis providing no falsifiable basis for asserting faith as a fact.

Superstitions ensure that the line between sanity and impending insanity is increasingly blurred, which is why it's important to value curiosity. We should tip our hats to curiosity since it's not only instinctively empowering but the perfect deterrent against superstitions masquerading as practical sporting norms. Curiosity challenges the idea that sincerity acts as a moral compass or as the primary benchmark for verifying faith. Just because we're sincere doesn't make our faith any more valid or real, so it's important to detach from the scourge of sincerity if spontaneity is to have any chance of evolving at all.

Consider the alternatives. What if we *sincerely* believe that we're not good enough or *sincerely* believe that superstitious omens suggest we're going to fail? What if Kayla the North American Bald Eagle which is mascot of English football club Crystal Palace FC was unable to fulfil its customary role? What if, through a dereliction of duty, Kayla failed to fly from one end of the football stadium to the other as is customary prior to every home game? If Palace were to lose, how long would it take before one of the causes attributed to defeat was placed at the talons of the hapless bird for breaking with tradition and seemingly affecting the luck of the team?

Fortunately, superstitious beliefs cannot penetrate scepticism and curiosity. Consider these eloquent words by author Terry Pratchett, *"It is often said that before you die, life passes before your eyes. It is in fact true. It's called living."* Given the simplicity of his surmise, it's worth asking why nature issues no similarly simplistic universal directives which compel us to subscribe to superstitious beliefs? Or, why, in the absence of such directives, do athletes voluntarily replace spontaneity with superstitious ideology? Consider as an example the following accolades attributed by ecstatic UFC fighter, Rafael dos Anjos, after relieving Anthony 'Showtime' Pettis of his World Lightweight crown in Dallas, Texas in March 2015:

"Jesus Christ, he can do all things. Man, it's such an amazing blessing when you came into a fight and [already] knew you were going to win because, as I said, Jesus, he's an amazing God and I knew I was gonna win before this fight happened. I knew that. He told me that."

What an extraordinary claim. Yet imagine if a stranger stopped you in the street to convince you they were forever hearing voices. Would you stop and listen with curious empathy? Would you embrace their words with a strange fascination or take to your heels and hightail it away from the scene as quickly as possible? Might you even suppose they were using drugs, schizophrenic, or clinically insane? Or what if there really is a fine line between madness and genius? What drives athletes to correlate the cause of success with the types of schizophrenic tendencies necessary to believe that supernatural voices are talking to them, guiding them, and meddling in terrestrial sport?

Where is the evidence that Rafael's God is a fan of mixed martial arts, or mentor to a stable of terrestrial MMA warriors, or partial to a cheeky flutter on the side? How did gifting Rafael the world lightweight title benefit God? Did God seek to avail of the fringe benefits of being credited with engineering the win, and was Rafael taking his god's name in vain by linking God to the UFC brand? Was he being sincere but sadly deluded? Or what of God's own dilemma if it was discovered that 'Showtime' Pettis was also a practising Christian? Might God then be faced with the unenviable task of choosing a favourite from two equally committed Christians?

Which one might God favour and why? Might Rafael's god end up drawing straws or tossing a coin in the interest of fairness? How does Rafael explain (since it was never mentioned) the seven professional losses on his fight record prior to that fight? Was he still in cahoots with God before those defeats or was God guilty of seven divine Freudian slips? His unswerving faith in an intermediary called God can justifiably be diagnosed as akin to acute schizophrenia due to the extent of the two-way conversation which he would have us believe had taken place between him and his invisible friend.

According to the superstition called Law of Attraction, there may be truth to his claim since thoughts seemingly have the power to manifest as physical things. Perhaps this indicates a placebo effect, whereby Rafael was so convinced that losing wasn't an option that his fervent belief in a construct called God proved partially responsible for incentivising his obsession to win. Where is the evidence to suggest that anything other than positive thinking bolstered his cause? The Law of Attraction is mere hypotheses and equally as invalid as every other superstition which works at roughly the rate of chance.

Rafael didn't execute any actions inside the octagon which he couldn't have done every bit as competently without the placebo effect of interacting with voices speaking directly to him from a supernatural realm. Despite appearing to work in his favour on this occasion, his sincerity was misplaced as, irrespective of his post-fight claim of *"I knew I was gonna win before this fight happened"*, the spectre of losing is always an option in competitive sport. The fate of all athletes is dependent on probability and chance. UFC Fighter, Rafael dos Anjos, chose a public platform to announce that God is a proponent of combative sport. Yet despite his sincerity, God has no explanatory power in the natural world.

Superstitious belief is a perfect example of human gullibility in terms of accepting faith as a reliable pathway to truth. Another form of superstitious gullibility is the indecipherable nature of luck. No athlete has proven, beyond all shadow of doubt, how luck intervening in sport would make the sport look any different to how it does now. The universal language of superstition is guilt, hence the impact of guilt throughout sport is palpable. We can easily measure the extent of the impact by simply asking the following questions: do athletes tend to feel less ecstatic at having won than perhaps they should, or experience more guilt at the idea of losing than is practical, necessary, or conducive to a healthy state of mind?

How long does the sense of elation last following a win when compared to the gut-wrenching sense of frustration and guilt which can linger for ages following a loss? Which feeling tends to stick with athletes longest? Is it the elation of winning or guilt of losing? Is the 'signature sin' of aspiring athletes the illusion of guilt of having lost, and why is losing accompanied by 'signature shame'? Nothing causes an athlete to consign their emotions into the hands of superstition, magic, or luck like trying to placate feelings of guilt and shame fuelled by human ego, despite the concept of ego teetering on the cusp of mere conceptual superstitious belief.

What makes otherwise rational and reasoning athletes swap spontaneity and curiosity for the mind-numbing lottery of lucky charms, omens, rituals, and spells? Why do others believe they can interact with supernatural agents which aren't only divine but seemingly cannot keep their noses out of sport? Consider the mind-altering highs which many athletes experience at the idea of having access to oracles in the sky who converse with them on sporting matters. Superstitionism *is* a religion. It is only our chosen brand of faith which sets us apart from the faith of our peers.

Superstitions are susceptible to cross-fertilisation. One example is Rafael dos Anjos' utilisation of theism, whereby he portrays God as a conscientious sports fanatic whom he can trigger at will. Superstitious guilt has transcended religion to permeate sport. Why not test this for yourself? Try to accurately pinpoint the very first time you came to accept that losing at sport felt comparable to committing a sin (sin is also superstition) as if you did something wrong or bad or should beat yourself up mentally for failing to succeed. Try to recall the first time you belittled your actions using demeaning self-talk to justify feeling shame for how poorly you performed.

What caused you to form such debilitating conclusions or arrive at assumptions so wide of the mark? Why do athletes accept that performing poorly, losing, or making mistakes carries a prerequisite for self-imposed guilt resulting in shame? Aspects of guilt and subsequent shame appear evident in the psychology of many athletes who seek to compete, and both factors remain an open wound for many, even to this very day. Modern consensus throughout sport suggests that terms such as 'punishment' are outdated and no longer practical in sport, yet punishment is the only appropriate term to adequately describe how athletes intrinsically beat themselves up for having lost.

What practical benefits can be gained from engaging in demeaning self-talk, and why embrace superstition as a pathway to perfection when, due to the delusion of sin, we are already hoodwinked into believing that every human on earth is fundamentally flawed from birth? This is a primary cause of human ego's ongoing search to experience relief using supernatural reasoning to justify the bizarre behaviours of sports elite.

Consider in contrast the actions of former England international player and football pundit Kieron Dyer who, when asked on *Sky Sports Soccer AM* if he was prone to superstitious beliefs, replied, *"I always put my left arm in my shirt before my right. Plus I put my left leg first into my shorts, [then] left sock on first, left boot [first], and I always step onto the pitch left foot first"*. It all sounded routine and unspectacular, yet that all changed the moment he acknowledged *deliberately* stepping onto the pitch left foot first as that action was clearly premeditated; but the search to uncover superstitious quirks among sports elite didn't end there.

On the very same episode of *Soccer AM* was a humorous snapshot of former Arsenal FC striker Joel Campbell's odd trait of hopping on to the pitch on one leg prior to each match. Also sat beside Kieron was Leicester City FC goalkeeper, Kasper Schmeichel, who said, *"I tap the crossbar twice."* Yet when asked if this action helped to improve any aspect of his game he rather sheepishly replied *"no."* At which point he was asked, *"Then why bother to do it at all?"* to which he replied, *"I dunno, it must be a superstition."* Why did Kasper and Kieron persevere with superstitious inclinations with no apparent rational?

Superstitions are only as transparent as the extent to which we are willing to prise open our beliefs and peek inside. The mechanics of memory is a non-stop phenomenon which remains neurologically active 24-hours a day. This means, prior to every human experience, we first engage with our brains to initiate memory of how to act and behave according to a premeditated list of demands. The generic mantra for all superstitions is *"to hell with the future, let's get on with the past."* Superstitions require a process of followership from competitors who are stuck in self-fulfilling cycles of faith which have religiously followed them from their past.

To verify this assertion, consider how often athletes feel susceptible to suffering losing streaks at specific venues, grounds, stadiums, or tracks. Or feel predestined to win prior to participating at specific events because their memory works overtime to remind them of their previous successful track record. Once an athlete's memory becomes exclusively tied to losing at specific venues or getting beat by specific opponents, it relives every previous experience of snatching defeat from the jaws of victory because, at an unconscious level (based on past experiences), it once again visualises it being so.

"It seemed like the stars were aligned. The guys in front started making triple and double bogeys, and it just felt like it was meant to be."

- Rory McIlroy, Golfer

Once an athlete is convinced that the planets have aligned to ensure they lose, their poor streak often continues as a result of first visualising the loss taking place in their mind. This was evident in an earlier scenario where elite golfer Rory McIlroy was unable to replicate the magnificent form he displayed on a Wednesday and Thursday when it came to a Friday. In response, the media coined the phrase 'Freaky Fridays' and, hey presto, a new superstition was born. Who says sport isn't psychological, as, by his own stark admission, Rory sought to defer to positive self-talk to reframe his thoughts with fresh impetus and inspire him to perform more consistently, irrespective of the day of the week.

Rory's stunning form on Wednesdays and Thursdays proved that neither talent nor form was holding him back. Instead, the only thing freaky about Fridays was allowing superstition to grow its own set of horns. Athletes often strive to emulate their sporting heroes. Every fighter, Gaelic hurler, triathlete, and cyclist carries a hero in the back of their mind and imitates their likeness and persona to become a little bit more like them. Mimicking our peers can be relatively easy. What is often more difficult is recognising how best to stay true to ourselves since human thoughts can be avid imitators. Imitation, however, flies in the face of nature's distinct organic laws.

The universe only seems to create originals. We can search the whole planet but never discover another like us; feel free to give it a whirl. Yet if we gazed into the eyes of our sporting contemporaries, I mean really deeply into their eyes, we'd discover extraordinary arrangements of intricate patterns which are encircled by rugged landscapes which eerily resemble the ghostly surface and craters of Martian terrain. These compositions are uniquely compelling, and one could almost feel justified by implying that our eyes contain blueprints of where human origins began.

It is of course a mere superstitious hypothesis, yet mystery and intrigue surround these astonishing configurations revealed by Armenian photographer and physics teacher, Suren Manvelyan. In an incredible set of photographs, he evokes curiosity by inviting us to ponder whether the eyes are truly windows to our soul (the concept of a soul is also superstition). So why not take a peek into what may be the origins of our past since the best form of awareness is experiential learning, i.e. experiencing things for ourselves. So have a browse through the photos and decide for yourself. Check out *Daily Mail* Article 1342468 entitled *Eyes resemble craters on Mars*.

If an image of an iris carries the potential to teach us anything, it's that behind every unique and spectacular composition of the human eye, and behind every strange and unique configuration of the human ear (no two sets of ears are identical), combined with the exclusivity of each set of fingerprints upon each unique set of hands we invariably shake, is seemingly confirmation that nature doesn't do replicas. This similarly applies to the intricate detail on every snowflake as it bobs and weaves its way down from the sky, and to every subtle nuance which distinguishes near identical breeds of mammals, birds, and fish.

The same sequence of non-replication applies to every leaf that falls from the branch of a tree, whereby every leaf and branch is totally unique; and that's exactly the point. It's that no snowflake, leaf, ear, eye, or set of fingerprints are identical since nature doesn't do replicas. Instead, given what currently can be observed, all that nature produces is utterly unique and physically (not supernaturally) immersed in its own holy trinity of birth, death, and replenishment on a continuous loop.

Perhaps the greatest question ever asked is what is the next question that needs to be asked? If nature's continuum of self-replenishing cycles has successfully sustained life on our planet for billions of years, then why in the 21st century are athletes so reluctant to embrace nature's tried and tested template? Why remain stubbornly transfixed in repetitive cycles of superstitious beliefs which have a demonstrable success ratio of zero? How can it be practical to hope, pray, and believe with as much faith and gusto as they can muster that their superstitions will work in the present and future, when no evidence exists that they worked in the past?

Why not simply allow superstitions to die? If such a template is good enough for nature, then why can't it work favourably for them or us? Why waste time and energy seeking to emulate sporting heroes by measuring *our* personal achievements against *theirs*? Consider the impact on an athlete's psychology of continuously seeking to replicate a process without any potential for the process to evolve.

> *"I wear red on Sundays because my mom thinks that's my power colour, and you know you should always listen to your mom."*
>
> - Tiger Woods, Golfer

Imitating our heroes is commonplace, or at least imitating the parts we can openly see, but how much do we know of our heroes' psychology or of what truly goes on in their mind? What inspires them to achieve the definitive margins which allow them to sustain high levels of success? Let's backtrack and revisit the tongue-in-cheek nature of Tiger's humorous quote which, on the surface appears innocuous. Yet, many golfing enthusiasts who were fortunate enough to witness his stratospheric rise to sporting prominence have debated his character trait of only wearing tee shirts or sweaters of bold, dynamic red during every final round at tournament events.

Many questions were asked as to whether Tiger's ritual of wearing bold, imposing red was due to being superstitious or instead if he had actively sought to impose a psychological edge on his rivals as part of his single-minded approach to engineering a win? Perhaps he just liked the colour red, or perhaps his methodology is best explained in the *Journal of Experimental Psychology,* where scientists from the University of Rochester suggested that the colour red possesses subliminal powers to manipulate subconscious thoughts into experiencing negative or positive states.

Did Tiger identify red as the 'secret sauce' to initiate game changing advantages over hapless opponents who had no choice but to succumb to the subliminal spectacle of being ingeniously exploited by red? Was bold red a practical innovation or did Tiger believe that forewarned is forearmed? The real crux of his genius, apart from his talent, lay in staying one step ahead of his peers. So was he playing mind games with his adversaries and if so, what possible insider information might he alone have been privy to that his rivals were not?

Was Tiger aware of the findings at Rochester University demonstrating that the cognitive impact of red's negative effects does not apply to those *wearing* red but only to those *seeing* red. This suggests a high probability that on many occasions he'd already won the day in terms of psychology in advance of a ball having ever been struck from an opening tee! This of course begs the question as to why his competitors did not follow suit and nullify his advantage by wearing matching red sweaters of their own?

Why was there such a lack of awareness amid golf's elite regarding the science of seeing red? Did professional pride stand in the way of acknowledging sports psychology as an integral component of competitive golf? Was it simply a matter of Tiger's individual branding? What gave him the edge in this psychological tussle? Was he aware of the findings of scientists at Durham University who theorised that teams and competitors wearing predominantly red coloured jerseys won more often than those wearing white or blue? They also theorised that the colour red signified intimidation and showed a direct correlation with the types of aggression and dominance frequently experienced in the animal world.

The scientists at Durham also suggested that the effects of red may arise from a deep-seated evolutionary response already hidden in the human subconscious for the sole purpose of placing adversaries onto the back foot. This methodology formed an integral component of Tiger's unprecedented success, whereby he appeared to have mastered a practical means to utilise the subliminal powers of red. Of course there were times too numerous to mention when red's effect didn't work and he was soundly beaten. Yet he persisted with his philosophy and appeared unwilling or simply unable to abort his allegiance to the power of red, believing it could work in his favour again the way it seemingly did in the past.

"Competitive golf is played on a five-and-a-half-inch course... the space between your ears."

- Bobby Jones, Golfer

During the latter stages of Tiger's career, he adopted a more pragmatic approach to competing due to an increasing susceptibility to persistent injury and poor form. These were prime factors in erasing the air of infallibility surrounding his persona up to that point, until bit-by-bit the fear of red, which he had previously instilled in the minds of his opponents, started to dissipate and lose its watertight edge. His downward spiral was further exacerbated by much publicised reports of infidelity, the distraction of which proved a contributing factor in destroying his aura of invincibility in the eyes of his peers.

The ensuing intrusiveness into his private life meant neither his reputation nor previous red aura remained intact. Hence, for the first time since he broke onto the professional golfing scene, Tiger's rivals saw beyond the subliminal effects of red, and with their psychology no longer impaired, they were finally confronted with the vulnerabilities of the man behind the myth. Suddenly, the 14-time major winner's fiercest rivals became 'blind' to imposing subliminal red and were no longer consigned to competing on the back foot. Instead, the chink in his previously impenetrable armour infused them with renewed optimism and hope.

A shift had occurred in his rivals' paradigm of thinking as they mentally downgraded his overwhelming aura of godlike status into something more akin to a mortal man; but how might *we* have coped with red's curious phenomenon? Would we have been any less prone to red's subliminal effect? Apart from his obvious golfing talents, Tiger's greatest stranglehold over other competitors on the final day of events was psychological, yet he had broken no rules of engagement. Instead we can learn a great deal from his psychological dominance, beginning with his pioneering approach to competitive golf.

Tiger seemed to manipulate the subliminal effect of red in a pragmatic manner and used it to stay ahead of his peers. Questions therefore arise as to *our* vulnerability to the subliminal effect of manipulative gurus playing us? How might our brains have reacted to a competitor wearing bold, imposing red if we were unaware of its potential effects? Would we be the players or the ones being played?

Tiger's most rewarding aspect of wearing red was the power to exploit the weaknesses in others without ever having to suffer seeing red himself. It all sounds reminiscent of a World War II tank commander who, while seated safely within the tank's armour, takes aim at approaching foot soldiers armed only with rifles, pea-shooters, and bayonets. In other words, Tiger's willingness to embrace sports psychology meant his opponents were engaged in an unfair fight.

Tiger Woods is the golfer of his generation, a genius of unparalleled talent, and perhaps the greatest golfer the world has ever seen. Yet, when his illusion of infallibility was destroyed due to much publicised infidelity, his affiliation with red was no longer enough to sustain the facade. Prior to his demise, many opponents were not even aware they had been suffering, just as superstitious beliefs can appear as such a comfortable fit to many athletes that it becomes easy to overlook the fact that they are merely illusions which they cannot hear, smell, taste, touch, or see.

The human psychology is equipped with enough nous and faculty to openly question the meaning of life. We reach out to the stars in abstract wonder of what lies beyond as we try to make sense of our place in the universe. We also practice bizarre sporting rituals which supposedly reach out to the cosmos on our behalf to attract good fortune so that we may experience applause, since applause is integral to an athlete's pathology. First though, what is meant by pathology in this specific context?

To explain with more clarity, consider this extract from a thought-provoking article in *The Spectator,* written by Matthew Parris and entitled *The Pathology of the Politician*. There are clear comparisons in the article which suggest that the pathology of politicians is akin to the pathology of elite protagonists of competitive sport. Simply swap the role of each protagonist and then watch as the pathology of politicians merges with the pathology of sporting elite.

"Politicians are not normal people, they are weird. It isn't politics that has made them weird: it's their weirdness that has impelled them into politics. Whenever another high-profile minister teeters or falls, the mistake everyone makes is to ask, what is it about the nature of their job [or] the environment they work in and the hours they work that has made them take such stupid risks. This is the wrong question, we should ask a different one. What is it about these men and women that has attracted them to politics?

On the whole, by and large and with any number of exceptions, individuals drawn to elective office are driven men and women. Dreamers, attention seekers, and risk takers [but] with a dollop of narcissism in their natures. Why wouldn't they be, they've self-selected? Elective office feeds your vanity and starves your self-respect. What then are the compensations for that, for those who choose this life [to] make it all worthwhile?

First [it's] a craving for applause, for being a somebody, for being looked up to.

Second [it's] a completely and unrealistic belief in your own good luck. You know the odds, you can calculate the statistical likelihoods, but for you it's going to be different. Someone up there is watching over you. You really do half-believe this. Even when all seems lost you tell yourself that maybe a miracle will happen. Thirdly, and this is truly weird, an awfully thick skin. All of this leads to frequent pain, frequent euphoria, a hopelessly optimistic estimation of your chances and an obsessive-compulsive drive to keep asking for more until something big and external to yourself finally tells you, like any addict, [that] you're half yearning for this to happen."

In other words, politicians, just like superstitious athletes, share an uncanny dependence on narcissism and luck. Matthew implied that it's not politics making them weird but instead it's their weirdness which has compelled them to remain in politics. So what does this say about athletes who believe that gods are real and have nothing better to do than to dabble in terrestrial sport, or believe that moonwalking onto a pitch to influence results isn't weird? Where does logic and reasoning fit into such a muddled sense of psychology given that, every time an athlete experiences 'dis-ease' (feeling ill-at-ease), there is an obvious threat to their wellbeing.

Every sports performance is neurological since the brain acts as the catalyst to how we think and feel we ought to perform, irrespective of whether we can or can't. Consider March 2015 and how, prior to a 1–1 draw between Italy and England, Italian goalkeeping legend Gianluigi Buffon was earning his 147th cap at 37 years of age. This was an incredible feat by any standard and not all athletes' standards are as high as Buffon's. Yet during an interesting turn of events, he chose to publicly question the impact of pressures being heaped on the already creaking psychologies of a young, inexperienced, and transitioning squad.

Buffon found himself embroiled in a very public changing of the old and trusted guard of Italian footballing elite. Such was the toxic nature of the exchange that former international coach Antonio Conte was forced to run a gauntlet of displeasure from irate fans for displaying the audacity to initiate change. In response he fired back with his own media salvo by imploring fans to *"open their eyes and grasp the reality of the situation [as] a number of players are taking their first tentative steps into international football. Please don't criticise them because it's not good for the players, it's not good for my job, and it's not good for Italian football."*

Buffon echoed his sentiments by stating, *"The last few days certainly haven't been*

264

boring but it's better to release this negative energy than to bottle it up as that leads to defeats." His assessment was more than just an interesting turn of phrase. His referral to bottling up negative energy highlighted the need to deploy mental energy in a creative and positive way to improve the wellbeing of all parties involved. Buffon drew attention to the negative effects of being overly critical, knowing this could lead to a downturn in self-expression followed by an upturn in harmful 'dis-ease'.

Once an athlete succumbs to sporting anxiety, their pathology is often the first thing to suffer, and as such, they will grasp at any alternative which helps them to experience relief. When the going gets tough, it's habitually easier to resort to the things they already know best. Often this means regressing into the comfortable rhythms and patterns of superstitious beliefs. Superstitions fill the vacuum that exists between what is conceivable, highly improbable, seemingly preposterous, and downright bizarre. Spontaneity on the other hand lends to fluidity and causes superstitious thoughts to flow through us unabated without damaging us on the inside.

Consider the thoughts of Irish boxer John Joe Nevin in an RTE documentary entitled *Reality Bites,* during which he expressed a wonderfully poignant outpouring of emotion and valuable insight into his 'go-to' superstitious beliefs which he habitually triggers to act as a safety net before entering the ring. The documentary highlighted his incredible appetite to overcome a horrifically violent physical attack which threatened to derail his highly promising career.

Following the attack, the devastating diagnosis was that the former Olympic silver medallist from London 2012 had sustained two broken legs. Incredibly, the speed by which John Joe returned to the boxing ring proved beyond all doubt that he was a fighter in every sense of the word. His explanation, however, caught many off guard as he presented a unique perspective on rehabilitation which included superstition as a contributing cause. He then gave the example of *"lighting a few candles, saying a few prayers, and visiting church every week."*

John Joe's post rehabilitation appraisal lends weight to the hypothesis that the need to alleviate doubt while experiencing mental respite and a sense of relief, is integral to sustaining superstitious belief. Yet perhaps the strangest dichotomy of all was hearing him talk about seeking solace in superstitious rituals, which themselves were ensconced in a superstition called God. It may also prove useful from this point onwards to subject every superstitious belief to the words of mentalist extraordinaire, Derren Brown, who stated at a sold-out show at The

Grand Opera House in Belfast that *"it's not enough to say that something is real simply because it cannot be disproved."*

Let's compare Derren's sentiment with the superstitious revelations of boxer John Joe Nevin during the *Reality Bites* documentary:

"Every time I box, I always go out and visit my grandparents' [graves]. I dunno, maybe it's a little superstitious thing that I have so that they'll look over me while I'm in the ring. If I don't go out, I feel like I'm missing something in the ring, but I feel when I go out there [to the graves] I'm safe then. Or I get the mother to ring up a special little priest that I believe in. Every time I do that, if I can't make it out to the graves or if I'm boxing abroad, I'll always get the father to go out and visit the graves or the mother will definitely ring that priest again for me. You know it's nice to believe in things like that and it drives me on and gives me strength I suppose."

John Joe engineered feelings of warm, cosy optimism by mixing emotion with large dollops of sincerity and sentimentality. Sincerity, however, is no guarantee against being dead wrong and Derren's earlier rationale challenges John Joe's belief in supernatural interventions by agents which he could not demonstrably hear, taste, touch, smell, or see. Despite sensing his grandparents, John Joe's superstitions typify the mindset of many athletes who carry sentimentality as a form of belief and find it easier to bask in the warm, cosy optimism of partial truths.

The scourge of sentimentality encourages athletes to nit-pick their way through imagination and trawl through their beliefs to extract only the parts which make them feel good. Superstitious beliefs are always emotive; imagine the effort required to prise John Joe away from his heartfelt rituals or to prise us away from ours, particularly when we consider that the strongest sedative known to ease sporting anxiety is simply to believe whatever we like.

To activate superstition is effectively gambling, and any form of gambling which we can't give up counts as an addiction. So when John Joe repeats his superstition, he is just as much an addict as the drug addict needing to administer his next fix or a smoker craving her next cigarette. Once he is predisposed to 'shooting up' on superstition for a sustained period of time, attempting 'cold turkey' and shedding his rituals may prove every bit as difficult as if he were attempting to shed his own skin.

This raises a question as to how athletes can unlearn superstition's addictive effects. Perhaps they can contemplate the following words spoken in an address entitled *Liberating Yourself from Society* by philosopher, writer, and eloquent speaker Alan Watts. To gain the full benefit of his intent, simply swap any references or rebuttals he aims at conventional education systems for the repetitive nature in which athletes are coached and conditioned to master any skill.

"Liberation is a kind of necessary evil and when the process of education (repetitiveness) has been completed, we need a cure for it. Education (repetitiveness) is like salting meat in order to preserve it for eating, but when you're ready to cook it and eat it, you need to soak some of the salt out.

So psychoanalysis is necessary when you finish with education (repetitive actions), so as to work out and resolve all of the damage and traumatic shocks that were done to you in the process. In sophisticated circles, one goes through [such a process], not because you're a mentally sick person, but because it's considered beneficial towards general mental health."

Alan's words provide a snapshot of the repetitive nature by which athletes are regularly conditioned to act, to such an extent that acting repetitively becomes their norm. Consider the hours spent in unrelenting practice during our primary education, as mathematical tables were drilled into us repetitively until the information became indelibly etched on our brains. Who can recall the relentlessness of learning 2 + 2 = 4 and 4 + 4 = 8 and so on, or the trauma of having to memorise Shakespeare's sonnets, or books from the Bible, or whatever scriptures or literal texts are uniquely cultural to you.

We not only internalised mathematical tables, but also learned to accept mind-numbing repetitiveness as an acceptable way of life, as if it were a living, breathing thing and integral to how we should aspire to learn. Sport mirrors our lives in microcosm, and how we are conditioned to approach life has a resounding effect on how we approach all matters relating to sport. Coaching often consists of endless processes of repetitive practice, with no thought whatsoever given to weaving ingenuity, creativity, or spontaneity into the fabric of how best to perform. This is clearly the downside of repetitive conditioning.

How many of us can recall, in our formative years, being encouraged to 'unlearn' the effects of thinking repetitively? Why were we not told that repeatedly activating a superstitious belief is the behaviour of a compulsive gambler? Why did no one use those actual words? Every punter who optimistically bets at a greyhound track, has a flutter on a racehorse, gambles at a casino, plays betting apps, crosses their fingers, or touches wood, hopes lady luck is smiling on them.

Every punter who hops on one leg onto a pitch, or wears lucky socks, or enters a place of worship in due reverence to a superstition called God and then engages in prayer is equally optimistic that lady luck will smile on them and here's why. It's because evidence for the belief that lucky socks can magically alter an athlete's fortune is equally as poor as that which exists for believing their performances are being guided by deceased family members or gods.

Every superstitious punter is a gambling addict and is willing to bet on faith and sentimentality dealing them the winning hand. It's the same with every punter who steps onto a track, into a ring, dives into a pool, bounds onto a court, or climbs onto a bike. Each and every one is a forthright gambler since their endeavours are influenced by probability and chance, both of which are too often mistaken for luck. So let's raise a glass in a posthumous toast to the intoxicating madness and human belligerence necessary to sustain a superstitious belief despite no falsifiable proof of which to speak.

It seems fitting to draw this curious superstitious odyssey to its natural conclusion; but in order to do the topic of superstition justice, I would like to recount this wonderful tale of human benevolence, selflessness, and goodwill. It is a tale with a hidden undercurrent but also the potential to penetrate our subliminal beliefs. It is a tale of far reaching consequence which tells how something much darker is mentally constraining athletes' penchant for exercising spontaneity, to such an extent that their true personalities rarely prevail.

There once lived a man who was widely acknowledged for inventing the art of making fire. One day, this marvellous man gathered his tools and set off to visit a tribe somewhere in the remote north, to a place where temperatures plummeted on a daily basis and each day appeared colder than the last. He was driven by an urge to aid humanity, so he lived and interacted with the tribespeople and patiently demonstrated the art of making fire. The tribe was intrigued by his amazing skills as he shared how to cook efficiently and how to best harness and channel heat from the flame. They were quick to recognise his value and sought to repay him however they could.

Without any prior notice, the man simply upped sticks and left as he did not seek applause nor was he in search of an inflated ego. He was merely concerned by the people's well-being and, having contributed to that cause, he swiftly moved on to another tribe where once again he selflessly began to share his incredible gift for

268

making fire. Once again the people were intrigued by the generosity of this curious man, perhaps a little bit too intrigued in the eyes of their spiritual gurus, who took a very keen interest in the man's continuing growth in popularity at the expense of their own. Yet the groundswell continued as onlookers flocked to witness the gift of fire offered so graciously by this seemingly miraculous man.

It was a process which led to his undoing, as those spiritual gurus became increasingly vexed as his popularity grew while theirs started to wane, so they secretly conspired against him and colluded to do away with him at the first opportunity; and that's exactly what they did. They poisoned the man, or stabbed him repeatedly, or perhaps it was torture, or crucifixion, or a merciless stoning or beating. Feel free to affix whichever ending you choose since this is a universal tale with ramifications for all.

After disposing of the man, the gurus grew terrified of the consequences if his adoring admirers were to find out and seek retribution. So once again they conspired to use all their craft and cunning against him even though he was dead. These holy men, who in the context of the story represent all denominations and non-denominations, concocted a masterstroke of unprecedented genius; so perfect in fact that it almost warrants tipping our hats to their ingenuity.

They agreed to commission the most beautiful portrait imaginable of this amazing man and mount it prominently above the altar in their beautiful temple, church, or chapel of whichever ilk; but their cunning plan didn't end there. Next they strategically placed the man's instruments of fire in a prominent position in front of the portrait for everyone to admire. Finally, the tribespeople were taught to worship the portrait and pay homage and due reverence to those instruments of fire, but their homage merged into a ritual which they felt duty bound to sustain for centuries and perhaps even to this very day.

Here's where the cunning plan of those conniving gurus paid dividends and where their shrewd manipulation of the grieving masses reached its zenith. The people were taught to revere and worship items which were defunct and obsolete; there was no longer any fire. Those devious gurus had captured the essence of the obsolete tools but had disposed of their glowing, sparkling, crackling, sizzling, blazing, and mesmerising majesty. You've got to hand it to those wily clergy, priests, rabbis, clerics, evangelists, ministers, or pastors for engineering a masterclass of such brilliance that it utterly bewildered the masses, many of whom even up to this very day still worship, tithe, pay reverence, fight, and kill to maintain the illusion of fire.

Sadly, their worship was cunningly assimilated and thereby diluted and also downgraded into dutiful rituals once the flame had been well and truly extinguished and its initial lustre had long-since petered out. This analogy is important to gain understanding of the impact of hanging onto obsolete beliefs. The painting couldn't transmit the mesmeric qualities of living, breathing fire, nor could it convey the heartfelt intent so graciously offered by the amazing man. It would be like trying to use an intermediary to transmit our intended emotions by way of an intimate kiss to someone we loved. Who among us can project our most intimate emotions using someone else's lips?

Despite their former artistry and past glory, once the objects were enshrined they could no longer disrupt physical reality. It's a curious tale with a familiar twist, similar to paying homage to obsolete superstitious beliefs as was earlier displayed by footballer Efe Ambrose, whose misplaced belief that Celtic FC was the beneficiary of divine intervention may seem admirable at face value, but beneath the veneer it tells us nothing at all. Even the mildest form of applied scepticism consigns Efe's God to the realm of superstition, which is already occupied by the equally revered portrait and obsolete tools of that fire making man.

So, just to recap: Efe's God was apparently nailed to a cross, while the man who brought fire was nailed to a plinth. Both were killed in pursuit of altruism and both resurrected through fable and myth to appear before you today in print. Yet despite both protagonists once seemingly interacting on earth for the purpose of altruism and due to the cunning manipulation of gurus, many of their acolytes in the 21st century are still psychologically locked in the grip of these ancient mythologies despite all sparks of absolute truth having long since petered out.

Many athletes believe that the superstition called God has a vested interest in personally disrupting the outcome of terrestrial sport. Efe claimed that a god supernaturally influenced his sporting outcomes, while footballer Tommy Elphick headbutted the goalposts as part of his superstitious ritual. One belief is theistic while the other is generic, yet both are so similar in nature that you couldn't fit a width of paper in between. When did wearing a pair of shorts inside-out or measuring a precise quantity of vegetables onto a plate carry supernatural credence and clout?

Why pretend it's normal to claim that an invisible god interacting in natural and observable reality isn't anything other than mere superstitious pie in the sky? Why are athletes so easily drawn to external saviours and to accepting extraordinary claims based on faith as their physical truth? Perhaps these illuminating words by author and former Jesuit priest, Anthony de Mello, may lend valuable insight regarding the impact of worshipping sentimental ideals which, despite being comforting, are devoid and bereft of life: *"If the worship isn't leading to fire, if the liturgy isn't leading to a clearer perception of reality, and if God isn't leading to life - where's the fire?"*

We can spend a lifetime being resolutely stuck in a belief and then die, never once knowing if it had any semblance of validity at all. So who is dousing your flames of spontaneity? Put a name to the guru behind the charade. What current means do athletes employ to uproot the effects of superstition or to uproot their need to experience applause? Where are the checks and balances in athletes' psychology to steer fragile mentalities away from dependency on superstitious beliefs? The most comical factor of human awareness is that the purpose of life is 'not to be dead'. This startling revelation does not imply being physically deceased, but refers instead to not switching-off to scepticism, inquiry, curiosity, or experiencing life at its spontaneous worst and best.

Any fool can believe and most probably do, but who taught us that the way to eradicate self-doubt was to bury our heads in fallacious ideals as a means of avoiding responsibility for how we perform? Why waste time and energy complying with superstitious rituals when they fail us so miserably? Is it because the only reason athletes subscribe to superstitions at all is that they believe there's something in it for them? Why do athletes blame themselves but not their beliefs when superstition and prayer fail to materialise? Who decreed that superstitions get to fly under the radar of falsifiable reasoning and get off scot-free?

Sport exposes the gambler in us all. Consider the well-heeled bookmaker who pockets exorbitant profit through mass saturation of innovative gambling apps. Yet gambling has flourished through countless millennia despite its reliance on probability and chance and its endless promotion of the superstition called luck. So why do sports itineraries in the 21st century fail to include compulsory discussions on the topic of luck, considering how many of us still cross our fingers in anticipation of which horse will cross the finishing line first?

Many of us enjoy a cheeky flutter on whether snow will fall on Christmas day. It is equally commonplace for optimistic punters to bet on the day, date, and time of when the biblical Jesus will return to earth. One opportunistic bookmaker even offered odds of 5000–1 for discovering aliens in a specified six-year period. Perhaps the biblical Jesus is the extra-terrestrial of which he implied?

Every superstition is accompanied by sport's most highly-prized gambling cohorts of chance, probability, and luck - 'the three amigos'. Gambling is only rivalled by prostitution and boxing as the oldest professions known to mankind, so it isn't going away anytime soon. Nor is superstition, as we are gambling every time we re-enact an unfalsifiable belief. In many quarters gambling is seen as harmful, but where do we draw the line between fearing that which is observably harmful, and the practice of causing needless and unwarranted harm to ourselves through unfounded superstitious fear? The justification for this question should be evident to anyone who has witnessed a fully grown adult fleeing in panic from a common household spider which is no bigger than their fingernail.

How did a tiny innocuous creature such as a spider gain such a stranglehold on their thinking that they abandoned all logical rationale in their desperation to experience relief? Ask them if they want to be scared of spiders and an overwhelming majority will say no. Ask most smokers if they would much rather quit and there's a high probability they will say yes. Sadly, the opposite of *willpower* is obstinate *won't power*, both of which are embroiled in a continuous battle for overall control of the mind. Their dilemma is circular, insomuch as any lack of control over willpower leaves them vulnerable to habits, whereas breaking free from habits requires them to exercise a greater sense of control over their own free will.

Consider the 2014 Commonwealth Games in Glasgow as disappointing news began to break to a large expectant crowd that two of British athletics' main sporting attractions, Mo Farah and Jessica Ennis-Hill, would not compete. Their withdrawal left organisers desperate to retain high profile British interest. Expectations were quickly restored, however, as pressure was thrust on the shoulders of 20-year-old 100-metre sprinter, Adam Gemili, to fly the flag for the UK. Adam comfortably won his semi-final heat and, as a result, British commentators gushed over his performance with plaudits and praise.

It wasn't long before Adam's performance was brought sharply back into focus by 200m and 400m four-time Olympic and eight-time World Sprint Champion Michael Johnson, as he critically evaluated aspects of Adam's semi-final win. In the wake of euphoria encircling Adam after progressing to the 100-metre final, one patriotic British pundit dared to suggest that Michael's analysis seemed a tad harsh. Yet, Michael had identified a glaring flaw in Adam's initial transition between bursting out of the blocks and being able to fluently increase his stride into a full-on sprint in one rhythmic motion.

When a champion with the calibre of Michael Johnson analyses a sprint, it is wise to listen, since sure enough with the benefit of action replays, even laymen could identify the flaw affecting Adam's sprint. If it wasn't corrected he could lose a percentage of initial speed. Fortunately, despite a few patriotic murmurings, the cameras vindicated Michael's analysis in stark contradiction to the blind spots of his British peers. *"He needs a smoother transition, but if he corrects that he can win a medal for sure,"* Michael confidently asserted. Shortly afterwards, as if he'd been listening to Michael in the studio, Adam corrected the flaw and stunned a highly competitive field which included three world-class Jamaican sprinters (not Bolt), to win a highly coveted silver medal in his first ever Commonwealth Games.

The Commonwealth fairy tale didn't end there, but instead unearthed a marvellous human story regarding 40-year-old competitor Steve Way, who became the centre of media attention after breaking the British Masters Marathon record with a personal best of 2 hours 15 minutes and 16 seconds. His achievement was incredible, inasmuch as he explained how seven years earlier he was a "fat bloke", while an accompanying media report unflatteringly saw fit to describe him as a corpulent sloth (charming eh!). Yet Steve wasn't phased in the slightest; instead he admitted to previously tipping the scales at a cumbersome 16 ½ stone, not to mention a twenty-a-day smoking habit.

After having struggled to sleep at nights due to a continual hacking cough, Steve talked of experiencing a form of epiphany, whereby afterwards he felt compelled to transition beyond his poor quality of life. He described his transition into becoming a bona fide competitor of long distance running as *"his personal quest to inspire couch potatoes everywhere,"* and he proceeded to milk his commonwealth experience for every soundbite it was worth. With the world's media hanging on every word, he was able to access a global audience and share how his positive mental stimulus acted as a transitional agent for change.

Steve's use of 'transitioning' as a key motivational driver to implement positive change bore a striking resemblance to that described in the previous chapter by neuroscience mind coach, Amy Brann, who waxed lyrical of the positive effects of neurological nudging as a practical means to achieve transformation and change. 'Nudging' refers to gently extending our current psychology beyond *can't do* beliefs by adopting a series of progressive actions which move us into the realm of *can do* beliefs. Ultimately, the real learning to emerge from both Commonwealth scenarios is of the meteoric effects which active transitioning can impose on a mediocre state of will.

It's important to sleep with one eye open to maintain vigilance since the idea of luck is a primary cause of every contingency experienced in sport. This hypothesis is enhanced by Commonwealth medallist Adam Gemili following his silver medal presentation ceremony when he stated, *"I'm speechless. I'm over the moon. Now the times will come, fingers crossed, [when] hopefully I have a decent career."* But let's backtrack just a tad to consider his optimism in more detail regarding his subtle reference to luck. How many of us noticed that, despite his burgeoning talent and medal winning transition from British hopeful to sprinting elite, his first words were directed at crediting luck?

It's hard not to deduce from 'fingers crossed' that Adam saw luck as instrumental to every unfolding chapter of his promising career. Yet given that luck is mere superstition, why isn't it evident in common consensus that luck is just probability and chance? What happens for instance when two athletes share the same genetics? Consider the Rio 2016 Olympics and the fate of two brothers who share the same genetics, family, upbringing, support mechanisms, training patterns and routines, and who travel together and share each other's company and counsel. Yet at the expense of his brother Jonny, Alistair Brownlee became the first triathlete to retain Olympic Gold in a gruelling triumph over a tough and testing Fort Copacabana course.

Alastair won gold on two occasions ahead of younger brother Jonny who improved on his own bronze medal showing at London 2012 by claiming Olympic silver this time around. Afterwards, in an emotional post-event interview, Alastair told the BBC of the torturous trials and tribulations he had to endure the previous summer, including lateral ligament reconstructive surgery on his left ankle. This made his incredible achievement at Rio seem even more outstanding and poignant than the time before. *"Every day has been so hard. I have woken up in pain every day; it has been so hard. I was pretty confident we would get first and second but I didn't know which way it would be. I just had the edge on Jonny, but he has killed me in training every day and I have been going through hell every day."*

Both siblings share the same genetics, domestic upbringing, training, and professional arrangements, so neither brother can justifiably be classed as 'luckier', and minus the red herring called luck muddying the water, both compete on equal terms based on the strength of their talent and willpower alone. Jonny knows how it feels to live with the scourge of comparisons after having lost twice to his brother at Olympic final events. The culture of comparisons, however, is prevalent in all sport, but not all athletes are as adept as Jonny at dealing with the demands of emulating their peers. Instead, many experience an overwhelming sense of anxiety, trepidation, and fear.

Superstitious paranoia tends to thrive best in anxious environments. Oddly, the only sports personality with whom athletes never get to compare is with themselves. Instead, from an early age, many feel pressured to emulate their peers and take up their mantle. As testament to sport's commonality of comparative language, consider the following throwaway comments: *"Are we witnessing the next Usain Bolt?"*, *"Is Katarina Johnson-Thompson the new Jessica Ennis-Hill?"*, *"This up-and-coming young jockey appears to bear all the hallmarks of a young AP McCoy"*, and *"Is this the new golden generation of English rugby stars we see before us?"* It seems no one is safe from the scourge of comparative beliefs.

The superstition called luck is primarily cultural. Every sport has its culture of unique rituals, traditions, and myths. What is your first recollection of experiencing culture, and can you recall if or when you signed up to its unspoken rules in terms of its privileges and constraints? Earlier, sprinter Adam Gemili and marathon runner Steve Way demonstrated a propensity to transition, but a similar propensity is also necessary to transition beyond superstitious beliefs, irrespective of whether they are cultural or just exist in our heads.

Who can deny that our predominant cultures still wield power and influence over our relationship with sport by adding cultural bias to every decision we make? We may choose to be proud of whoever we are, or where we are from, or how we arrived at being us, yet the person we've become still operates in accordance with our culture's indoctrination of us. In contrast, the act of being spontaneous requires space to flourish, free from the constraints and customs prescribed to us by somebody else.

We are born *of* a culture, but we are not *the* culture. We can still appreciate having experienced the best and worst of what our culture has to offer while learning to differentiate between cultural quirks and superstitious traits. This affords us the space to drop whatever part of culture is inappropriate for us. So welcome to the world of cultural disentanglement, where simply being cultural does not imbue superstition with any divine right or special dispensation to represent us. Just because we are born into a culture does not mean that the culture has ownership of us.

Every culture has language colloquialisms which inadvertently control our emotions via our brains. One example is the globally recognised cult of 'my'. The word 'my' is the cause of much sporting anxiety and a perilously false indicator of truth. Claims such as my culture, my superstition, my fault, my team, my tradition, my habit, my religion, my responsibility, my expectation, my mistake, my culpability, and my problem are commonplace. Throughout the annals of history, what used to be viewed as an innocuous word has somehow grown horns and a set of legs. It's as if culture and superstition are part of our physical anatomy and we're joined at the hip. Every time we add 'my' to a sporting scenario we slip closer to the domain of the clinically insane as it becomes increasingly difficult to tell either apart.

It requires checks and balances to prevent the culture of 'my' from strengthening its alliance with superstition, and to avoid falling into the trap of believing that superstition is part of us. Once we validate 'my' as being of substance, or attach 'my' to a physical object, or give rise to the claim that a ritual is 'mine,' then shedding our habits, rituals, or compulsions becomes tantamount to the shedding of our skin. The word 'my' carries negative 'I' connotations as is evident by the misuse of emotional sentiments such as, *"My performance was terrible today,"* which most athletes recognise as meaning, *"I was terrible today."*

"My performance wasn't up to scratch" is another prime example of a negative 'I' connotation, whereby athletes feel unable to draw a distinction between the performance and the performer, and instead assert *"I wasn't up to scratch."* This cuts athletes no slack to detach emotionally, or to create mental separation between themselves and the performance, or to look beyond the performance and analyse it objectively without feeling damaged on the inside.

Consider the impact of this troubling quote: *"There is no such thing as the present, only the past being repeated over and over again."* If this is true, what a dangerous precedent it sets since imagination is a breeding ground for exaggerated truths. This was well illustrated at the 2014 Champions League Final in Lisbon as reporter Graeme Bryce offered an interesting summary of Real Madrid's footballing superstar, Gareth Bale, who had scored what, for many, was the killer goal of the tie to finally break the dogged resistance of Atletico Madrid.

Graeme's article read, *"Then came the moment fate decided that Real's No 11 should score in the 11th minute of extra time."* Gareth later summed up his amazing experience using similar conspiratorial overtones: *"A few thoughts crept into my mind. Missing chances - it happens. Sometimes you don't get the rub of the green but you have to keep persisting. Keep going and you may get that one chance that will make the difference."* What are we to make of Graeme describing *"the moment that fate decided"* or the superstitious overtone of Gareth's reference to *"rub of the green"*? What was Graeme insinuating by mentioning that *"number 11 scored in the 11th minute"*?

Let's pause for a moment to confirm that we read that correctly. Was Graeme drawing a direct correlation between the shirt's number being eleven and Gareth scoring in the eleventh minute? Was his observation deliberate or purely coincidence, and if it wasn't coincidence then what does drawing such a random association achieve? Was it that, despite all the footballing talent on parade that particular day, something supernatural had occurred to influence the outcome? Was he implying that, despite all the bases being covered during Real's stringent pre-match preparation routines, in the end their fate was decided by superstitious constructs such as fate, destiny, fluke, and luck?

It seems as plain as the nose on our face that this was exactly what was being implied. Athletes often concede to superstitious bias based on the premise that something unobservable but seemingly intelligent is proactively guiding their sporting careers. As such, many lose any impetus to apply scepticism and curiosity to their beliefs. Both Graeme and Gareth appear to suggest that superstition and luck are alive and well and still prominently positioned at the forefront of the minds of sporting elite. This is why it's important to introduce conversations about luck into every contingency of sport, not just as a convenient get-out clause which athletes only see fit to trigger when they're in trouble and prepared to grasp at any conceivable means to bail themselves out. Nor should luck be used as an excuse to pass the buck when things go awry and they need a scapegoat to blame.

Gareth's post-match analysis highlights the impact of self-talk and demonstrates that right at the forefront of his psychology were thoughts about luck. So what can we learn? How about that it's time to decide on whether we actually care if our beliefs are true, rather than display the audacity and artistic licence to imply that any given performance can be altered by luck. How do lucky interactions come about? Is it with aid of telepathy or by way of a 24-hour hotline to a supernatural ear in the sky? If so, how wide off the mark or near to the knuckle is the gist of the following satirical quote? *"Welcome to Telepathics Anonymous. Don't bother introducing yourselves."*

Is some form of telepathy occurring between athletes and luck? How else could luck know when to intervene? Or perhaps we'd be better off channelling time and energy into eradicating the cause of superstitious beliefs by considering a phenomenon called the 'Law of Reversed Effort', otherwise known as the

Backwards Law. This astonishing law by Émile Coué suggests that imagination is the language of an unconscious mind and so acts as our principal source of awareness. Coué also suggests that imagination is more powerful than willpower, given willpower exists at the behest of our thoughts.

Before we rise from a chair we already imagine ourselves being somewhere else. Before we kick a ball towards the goal, aim a punch at an opponent, or manoeuvre ourselves through the field from fourth position to third during a race, we have already imagined (visualised) the outcome. Coué's law shares correlation with the pseudoscientific superstition called Law of Attraction, as both supposedly share the potential to transition thoughts into physical things. According to Coué, everything we experience is a manifestation of an imaginative process of thought, and those thoughts have the potential to become more potent than willpower itself.

Sports motivation begins with imagination, as does demotivation and self-denigration. Coué's Law of Reversed Effort suggests that once a thought becomes lodged in our imagination, it persists unless or until it is duly dispersed, released, or mentally displaced by another thought. This is one of the reasons dreamers procrastinate. Dreamers struggle to curtail continuous flows of creative thinking with diversionary thoughts which are more conducive to pressing tasks and matters at hand.

Athletes who subscribe to superstitions are acting imaginatively and are effectively dreamers. Then again, it's hard to be unimaginative since the brain doesn't switch off to creativity; which is why it's imperative that athletes don't drop their guard. Don't take my word for it! Instead, try being unimaginative for a change and you may find it requires a great deal of imagination to think unimaginative thoughts. Coué also suggests that when imagination and will dually align, they increase the effect of the other's potency.

All of us are aware of Coué's peculiar Law of Reversed Effort, but in order to reacquaint our minds with its effect, consider the feeling of slowly drowning. No really! Visualise the sense of slowly drowning, along with the emotions of slowly drowning and the accompanying sense of panic which naturally ensues as we frantically scramble to stay afloat. Perhaps by now we're beginning to recognise that the more we struggle the faster we sink. Yet by reversing the effort required to struggle and wilfully submitting to the serenity of being submerged by allowing our arms, legs, and bodies to go limp, we begin to float. By supplanting perspiration with relaxation, we are able to stay afloat and survive.

Coué's Law of Reversed Effort is evident in further scenarios such as being asked by a friend, when our mind is preoccupied, to recall someone's name, or the lyrics to a song, or the punchline to a joke, etc. Yet every time we are asked, despite our best efforts, the answer completely escapes our mind. Our inability to remember lends to frustration and increased anxiety as we wrack our brain in vain, attempting to summon the elusive information to the forefront of our mind. Why does it appear that the harder we try to remember, the harder it becomes? Yet once we actively stop trying to remember, our thoughts drift into a state of serenity until, almost by magic, those elusive answers come flooding back.

Once we stopped trying so bloody hard to remember, almost instinctively our power of recall returned. Coué's Law of Reversed Effort refers to a process where reversing all previous efforts to remember increases our chances of experiencing recall and decreases the likelihood to forget. Coué also suggests that the conscious mind is awash with inaccurate memory and this accounts for the existence of neurological filters which help to screen against indiscriminate views. He suggests that the unconscious mind has impeccable memory which records every detail of every event we experience throughout our lives.

Coué's Law of Reversed Effort is part of a much wider hypothesis. Yet it remains interesting nonetheless, as any form of study which suggests that imagination has the power to outrank our will is a natural bedfellow of the idea that superstitious *won't-power* can outrank practical *willpower,* and these are perhaps reasons why athletes are prone to re-enact superstitious beliefs.

"It turns out that an eerie type of chaos can lurk just behind a façade of order, and yet deep inside the chaos lurks an even eerier type of order."

- Douglas R. Hofstadter, Professor of Cognitive Sciences

Consider this marvellous quote by writer Havelock Ellis: *"A man must not swallow more beliefs than he can digest."* It bears a striking resemblance to Coué's assertion that the human brain cannot accept two separate thoughts at the same time. This an interesting observation insomuch as it may be a contributing factor to why so many coaches and athletes ignore the clear dichotomy which exists between rational and irrational propositions such as wearing lucky numbers as a prerequisite to securing a win. Or as to why footballer Efe Ambrose believes that his god favoured Celtic FC in the Scottish Cup final, simply because he couldn't envisage it not being so.

Superstition enthrals the imagination with enchanting deceptions designed to throw scepticism off its track; but why not simply reverse the effort required to keep us locked into superstitious states? Why not focus our efforts on embarking upon our own unique journey of uncharted truth, as if we were the first people ever to exist on planet Earth? Imagine how that would look. We'd have no blueprints to follow, customs to uphold, protocols to adhere to, peers to impress, or need for applause. Nor would there be any cultural superstitions to curtail spontaneity or immerse us in guilt.

We'd be pioneers of spontaneity; whereas currently spontaneity struggles to flourish in environments where superstition persists. We'd be open to redefining winning but also keen to explore the prospect of losing as no more than a symptom of probability and chance. We'd have no recollection or foreknowledge of luck. So why do athletes embrace superstition but remain apathetic towards scepticism when it comes to transitioning beyond their beliefs? Perhaps author Raymond Lindquist's insightful sentiment, *"Courage is the power to let go of the familiar"* is somewhat prophetic as only through courage to let go of the familiar are we free to commence thinking anew.

"A man who wants to lead the orchestra must turn his back on the crowd."

- Max Lucado, Author

Superstitious beliefs are primarily cultural, as is conceding to fear of the unknown. What superstitious athletes actually fear, however, is the idea of losing what is already known. The human psychology is a seeker of context, hence we'd much rather believe something than admit to knowing little or nothing at all. Perhaps the most proficient skill of all human rationale is our ability to 'make stuff up', an example of which is the added complexity required to justify superstitious charades. Yet, Coué's Law of Reversed Effort suggests we are thinking too much.

Life is a humbling yet stirring encounter, so why not learn to embrace it for what it is? Why over complicate sport with superstitious complexity? It is said that a candle loses nothing by lighting another candle. Athletes also lose nothing by illuminating their understanding that extraordinary claims require extraordinary evidence, since that which they assert without evidence can also be dismissed without evidence. Superstitious beliefs don't exist in a vacuum. So I issue a challenge to every athlete currently prone to superstitious beliefs. Try practicing scepticism for a change, just to throw superstition off your scent.

"The saviour who wants to turn men into angels is as much a hater of human nature as the totalitarian despot who wants to turn them into puppets."

- Eric Hoffer, Philosopher

Human evolution is prone to regenerate of its own accord as nature continues along its tried and tested cycle of birth, death, and replenishment. Superstitions have orchestrated the human psychology for time immemorial, and right at the forefront sits our fear of mortality. Here are some examples of this type of fear, as researched by former homicide detective and forensic coroner Garry Rodgers, who published an article in *The Huffington Post*.

Coins on the Eyes: *'Many people die with their eyes open. It can be a creepy feeling to have the dead stare at you and it was thought the dead might be eyeing someone to go with them. Coins were a practical item to weigh down the eyelids until rigor mortis set in. The most famous set of eye coins is the two silver half-dollar coins set on Abraham Lincoln, now on display in the Chicago Historical Museum.'*

Remove a corpse, feet first: *'This practice dates back to Victorian times. It was thought if the corpse went out head first it'd be able to look back and beckon those standing behind to follow.'*

Hold Your Breath: *'Another popular superstition is that you must hold your breath while passing a graveyard to prevent drawing in a restless spirit that's trying to re-enter the physical world. That might be a problem if you're passing Wadi-us-Salaam in Najaf, Iraq [as] it's the world's largest cemetery at 1,485.5 acres and holds over five million bodies.'*

Many of us have heard the common superstition of people dying in groups of three. This has since been upgraded with a modern twist, whereby it's now said that *celebrities* die in threes. Oddly, there's a consistent correlation between death and the number three. All superstitions are tinged by an air of mystique. Some are positively exhilarating, while other examples carry shadowy undercurrents of an unspoken reality where athletes view the prospect of disclosing their superstitions as strictly taboo. So how about us? How good are we at applying scepticism and curiosity to our superstitious beliefs?

How capable are we of regenerating the superstitious beliefs which keep us locked in a state of arrested development, compared to nature's cycle of regeneration and replenishment? Perhaps, by way of measurement, it's worth considering the next time someone ruffles our hair or shakes our hand after meeting again for the first time in ages, that the *us* they are greeting has regenerated from the person they once knew. Despite looking similar, the surface layers of our skin continued to regenerate once every 2 to 3 weeks, our hair also kept growing at an estimated 1cm every month, while our eyebrows and eyelashes renewed every 6 to 8 weeks.

Since we last met, the cells in our intestine died and replenished every 2 to 3 days, while our fingernails grew an estimated 3.4mm every month and our toes grew full nails every 10 months or so. It's quite an extraordinary transformation, yet our regeneration didn't end there. Our tongue, which has around 9000 taste buds to help us detect sweet, salty, bitter, and sour flavours, renewed itself every 10 - 14 days. This incredible process of regeneration and replenishment can even improve the condition of the liver of some heavy drinkers, as liver cells only have a lifespan of around 50 days.

David Lloyd, a liver consultant and surgeon at Leicester Royal Infirmary explained, *"Thanks to its rich blood supply, I can take 70% of a person's liver away in an operation and around 90% of it will grow back within 2 months."* Even the cells on the surface of our lungs renew themselves every 2 to 3 weeks. So in summary, the human body is replenished by regeneration, and along with each regeneration cycle we are being renewed and can no longer lay claim to being exactly who we once were.

Human psychology appears less accommodating when it comes to replenishing old beliefs with new beliefs. This is not in keeping with comparable aspects of human behaviour since we regularly discard old clothes and periodically replenish our car by exchanging old for new. We replenish past friends and acquaintances with new friends and colleagues, and deceased family members with the birth of new members. Yet we struggle to discard and replenish outdated, unfalsifiable superstitious beliefs with any regularity, if at all.

So what about sport? It's egotistical to believe we can summon the supernatural to intervene in terrestrial affairs. Such is our arrogance that we choose to ignore nature's evolutionary template of birth, death, and replenishment on a loop. Yet if this cycle is good enough for nature, then why not apply it to superstitious belief? How can an athlete's superstitious psychology transition beyond delusionary mental constructs (effectively placebos) which keep them locked in the past, unless those delusions are allowed to wither and die? Perhaps it's a dichotomy best described by author Anthony De Mello, who shared the following anecdote:

The disciple said: *"I have no idea what tomorrow will bring, so I wish to prepare for it."*

His teacher replied: *"You fear tomorrow not realising that yesterday is just as dangerous."*

Few have managed to capture the overall tenet of the restrictive nature of superstitious beliefs better than actor Will Rogers who warned: *"Don't let yesterday use up too much of today."* There is nothing 'super' about superstitious beliefs, nor is faith a virtue when it lacks the contingency to ensure that a falsifiable end-game to ignorance is always in sight. It's important to implement practical timescales as to how long it is reasonable to keep on believing in illusionary constructs which can't be observed.

To illustrate this assertion, I draw your attention to a humorous interview I conducted with former Watford, Aston Villa, and England Manager Graham Taylor at a conference in Belfast. I asked for an example of any superstition he'd witnessed first-hand. In response, he laughed heartily and began to recount a story which I'll make no attempt to analyse. Instead, I'll happily share exactly what he said since it made me smile and may do so for you.

"There's been so many. The thing is, you don't always know exactly because they don't tell you. You learn it when you observe them before a game. There was one, I can't give you this player's name but he insisted on walking around the dressing room naked, bollock naked and that was what he wanted to do. He walked right round the dressing room with no clothes on and then he got changed. He said it was his superstition; I never believed him but I'll tell you what, he was a good player.

I think some players are that way [feel they have to trigger their superstitions before they can perform]. I'd have to say myself, for home games at Watford, my routine was always to go down to the game on the Saturday morning, down to the ground. Then I always wanted to go back home and relax in a warm bath so I felt relaxed, and then I got changed and went back down to the ground and, I have to say, those were the most successful periods probably in my whole life."

Printed in Great Britain
by Amazon